Walking Into Colorado's Past

50 FRONT RANGE HISTORY HIKES

By Ben Fogelberg and Steve Grinstead

WESTCLIFFE PUBLISHERS
westcliffepublishers.com

International Standard Book Numbers
ISBN-10: 1-56579-519-9
ISBN-13: 978-1-56579-519-8

Editor: Jenna Samelson Browning
Designer: Angie Lee, Grindstone Graphics, Inc.
Production Manager: Craig Keyzer

Published by:
Westcliffe Publishers, Inc.
P.O. Box 1261
Englewood, CO 80150

Printed in China by: C&C Offset Printing Co., Ltd.

Library of Congress Cataloging-in-Publication Data:
Fogelberg, Ben.
 Walking into Colorado's past : 50 Front Range history hikes / by Ben Fogelberg and Steve Grinstead.
    p. cm.

Includes bibliographical references and index.
ISBN-13: 978-1-56579-519-8
ISBN-10: 1-56579-519-9

1. Historic sites--Front Range (Colo. and Wyo.)--Guidebooks. 2. Hiking--Front Range (Colo. and Wyo.)--Guidebooks. 3. Hiking--Colorado--Guidebooks. 4. Front Range (Colo. and Wyo.)--Guidebooks. 5. Front Range (Colo. and Wyo.)--History, Local. 6. Colorado--Guidebooks. I. Grinstead, Steve. II. Title.
 F782.F88F64 2005
 917.88'6043--dc22
                          2004027903

For more information about other fine books and calendars from Westcliffe Publishers, please contact your local bookstore, call us at 1-800-523-3692, or visit us on the Web at westcliffepublishers.com.

Please note: Risk is always a factor in backcountry and high-mountain travel. Many of the activities described in this book can be dangerous, especially when weather is adverse or unpredictable, and when unforeseen events or conditions create a hazardous situation. The authors have done their best to provide the reader with accurate information about backcountry travel, as well as to point out some of its potential hazards. It is the responsibility of the users of this guide to learn the necessary skills for safe backcountry travel, and to exercise caution in potentially hazardous areas, especially on glaciers and avalanche-prone terrain. The authors and publisher disclaim any liability for injury or other damage caused by backcountry traveling or performing any other activity described in this book.

The authors and publisher of this book have made every effort to ensure the accuracy and currency of its information. Nevertheless, books can require revisions. Please feel free to let us know if you find information in this book that needs to be updated, and we will be glad to correct it for the next printing. Your comments and suggestions are always welcome.

Cover Photo: *The Vindicator Valley Loop displays many relics of Colorado's mining past.*

Previous Page: *An old sawmill at the Meyers Homestead*

Above: *Spectacular vistas await hikers near the Fourth of July mine.*

Below: *Vindicator Valley mining structure near Victor*

Contents

Introduction

Nothing—absolutely nothing—beats a walk in the wilderness. It's that feeling of escaping into Colorado's open spaces that was the inspiration for this book. But there was another inspiration as well. While walking along a trail, any trail, you also can't beat the sense that you're hiking into history: the sense that before you, history was made, right where your own feet are landing today. Ironically, that connection with the past and that feeling of mystery—knowing that someone was here long before— is as rewarding to me as the feeling I get when I think I may be walking where no one has *ever* walked before.

The history hidden among Colorado's mountains is legendary, and for good reason. A wealth (sometimes literally) of stories is waiting there: gold mines, silver mines, long-vanished mining camps, fire lookouts, homesteads nestled among high peaks. One of my all-time favorite hikes is the trail that goes straight up the flank of West Spanish Peak (Hike 49) to the site of a mine that nature is fast reclaiming in its wind-raked alpine setting high above timberline.

But anyone who knows me knows that I'm a contrarian. I like bad weather. I'll tell you that the plains of Kansas are just as beautiful as the peaks of the West, and I'll mean it. Point me one way and I'll likely look the other. And so I have to put in a word for the Colorado hikes that go down, not up.

In putting this book together with Ben, I've discovered that I have a soft spot for Colorado's canyons. These scenic stretches of river hold so much history, and trails that often see far less foot traffic than the classic paths up to the high-altitude mining camps. A walk or bike ride into Picketwire Canyon (Hike 45) doesn't just take you along one of the most scenic stretches of the Purgatoire River. It takes you to Apishapa rock art etched into canyon walls. It takes you to a Hispanic mission and the graves of those who died there. It takes you to the walls and foundations of settlers' homes, and it takes you to the footprints of dinosaurs. Now *that's* history, and no mountain hike can do all that.

Still, there's just something about a silver mine clinging to a high peak…

Here's to my hiking partners: Pete Allen; Minor Davis; Pat Fraker; Doug Giffin; Kim Grant; Leigh, Seth, and Emma Grinstead; Rosie and Will Grinstead; Chris Hilliard; Julie Johnson; Amanda, Julie, and Lindsay Moorman; and Andy Stine. Thanks, Andy, for your great hike ideas and your inexhaustible research. An overdue thank-you to Bill Durrua for the long-ago Lost Creek camping trip that may very well have planted the seed for this book. Thanks, Julie Fletcher, for all your help on the home front. Much respect to the great staff at Westcliffe Publishers for liking the book's concept and seeing it through.

Thanks to my parents, Will and Rosie Grinstead, for showing me the West. And most of all, thank you, Leigh, for letting me use your camera. And your bike. And your car. And for the child care and all the advice. I still owe you a lens cap.

—*Steve Grinstead*

Opposite: *Forest Canyon, Rocky Mountain National Park*

My father and I reached timberline on Longs Peak well before dawn. We followed the trail west over rocky terrain mottled by wind-twisted shrubs, our vision limited by the range of our headlamps. A cold easterly wind forced us to don gloves, jackets, and hoods. We kept warm, but the layers of Gore-Tex and fleece muffled our conversation. So we marched in silence as the sun rose at last, our eyes drawn to the single-file line of hikers ahead. Their own flashlights and headlamps glowed in the distance as they ascended, giving the scene a pilgrimage-like aspect.

As we walked, I remembered a story Dad had told me when I was young. Around 20 years ago, he had been hiking Longs alone—something I don't recommend—when he encountered a hiker having a heart attack. After getting someone with first-aid experience to try to help the man, Dad ran back down to the trailhead and notified the forest rangers. Within minutes he was on the trail again, toting a stretcher. Tragically, the rescue party didn't reach the victim in time. My father reached the summit that day, though the achievement meant both more and less than he thought it would.

Dad's story—which for me has become part of Longs Peak lore—occurred to me often as I composed my half of this book. For me, every hike is a pilgrimage into the past. Every mountain, mesa, canyon, and plain in Colorado has its own story. Some are tragic, some triumphant. When I hike with my family, I tell Dad's story and add some of my own. And the more American Indian trails, abandoned silver mines, airplane crash sites, and pioneer homesteads I find, the more I realize that Colorado's wild places are more than scenic wonders. They are historical treasure troves. I hope your family enjoys these trails and tales as much as mine does.

I'd like to thank my father, Dan Fogelberg, who hiked more than a hundred miles with me during a single summer and took photos for about half of the hikes in this guide. My stepmother, Robyn Fogelberg, kept us going by preparing innumerable lunches. I am indebted to my good friends Paul Johnson, Kevin Weed, Kelley King, Ian Hooper, Lorri Frisbee, Christy Hansen, and my brother-in-law Brandon Wright for their company on the trails. Modupe Labode gave expert advice on the manuscript, and Andy Stine helped identify potential hikes. My mother, Marilyn Fuqua, and my grandparents, Dale and Ardyce Myers, introduced me to many of the Rocky Mountain National Park trails in this book. Dozens of employees and volunteers at state parks, national forests, libraries, and museums helped out along the way. And I could not have done the book without encouragement from my wife, Marcia, and my son, Noah.

—Ben Fogelberg

To Leigh, Seth, and Emma: Thank you for being my partners in this project. You helped me more than you'll ever know.

—S.G.

To my wife, Marcia, and my son, Noah, for reminding me that my family is the only compass I need.

—B.F.

Opposite: Longs Peak at sunrise, Rocky Mountain National Park

8

How to Use This Guide

Coloradans define the "Front Range" in many ways. In this book, we take the broad view. All of the hikes in this guide are easily accessible from the urban corridor that stretches north to south along the eastern slope of the Rocky Mountains from Wyoming to New Mexico. Most trails are within an hour and a half's drive from one of eight major cities or places: Fort Collins, Rocky Mountain National Park, Boulder, Denver, Colorado Springs, Pueblo, La Junta, and Trinidad.

Most of the hikes follow trails within open space preserves, national forests, state parks, or other places people often think of as "the wilderness." In recent years, public land stewards have chucked their "return the land to its natural state" philosophy in favor of policies that recognize the record of previous human use. You'll find everything from perfectly preserved homesteads and ranches to ancient rock art, ruined cabins, long-abandoned gold and silver mines, and a wrecked B-17 bomber.

Each hike begins with a short story that places the trail's historical resources in context. Contact information, trail distance and difficulty rating, starting and maximum elevations, map references (keyed to DeLorme's *Colorado Atlas & Gazetteer*), approximate hiking time, and helpful icons follow every narrative. You will also find driving directions from the nearest urban area ("Getting There"), planning tips ("Good to Know"), and a trail description ("The Walk").

Having fun at the Holzwarth Trout Lodge in Rocky Mountain National Park

DIFFICULTY RATINGS

We rated our hikes according to relative difficulty. These ratings are subjective. Actual difficulty will vary according to your fitness level and experience. Generally, easy hikes are short with well-defined paths and minimal elevation changes. Most of them are suitable for families with young children. Moderate hikes are longer and might have steep sections but are still suitable for active adults and older children. Difficult hikes have substantial elevation changes and are only recommended for experienced, physically fit hikers.

ICONS

The following icons provide useful information about each hike at a glance:

ruined or preserved homesteads, dwellings, or ranch structures

American Indian history or resources such as rock art, petroglyphs, or game trails

mines, mining structures, and related machinery

ruined dams, irrigation ditches, conduits, or reservoirs

fire lookout tower

historic buildings designed by 20th-century architects

railroad grades, tracks, rolling stock, or related structures and machinery

historic cemetery or gravesite

dinosaur tracks and/or fossils

remains of a stagecoach station and/or route

suitable for families with young children

mountain bikes allowed (see "Good to Know" sections for specific regulations)

dogs allowed (see "Good to Know" sections for specific regulations)

VISITING HISTORIC PLACES

The historic places described in this book, most of which are protected by state and federal law, should be treated with respect. Left alone, they will continue to bring visitors closer to the history they represent. For your safety and for their protection, do not enter historic buildings or structures unless they are open to the public for interpretation. Be especially wary of abandoned mining areas and equipment. Always stay on the trail and keep an eye on children and pets. Never touch Indian rock art (the impact of your touch and the oils in your hand can deteriorate them), and do not touch or remove historic artifacts. By leaving these resources as we find them, we can preserve their legacy for future generations.

And remember, any time you're hiking, please respect private property.

HIKING IN COLORADO

A note of caution on Colorado's altitude and weather: The lowest hikes in this book begin about a mile above sea level, many end above timberline (about 11,000 feet), and some go above 14,000 feet. Bring plenty of water, use sunscreen, and walk at a comfortable pace. Headaches and nausea are signs of altitude sickness. If you experience these symptoms, head back down the trail and drink more water.

Colorado's abundant sunshine and mild climate allow hiking all year long. Still, you should prepare for all weather conditions, even in the summer. Afternoon thunder and lightning storms can be dangerous, especially above timberline. And at Colorado's highest elevations it often snows in July.

Regional Map

CONTENTS

Right: *One of the historic mines at Waldorf*

Above: *Grand Lake during the annual summer regatta.*

Left: *Site of the Crags Mountain Resort ruins near Boulder*

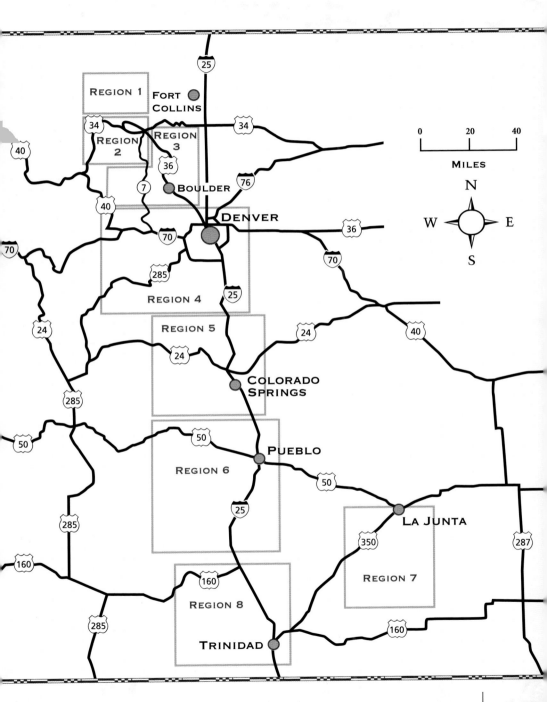

REGION 1
Fort Collins

The Pingree Valley Loop offers views of the Comanche Peak Wilderness and an up-close look at the Ramsey-Koenig Ranch.

Fur trader Antoine Janis (seated) with Oglala Indian leaders, circa 1877

CONTENTS

15

Montgomery Pass

CACHING IN ON THE POUDRE

In 1889, teenager Norman Fry traveled alone from London to Larimer County, Colorado, via one boat, three trains, and one full measure of fortitude. The trip took two weeks. He arrived a greenhorn, but a lifetime of demanding and rewarding labor on the Cache la Poudre River seasoned the Englishman into the region's savviest old-timer. As such, he might have been the best source for information on a decaying, remote, and little-known cabin in the Poudre Canyon—and the people who might have built and used it.

Upon his arrival in Fort Collins, Fry learned from new friends about the fur trappers who gave the Cache la Poudre its name. According to legend, a brigade of French-speaking mountain men stashed, or cached, barrels of gunpowder (*poudre*) in a riverbank sometime in the 1820s. True or not, the story reflected the real presence of French Canadians on the Poudre River in the early to mid-1800s. Working with American Indian wives who helped to scrape, tan, and soften beaver pelts for sale, men such as Antoine Janis trapped the entire Poudre watershed. After the market for beaver pelts disappeared, a few of the newcomers built cabins along the river and lived off the land.

Locals also gossiped about George Pingree, a former trapper who helped build the local railroad tie industry. In the 1870s, the Union Pacific needed timber for the portion of its transcontinental railroad that traveled through Wyoming. Several years before Fry came to the area, tie contractors Isaac Coe and Levi Carter hired Pingree to show them the way to the best timber country (for more on Pingree, see Hike 2). Once they settled on the upper Poudre, they built a road from present-day Rustic to Cameron Pass—part of the route of today's CO 14—to facilitate transportation. The river, clogged with logs being sent downstream, became known for a time as the Tie Highway. According to Fry, "the 'tie boys' had cabins and camps up every gulch along the Poudre, and their numbers must have run in the hundreds."

Fry arrived too late to participate in the tie-cutting frenzy, but he got there just in time to help establish the mining and ranching industries. He was one member of a small group of pioneers who homesteaded or purchased mountain meadows along the Poudre and the streams that feed into it. Too young and too green to claim a homestead in 1889, Fry worked for other families until he had gained enough experience to establish his own place. These years introduced him to people who became such fixtures on the territory that geographers named lakes, streams, and mountains after them.

John Zimmerman, a Swiss-born Minnesotan, settled his family in a location just below Cameron Pass in 1881, possibly near today's Zimmerman Lake and Montgomery Pass Trailheads. Finding winter too severe, he moved down the river and built a permanent home while searching for gold. He found it near present-day Rustic and then built a stamp mill to process the ore. Fry found work hauling lumber from

Zimmerman's homestead, which was near the mill site. The discovery caused a sensation in Fort Collins and prompted the local newspaper to declare, "Larimer County is destined to be the richest mining country in the state." For a while, would-be miners sank prospect holes all over the area, and a little town called Poudre City, complete with a saloon, hotel, and several cabins, sprang into being. But the high cost of transporting the low-grade ore to big-city smelters doomed the infant industry to failure.

In his autobiography, Fry claimed that in 1890 rancher C.B. Andrews owned "everything above the Zimmerman place," which would have included river valley property between Kinikinik and Cameron Pass, but the property probably consisted of a much smaller area. The fact remains that Andrews and subsequent ranchers in the area ran cattle in the high country surrounding the upper Poudre. It is possible that during the summer, cows grazed as far away from the home ranch as the big meadow east of Montgomery Pass. If so, cowboys might have constructed a line camp to store equipment and to shelter themselves from the alpine cold while tending the far-flung pasture.

Though Fry does not mention line camps in his book, he does explain how he helped build mountain cabins that resemble what the ruins on Montgomery Pass might have looked like. After cutting the "green and yellow pine" logs to size with an ax, he "used a tripod and one of the work mules on a block and tackle to pull the logs into place."

By 1899, Fry had learned enough from his assorted odd jobs. He "proved up" on a homestead in Sheep Creek Gulch—near the old Poudre City site—and went into the ranching business for himself. Those were busy years. "My cattle were increasing in numbers, and there seemed to be a lot to do," he wrote. "Fences to build, ditches to improve, a bridge to put across the river, and outside work to bring in a few dollars."

"I was able to get a contract to deliver beef to the men working up at Chambers Lake," he added, citing one such job. The reconstruction of the lake's washed-out dam exemplified water management in the Poudre River basin. Located 5 miles downstream from the Montgomery Pass Trailhead, Chambers Lake was named for a fur trapper who was killed by American Indians on its shore. Nine hundred years ago, an earthquake caused a landslide that backed up the area's streams. A ditch company enlarged the lake for irrigation purposes in 1887. Its dam promptly failed, sending a wall of water down the Poudre River that wrecked every bridge between the lake and Fort Collins. Crews have fixed and enlarged the dam five times since then. The completion of other water projects, including the Grand Ditch (see Hike 6), Skyline Ditch, Michigan Ditch, Joe Wright Reservoir, and the Laramie-Poudre Diversion Tunnel, make the Cache la Poudre the most heavily managed river in Colorado.

A hiker reaches 11,227-foot Montgomery Pass.

LOCATION:	Roosevelt National Forest and Colorado State Forest
DESCRIPTION:	This short, steep trail leads to the ruins of what was probably a rancher's line camp and continues above timberline to Montgomery Pass and alpine views.
DISTANCE:	3.6 miles, out and back
HIKING TIME:	2 hours
RATING:	Moderate
TRAILHEAD ELEVATION:	10,050 feet
MAXIMUM ELEVATION:	11,227 feet
MAP:	*Colorado Atlas & Gazetteer*, p. 18, D3
CONTACT:	Canyon Lakes Ranger District, (970) 295-6700, www.fs.fed.us/r2/arnf/

GETTING THERE:	From Fort Collins, take US 287 north past Laporte to Teds Place. Turn left (west) on CO 14 and go up the canyon 57.4 miles, almost to Cameron Pass. Stop at the Zimmerman Lake Trailhead parking lot on the left, just past Joe Wright Reservoir.
GOOD TO KNOW:	The Zimmerman Lake Trailhead parking lot has restrooms. The Montgomery Pass Trail is good for cross-country skiing, but cabin ruins might be buried in the snow.

We may never know who built the old ruined cabin near Montgomery Pass. Perhaps it's better that way. Today's hikers and history buffs recognize it for what it is: a symbol for all the people—trappers and their American Indian allies and enemies, tie boys, ranchers, homesteaders, and water project crews—that have shaped the upper Poudre River's history.

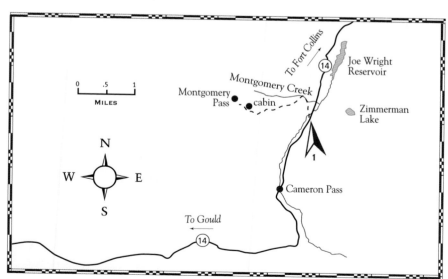

Barbed wire remnants on Montgomery Pass indicate the extent of high-country cattle grazing.

THE WALK

To find the trailhead, locate the Montgomery Pass sign on the north side of the Zimmerman Lake Trail parking lot. Carefully cross the highway and walk north along the road until you come to the trail.

Follow the trail north to Montgomery Creek, and then continue alongside it for a short distance. The trail diverges from the creek and becomes steep as it heads west up the mountain through dense Douglas fir and Engelmann spruce.

At about 1.3 miles, two blue diamond-shaped signs nailed high on a tree direct cross-country skiers southwest to the "bowls" and northwest to the pass. The site also marks the boundary between the Roosevelt National Forest and the Colorado State Forest. The cabin ruins are just north of the sign in a small clearing.

After investigating the ruins, continue on the main trail toward the pass. The trail becomes undefined as it goes above timberline. As you emerge from the forest, continue northward into the alpine meadow and look west for the Montgomery Pass sign. Remnants of barbed-wire fences indicate this meadow's use for cattle grazing.

The view from the pass is stunning. Brave the wind and climb a nearby mountain for an even better vantage point. Look northwest for a view of North Park, home to innumerable cattle and moose, and south for a view of Zimmerman Lake and the Never Summer Mountains.

Return by the same route.

Pingree Valley Loop to the Ramsey-Koenig Ranch

"LET ME LIVE BY THE SIDE OF THE ROAD..."

Late in life, Hazel Koenig told an interviewer that she enjoyed living in Pingree Park because of its isolation. She loved her mountains, the wildflowers, and the solitude that comes with life at 9,000 feet above sea level. But try as she might to keep the world at bay, civilization's problems eventually caught up to her and marked her life with tragedy.

Hazel's father, Hugh Ramsey, homesteaded Pingree Park in the mid-1890s. Attracted by the beauty of its open meadow, meandering stream, and surrounding snowy peaks, he and his brother filed on adjacent 160-acre parcels. Ramsey and his wife, Drusilla, made a living any way they could, but started out by harvesting trees that had been charred by a recent fire. Combining pioneer hardiness with an entrepreneurial spirit, Hugh hand-dug a mile-long irrigation ditch that routed water to his sawmill's waterwheel. He used the lumber for ranch buildings and sold the rest in the nearest town.

South Fork of the Cache la Poudre River, Pingree Park

Ramsey-Koenig barn on the Pingree Valley Loop

Ramsey's timber business followed a precedent set 25 years earlier by the valley's namesake. George W. Pingree settled near the town of Rustic in the late 1860s after serving briefly with Company H of the First Colorado U.S. Volunteer Cavalry. In 1868 and 1869, he operated a tie camp on the South Fork Cache la Poudre River in the Pingree Park area. Working with 30 to 40 other men, he cut and hauled ties for the Union Pacific Railroad. The men, who called each other "tie hacks," floated timber down the Poudre on the spring runoff to Laporte. Freighters hauled the ties in ox-drawn wagons overland to Tie Siding, Wyoming, for pickup by the UP construction crews.

The timing of Pingree's military service suggests, but does not prove, that he participated in the infamous Sand Creek Massacre. On November 29, 1864, Colonel John M. Chivington led the Third Colorado and elements of the First from Denver to the Eastern Plains north of present-day Lamar. He and his men, minus a few holdouts, attacked a peaceful village of Cheyenne and Arapaho people, killing and maiming more than 160 men, women, and children assembled under a white flag of surrender. Three weeks later, Lieutenant Joseph A. Cramer—who had refused to participate in the slaughter—wrote a letter to Major Edward Wynkoop revealing the atrocities committed by the cavalrymen. He indicted Chivington and listed the units that were present, including "parts" of Pingree's H Company. Larimer County historian Ansel Watrous, writing in 1911, flatly states that Pingree "was with Kit Carson for many years and during the Indian troubles of 1864–65 was with Col. John M. Chivington's command, participating in the battle of Sand Creek."

Misfortune of a less violent but equally heartrending kind touched Hazel and her family in the decades following settlement in Pingree Park. In 1907, a diphtheria outbreak reached their home, despite its seclusion. The bacterial disease, which mostly affected children under five and adults over 60, robbed Hugh of a son and

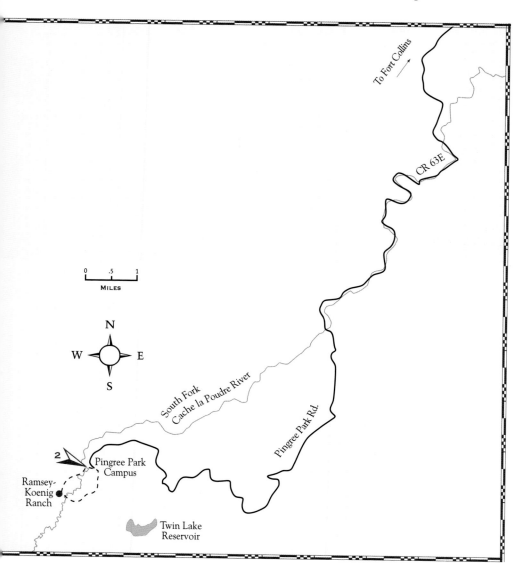

two young daughters before taking his wife. Just 11 years old, Hazel took over all of the domestic duties.

Six years later, Hazel married one of the men who helped her father construct Twin Lakes Reservoir (visible from the B-17 Bomber Crash Site Trail, see Hike 3). Like his father-in-law, Frank Koenig earned a living by becoming proficient at several trades. He ran cattle, kept chickens, sold milk, and rented cabins to tourists. After Rocky Mountain National Park opened in 1915, he became one of its first rangers.

Hazel Koenig

Tragedy struck Hazel and her family again in 1920. This time, whooping cough —a highly contagious disease that killed thousands of young people in 19th-century America—claimed Frank and Hazel's twin children. They buried Columbine and Dwayne in a private hillside cemetery behind their home. Five sculptures of white lambs mark the spot today.

In 1974, the Koenigs sold part of their Pingree Park homestead to Colorado State University. Students in the College of Natural Resources come to the park every summer for a four-week hands-on field session. The homestead, preserved in partnership with the Colorado Historical Society's State Historical Fund, reminds students and hikers alike of the hardships endured by the park's pioneers.

Today, visitors who peek inside the Koenigs' home will find a framed poem on the wall labeled "Sayings that Hazel liked." The first two stanzas of "House by the Side of the Road" by Sam Walter Foss read:

There are hermit souls that live withdrawn
In the peace of their self content
There are souls like stars that dwell apart
In a fellowless firmament

There are pioneer souls that blaze their paths
Where the highways never ran
But let me live by the side of the road
And be a friend to man.

Hazel claimed to enjoy her solitude, but the poem tells a different story. It is hard to imagine that the mountains and wildflowers, spectacular as they can be in this mountain paradise, could compensate for her losses.

LOCATION:	Pingree Park Campus, Colorado State University
DESCRIPTION:	The Pingree Park Loop, sometimes called the Valley Walk, leads hikers along the South Fork Cache la Poudre River and through Colorado State University's mountain campus to the historic Ramsey-Koenig Ranch.
DISTANCE:	2-mile loop
HIKING TIME:	1 hour
RATING:	Easy
TRAILHEAD ELEVATION:	9,065 feet
MAXIMUM ELEVATION:	9,065 feet
MAP:	*Colorado Atlas & Gazetteer*, p. 19, D6
CONTACT:	CSU's Pingree Park Campus, (970) 881-2150, www.pingree.colostate.edu/

GETTING THERE:	From Fort Collins, take CO 14 west up the Cache la Poudre Canyon to Pingree Park Rd. (CR 63E, mile marker 96), which is gravel but is well maintained. Turn left and follow it 16 miles to Pingree Park. Turn left at the entrance to Colorado State University's Pingree Park campus and stop at the nearby Stormy Peaks Trailhead parking area.
GOOD TO KNOW:	The trail traverses Colorado State University's Pingree Park Campus and Conference Center. Be courteous to the students and please respect their privacy and property. Restrooms and water might not be available on campus, depending on the time of year. Dogs are not allowed on campus.

THE WALK

Begin at the trailhead opposite the Stormy Peaks Trail parking lot. Hike south past the ropes course through a truncated forest of charred tree stumps burned in the 1994 Hourglass Fire to the right bank of the Poudre's south fork. Cross the stream on a long, winding wood bridge and continue south past a memorial to the crew of a B-17 bomber that crashed nearby during World War II (see Hike 3). Keep going past the softball field, recreation hall, and dining hall. After passing one more building, veer right and go around the west side of the South Dorm. The Ramsey-Koenig Ranch portion of the trail begins just south of the dorm.

Continue south to the Pingree Park Museum, which was the Koenigs' last home on the ranch. Peek inside if the door is unlocked, but do not disturb the artifacts on view. Just past the homestead is a trail leading west to the assay shed, carriage shed, and family cemetery where the Koenigs' twin children are buried.

Return to the main trail and go south to see the dugout, restored barn, schoolhouse, and other structures. After entering a meadow, turn left on a trail leading east across the stream. Follow it to the east side of the valley where it joins a dirt road near an oversize wooden bench that offers a view of damage caused by the Hourglass Fire on the opposite side of the valley. Continue north along the road, past several private cabins and back toward the ropes course and the Stormy Peaks Trail parking lot.

B-17 Bomber Crash Site

B-17 DOWN: TRAGEDY ON THE HOME FRONT

On October 18, 1943, at 10:45 p.m., Mrs. Albert Chandler saw an airplane flying low over her Larimer County ranch. Moments later she heard a "violent explosion." Sheriff Ray Barger took her report and issued a warning through the *Fort Collins Express-Courier* the following day. He announced that Lowry Field in Denver (later known as Lowry Air Force Base) had informed him that a B-17 bomber was missing and asked the public to stay off the roads so the Army could reach the crash site without fighting traffic. But traffic was the least of Sheriff Barger's concerns. Initial reports indicated that the plane had crashed "somewhere in or near the northeastern tip" of Rocky Mountain National Park with eight men on board. He knew that vehicles would be useless in the search area. The recovery team would have to fight through dense forests and deep snow on horseback up the sides of 11,000-foot peaks. The search began on October 20 at 5 a.m.

Nine years earlier, the U.S. Army Air Corps had drawn up a military aircraft wish list. Near the top were vague specifications for a long-range bomber capable of defending Alaska, the Panama Canal, or Hawaii from mainland bases. Boeing produced the four-engine B-299, later dubbed the B-17. With a 103-foot wingspan it was the largest military airplane of its time. Noting the massive aircraft's four blister-type machine gun turrets, journalists called it the "Flying Fortress."

At first, the plane didn't live up to its name. When World War II broke out, the United States sent 20 B-17s to its ally, Great Britain. Many of the planes that survived attacks from Luftwaffe fighters crashed on their own. Royal Air Force officers noted that the B-17's poorly positioned manual machine guns couldn't defend against attacks from the rear and sometimes froze up at high altitudes. American pilots encountered the same problem in the Pacific against Japanese Zeros. Boeing corrected the flaws by putting a turret in the tail and increasing the mobility and firepower of the remaining guns. The updated Fortress carried a crew of 10, weighed 54,000 pounds, and was armed to the teeth with turrets on the nose, tail, midsection, and canopy. By 1943, American generals could (and did) unleash waves of more than 200 B-17s upon German industrial targets and expect a very high percentage to return.

Battling wind and snow, Sheriff Barger and 20 men set out on horseback from John Derby's ranch in the Mummy Range while planes scouted the area from the air. Later, they learned that local ranchers Vernon Spencer and

B-17 landing gear and engine cowling

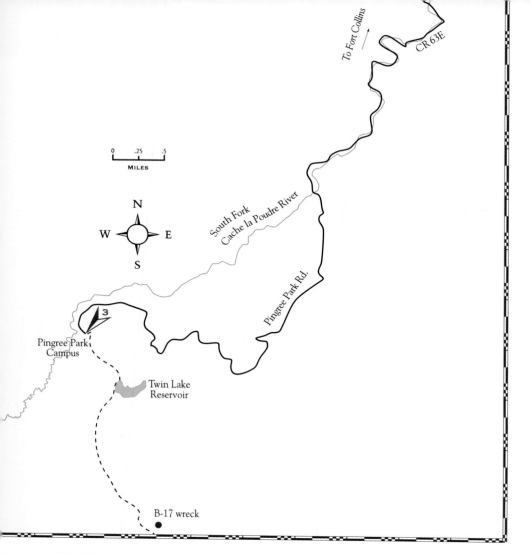

Chris Hyatt, who had set out ahead of the search party, had discovered wreckage and at least five bodies just below timberline near Stormy Peaks Mountain. Barger's team urged their horses to within a mile of the site and continued the rest of the way on foot.

While Barger, a few Lowry soldiers, and several volunteers located the flyers' bodies and carried them back to the horses, forest rangers Norman Griswold and Lynn Coffin controlled a 1.5-acre fire that had started when burning fuel had sprayed the forest's undergrowth and trees. They left the B-17's tail assembly, engines, and some melted parts in place. The *Express-Courier* described their work as "tedious and grim."

It took two days to remove all eight bodies and return them to Lowry Field. Newspapers failed to explain the accident's cause. Perhaps the plane lost its way in the storm. Maybe it succumbed to mechanical failure. Whatever happened, one thing is certain. Its crew died at the same time that U.S. soldiers were fighting and dying in Italy, Wake Island, and elsewhere. The wreckage near Stormy Peaks Mountain must be regarded as one more place where young men died in service to their country.

LOCATION:	Pingree Park and Comanche Peak Wilderness Area
DESCRIPTION:	This often steep, sometimes narrow trail gains almost 1,200 feet on its way to a World War II bomber's crash site.
DISTANCE:	5.8 miles, out and back
HIKING TIME:	4 to 5 hours
RATING:	Difficult
TRAILHEAD ELEVATION:	9,065 feet
MAXIMUM ELEVATION:	10,225 feet
MAP:	*Colorado Atlas & Gazetteer*, p. 19, D6
CONTACT:	Canyon Lakes Ranger District, (970) 295-6700, www.fs.fed.us/r2/arnf/
GETTING THERE:	From Fort Collins, take CO 14 west up the Cache la Poudre Canyon to Pingree Park Rd. (CR 63E, mile marker 96), which is gravel but is well maintained. Turn left and follow it for 16 miles to Pingree Park. Turn left at the entrance to Colorado State University's Pingree Park campus and stop at the nearby Stormy Peaks Trailhead parking area.
GOOD TO KNOW:	No facilities are available at the trailhead. Restrooms and water might be available at the Pingree Park Conference Center on campus, depending on the date. Special regulations protect the Comanche Peak Wilderness Area: No mechanical equipment is allowed, including bikes; no camping is allowed within 100 feet of lakes, streams, or trails; and dogs must be leashed at all times.

THE WALK

Begin at the Stormy Peaks Trailhead and hike 0.7 mile to the Twin Lakes Trail junction. Take the Twin Lakes Trail 0.2 mile to the reservoir. Go around the reservoir's west side, hopping several fallen trees as you go, and continue 0.6 mile south through a recently burned aspen forest to a fork in the trail (at this writing, an arrow made of large stones pointed out the correct path). Take the left fork and continue south up a steep hillside another 0.2 mile, pass three posts planted in the middle of the trail, and continue uphill another 0.2 mile to a sign marking the Comanche Peak Wilderness Area boundary. Go up the hill, paralleling an irrigation ditch. At the top of the hill follow the trail alongside the ditch. At a wooden sluice box (0.5 mile from the wilderness boundary), turn left and follow the narrow trail over a creek about 0.1 mile to a small clearing in the woods. Look for a side trail that leads south into the woods and up the mountainside (again, an arrow made of stones pointed the way). Follow this trail 0.3 mile to a large boulder field. Pieces of the bomber, including the tail section, engines, landing gear, and other parts, are scattered over the entire area.

Return by the same route.

Rocky Mountain National Park

The East Face of Longs Peak reflected in a tundra pool

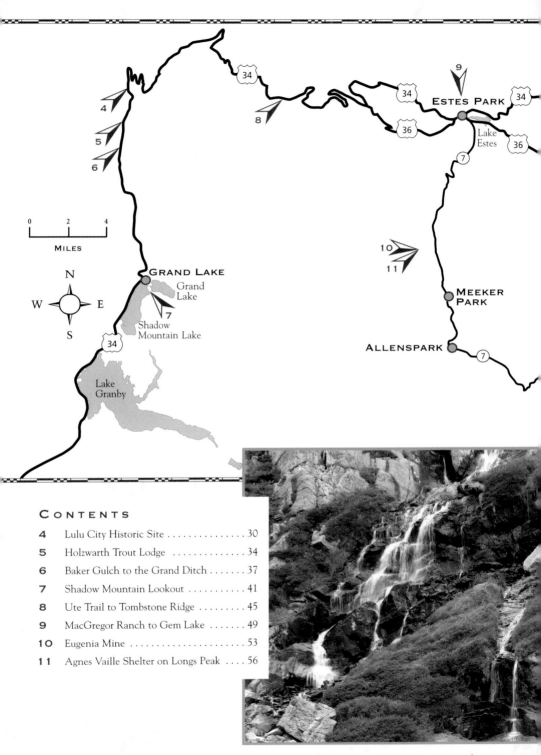

CONTENTS

Waterfalls by the Longs Peak Trail

Lulu City Historic Site

SHIPLER'S SEARCH

Joseph Shipler had a knack for finding things. In 1874, Fort Collins relocated a cemetery to make room for a new post office on the corner of College Avenue and Oak Street. Shipler, employed as a contractor and builder at the time, helped a crew locate six unmarked graves, disinter the remains, and transfer them to a new cemetery on the outskirts of town. The graves belonged to soldiers who had served at Camp Collins, the Army post established in 1865 to protect the Denver-to-Laramie stage route and emigrant trail from attack by American Indians and thieves. While digging up one of the graves, Shipler found a bottle containing a note identifying the deceased occupant. The unknown author wrote:

> I am really sorry to be pained with the duty of announcing the death of hospital steward, W.W. Westfall, which sad event transpired on the 8th day of November 1865 at the hour of 6:20 p.m. at this place. Poor Westfall took ill on the morning of the 3rd of November, '65 and after having suffered the most excruciating agony from typho-gastro-interic disease, died.

Lulu City in 1889, five years after its abandonment

Shipler Cabin ruins

By connecting a name with one of the unmarked graves, Joseph Shipler's discovery linked the cemetery to the town's infancy as a military post. It also restored honor to the hospital steward, who had died serving his fellow soldiers and his country.

After serving a term as Fort Collins's first town clerk, Shipler decided to put his talent for finding things to better use. On July 10, 1875, Alexander Campbell and James Bourn discovered silver near the headwaters of the Colorado River (called the Grand River at that time). Their Wolverine silver mine attracted the attention of other northern Colorado fortune seekers, including Shipler. By 1879, enough people had come to the area to warrant the establishment of a town.

Benjamin Franklin Burnett, one of the area's first prospectors, founded Lulu City in 1879. Most historical accounts say he named the town after his daughter. Shipler joined the rush, too, but chose to live south of Lulu, near his mines. He and three other men located claims, including the North Star, Southern Cross, and Tiger mines, on or near a peak now known as Mt. Shipler. They built a log cabin at the mountain's base and called it Camp Coon. After staking at least two more claims, the men built a second cabin and settled down to work.

Lulu City thrived on hope and boosterism. In 1880, one newspaper called the town a "coming metropolis...lively in prospects and prospectors." The town boasted a post office, stores, hotels, saloons, a red-light district, and, wrote Kenneth Jessen in *Ghost Towns: Colorado Style*, "a peak population of several hundred."

According to legend, that optimistic population figure included a grizzly bear named Three-Toed Jim. The bear had been raiding Lulu's greater metropolitan area for some time before residents took action. Someone shot the bear but it got away. On subsequent raids, the maimed animal left distinctive footprints: One of its paws was missing a toe. Luluites eventually ensnared him in a sturdy log trap baited with rotting meat. Today's hikers will find two deteriorating log structures at the Lulu City site. Careful observers may still find claw marks inside one of them.

Lulu City never lived up to its residents' expectations. Most of the miners had abandoned the place by 1884. Poor-quality ore, high transportation costs, and severe winter weather defeated all but a few intrepid diggers. Joe Shipler was one of them. In 1914, a Colorado Mountain Club group hiking the Kawuneeche Valley found the Lulu City area deserted except for "an old miner, Mr. Shipler, who had several mining claims in the region, and from whom the park as well as a mountain looking down upon it got its name."

Watch for inquisitive marmots among the rocks

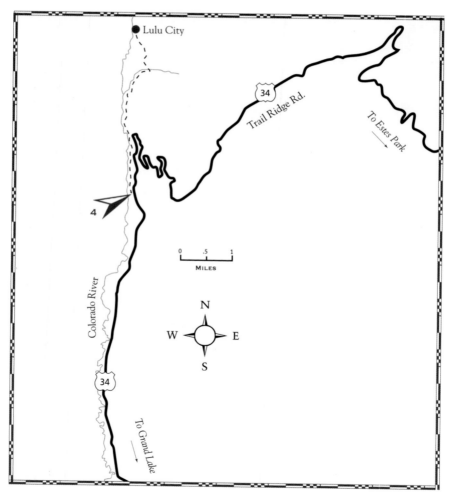

LOCATION:	Rocky Mountain National Park
DESCRIPTION:	This relatively level trail parallels the Colorado River near its source and leads through dense forest and occasional meadows to the site of Lulu City, a once-promising but long-abandoned mining town.
DISTANCE:	7.4 miles, out and back
HIKING TIME:	4 hours
RATING:	Moderate
TRAILHEAD ELEVATION:	9,000 feet
MAXIMUM ELEVATION:	9,600 feet
MAP:	*Colorado Atlas & Gazetteer,* p. 28, A4
CONTACT:	Rocky Mountain National Park, (970) 586-1206, www.nps.gov/romo/
GETTING THERE:	From Estes Park, take US 34 or US 36 to Rocky Mountain National Park and follow the signs to Trail Ridge Rd. (US 34 is Trail Ridge Rd. inside the park). Usually open from Memorial Day through mid-October, this scenic alpine byway connects Estes Park to the Kawuneeche Valley on the west. It ascends to a peak elevation of 12,183 feet and offers unparalleled views of glacier-carved mountains. Follow Trail Ridge Rd. for about 30 miles over the Continental Divide at Milner Pass to the Colorado River Trailhead. The parking lot is on the west side of the road.
GOOD TO KNOW:	Restrooms and several picnic tables are available at the trailhead. Dogs are not allowed on trails or in areas not accessible by automobile. Bikes are not allowed on the park's trails.

THE WALK

The Colorado River Trail leads north along its namesake waterway. Hundreds of miles downstream, the river carries rafters through the Grand Canyon, but here it trickles and meanders over sandbars and smooth stones. Social trails lead to its banks, while the official path goes up a slight rise and then levels out. At 0.5 mile the Red Mountain Trail branches left across the river to backcountry campsites. Continue north 1.8 miles to the two decaying Shipler cabins. You will pass several talus slopes on the way, one of which stands out because of its yellow color. Created by Joe Shipler and his fellow prospectors, this tailings pile came from one of several Mt. Shipler mines opened after 1879. Look for a side trail leading west about 10 yards to a rusted ore cart.

The trail gets steeper as it goes north past the cabins. At 3.2 miles it forks right to the Little Yellowstone Canyon. Take the left-hand trail down the hill 0.2 mile to the Lulu City site. Explore the area for stacked and rotting logs, which are all that remain of this once-ambitious "city."

Return by the same route.

Holzwarth Trout Lodge

MINING THE TOURISTS

It just made sense. With so many more tourists coming by automobile into Rocky Mountain National Park to learn how to hunt, fish, and ride horses, someone had to teach them—and someone had to put them up for the night and feed them. John Holzwarth had homesteaded near Grand Lake for 10 years in the 1880s and was back again, living off the land; he knew all the ropes of hunting, breaking horses, and pulling trout out of Grand County's streams. And Sophia Holzwarth's meals were known to please. With their three teenage children they had a ready supply of day labor to keep things running smoothly. The Holzwarth Trout Lodge was born.

The "Mama Cabin" at the Holzwarth Trout Lodge

John Holzwarth was 14 when he came to the United States from Germany. He worked at a bakery in St. Louis but was treated cruelly by his boss. He made his way to Denver, where he met Sophia, and they married in 1894. The couple ran a saloon together in Denver, but the onset of Prohibition in 1916 brought their venture to its knees.

So they started over. They moved to the Grand Lake area that John remembered so fondly, taking on a remote homestead of 160 acres in the Kawuneeche Valley alongside the north fork of the Grand River (today's Colorado River). With his teenage son Johnnie, Holzwarth built a sod-roofed cabin, nicknamed the "Mama Cabin" after Sophia "Mama" Holzwarth. Over the years they improved the one-room shelter and expanded it into a respectable house with the kind of kitchen Sophia could work her magic in. The Holzwarths started raising cattle, too, building a sawmill and a barn and reclaiming meadows from the beavers to grow hay for the cattle ranch they saw in their future. Then a serious haying accident left John "Papa" Holzwarth permanently unable to keep up the pace he had set for himself. He took up taxidermy and tried to get by, but something had to give.

This was 1919. By that time, mass-produced automobiles meant greater numbers of visitors coming into the country's national parks, until then the domain of those traveling on foot and on horseback. Fall River Road opened in 1920, joining Grand Lake and Estes Park and bringing curious auto drivers intrepidly rolling through the valley. The Holzwarths saw a ready clientele for a dude ranch. They decided to open up their spread as a trout lodge to capitalize on the discovery of the valley by the traveling world at large.

John and Johnnie Holzwarth built rental cabins to house their guests. The Holzwarths charged $2 a day for three meals and a horse, or $11 for a week's stay. Guests enjoyed Sophia's masterful feasts in the Mama Cabin as she served up venison, grouse, chicken, and, of course, trout, all cooked on the stove she had ordered from the Montgomery Ward catalog and supplemented with fresh-baked treats. John even had a still; this was during Prohibition, but he shrewdly registered his still with the government and thus could legally make enough for "personal" use. Given all these amenities, some guests stayed for a month.

By day, John and Johnnie Holzwarth took guests hunting and fishing. Select guests who were deemed skilled enough could even wander about at will on their rented horses. Young Johnnie made a second living as a trapper as the guest ranch gradually took shape, but soon the Holzwarths had all the business they had ever dreamed of. In 1929 they opened a larger, more modern lodge closer to the road. They christened the new lodge the Never Summer Ranch.

Fall River Road brought auto tourists into Rocky Mountain National Park, but Trail Ridge Road made it easy. Opening in 1933, that road extended Fall River Road's reach and brought unprecedented numbers of drivers into the park. But with newly opened opportunities for seeing such a greater swath of the park, a riverside trout lodge was less of an attraction. After John Holzwarth's death on Christmas Day, 1932, the Holzwarth family had scaled back its offerings—even Sophia's home-cooked meals. Still, the family kept the business going for decades thereafter. In 1973, no longer a young man by any stretch, Johnnie Holzwarth sold the ranch property to the Nature Conservancy in an effort to ensure its preservation. The national park bought the ranch from the conservancy a year later, with the promise that it would remain intact for visitors to appreciate.

The buildings of the Never Summer Ranch are long gone—removed amidst mid-century efforts to return the park to its "primitive" state. But the buildings of the trout lodge remain, including the Mama Cabin. The Mama is still stocked with furniture, china, linens, a stove, and the occasional deer-hoof gunrack and footstool to remind visitors that this was once the focal point of a cozy hunting and fishing lodge run by a family who knew how to seize a good opportunity in the valley they loved.

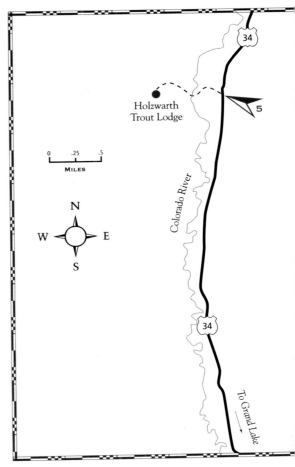

LOCATION:	Rocky Mountain National Park
DESCRIPTION:	An easy walk offers scenic wonders and a stroll into the past of a historic trout lodge.
DISTANCE:	1 mile, out and back
HIKING TIME:	1 hour
RATING:	Easy
TRAILHEAD ELEVATION:	8,900 feet
MAXIMUM ELEVATION:	8,920 feet
MAP:	*Colorado Atlas & Gazetteer*, p. 28, B4
CONTACT:	Rocky Mountain National Park, (970) 586-1206, www.nps.gov/romo/

GETTING THERE:	On US 34 (Trail Ridge Rd.), drive about 9 miles north of the Grand Lake Village turnoff to the sign for the Holzwarth Trout Lodge; turn left into the parking area.
GOOD TO KNOW:	The parking area is paved, and handicap-accessible parking is available. There are toilets and many shaded picnic tables. As with all Rocky Mountain National Park trails, no pets or bicycles are allowed on the trail. Pets on a leash are allowed along roadways and in the parking and picnic areas. At the trailhead is one of the oldest surviving buildings in the valley, the cabin of homesteader Joseph Fleshuts. Fleshuts built the cabin around 1902 and left the valley nine years later, never to return.

THE WALK

The trail to the Holzwarth Trout Lodge is an easy, wide pathway through a breathtaking meadow that lies at an elevation of about 9,000 feet along the base of the Never Summer Mountains. The meadow is a popular gathering place for elk, deer, and even moose. The trail crosses the Colorado River (at this point a stream), and markers all along the path discuss the human and natural history of the region.

A view from the trail to Holzwarth Trout Lodge

After a 0.5-mile stroll you'll walk into the woods and find the cabins, tent house, taxidermy shop, icehouse, and woodshed that made up this early 1900s trout lodge. During summer, rangers share the lodge's history and lead tours of the buildings, which are furnished and remarkably well preserved. An old laundry washtub, period clothes to wear, and a wooden horse for lassoing help kids and grown-ups all get a taste of early dude-ranch life.

Baker Gulch to the Grand Ditch

STEALING WATER FROM THE WEST

"Grand Ditch" might sound like an oxymoron, but the name honors one of the most ambitious efforts to coax water away from Colorado's Western Slope. The ditch is indeed grand in scale: This 14-mile artificial waterway stretches along the ridges of the Never Summer Mountains, offering picturesque views of the valley below and the peaks of Rocky Mountain National Park beyond. Gouged out of the mountainsides before and after the 1915 creation of the national park and visible from great distances, the horizontal band of the Grand Ditch carries western snowmelt across the Continental Divide toward the thirsty farms and communities of Colorado's Front Range.

After traversing their stretch of the Never Summers, the waters of the Grand Ditch ultimately flow down into the Cache la Poudre River and from there to Fort Collins, Greeley, and beyond. First called the Grand River Ditch because it took (some would say stole) its water from the Western Slope's Grand River, its name was tightened to Grand Ditch after that river was renamed the Colorado.

Sensing an opportunity to capture the snowmelt of the high peaks and send it down to Larimer County's farms, the Larimer County Ditch Company incorporated in 1881 to do the job. Work crews wielded shovels, picks, and wheelbarrows, and the company established "ditch camps" for its workers along the way. Crews of Japanese joined the fray, willing to perform such backbreaking, high-altitude work given the opportunity to literally carve out new lives for themselves in the West. The gangs dug a series of canals to shift the runoff of melting snows toward La Poudre Pass (in

the northwest corner of today's Rocky Mountain National Park) and into the eastward-flowing Long Draw Creek, which then emptied into the Poudre.

In 1890 the first of the diverted water flowed eastward across the pass. After that, workmen extended the ditch bit by gouged-out bit. With each new section, a little more water coursed down to the plains. In the

The Grand Ditch

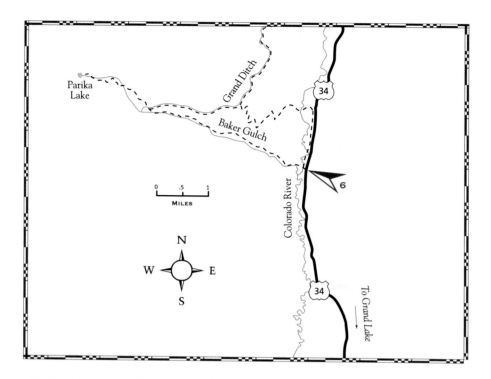

1890s, with Eastern Plains farms and communities booming in every direction, more and more water was critical to sustain that growth. For more than 15 years, beginning in 1894, the crews carved out a new section of the ditch with every summer season.

After 1911, with the ditch well beyond the remains of Lulu City (see Hike 4) and with many creeks now feeding into the waterway, workers simply maintained what had already been dug and only occasionally extended the ditch. Still, it crept ever southward. A right-of-way agreement allowed the company to continue building it even after the 1915 creation of the national park. In 1936, at Baker Creek, the last crews completed the southernmost stretch of the canal, 14.3 miles south of the spot where other crews had begun 55 years earlier. By this time, machinery could sometimes take over where shovels and picks left off.

Through the decades, the crews digging the ditch simply tossed the dirt and loose talus over the side, giving the canal its scarlike profile as it traverses the Never Summers. The ditch was grand in ambition and brash in its execution. But water-diversion projects like the Grand Ditch—projects that often led to scarring, erosion, and landslides—can take some of the credit for helping convince Rocky Mountain National Park's stewards and others to seek alternative means of getting farmers the water they needed to survive. After all, as they watched the ditch snake its way south, they saw the transformation of a landscape.

LOCATION:	Rocky Mountain National Park and Never Summer Wilderness
DESCRIPTION:	A steep wilderness hike takes you up a scenic gulch to one of the most ambitious water-diversion projects in the West's history.
DISTANCE:	8 miles, out and back (to the Big Baker Creek waterfall)
HIKING TIME:	5 hours
RATING:	Moderate to difficult
TRAILHEAD ELEVATION:	8,900 feet
MAXIMUM ELEVATION:	10,320 feet
MAP:	*Colorado Atlas & Gazetteer*, p. 28, B4
CONTACT:	Rocky Mountain National Park, (970) 586-1206, www.nps.gov/romo/

GETTING THERE:	On US 34 (Trail Ridge Rd.), go 8 miles north of the Grand Lake Village turnoff to the sign for the Bowen-Baker Trailheads; turn left into the parking area.
GOOD TO KNOW:	The parking area is paved, and handicap-accessible parking is available. The area offers toilets, many shaded picnic tables, and a few cooking grills. Just off the parking area and along the edge of a huge meadow is a beautiful fishing stream with brook and brown trout. Fishing is permitted with a license.

No bicycles are allowed on the trail, but horses are. Dogs must be under voice control or leashed at all times. Camping and campfires are permitted more than 100 feet from lakes, streams, and trails. No camping is permitted within 0.5 mile of Parika Lake.

From the trailhead, you can see the long horizontal scar of the Grand Ditch as it traverses Baker Mountain and Mounts Stratus, Nimbus, and Cumulus, from south to north. Although the bulk of the hike lies within the Never Summer Wilderness, the trailhead is in Rocky Mountain National Park. This lovely and mountainous southwestern section of the park sees much less traffic than the more spectacularly rugged terrain of the eastern section, closer to Estes Park.

THE WALK

From the trailhead, it's about 3.5 miles to the Grand Ditch. Leaving the trailhead, cross the stream and go right (west) to continue on the Baker Gulch Trail. After crossing a sprawling meadow favored by elk, moose, and deer, follow the signs to stay on the Baker Gulch Trail. At 0.5 mile, a gate marks the beginning of the Arapaho National Forest and the Never Summer Wilderness.

Here the hike gets steadily steeper. The trail traces a stream upward as the stream meanders down Baker Gulch from tiny Parika Lake, which lies at the end of the trail. Nice campsites are tucked into the forest along the way. You'll pass several waterfalls,

A strenuous hike up Baker Gulch rewards you with expansive views of Rocky Mountain National Park.

plus a colorful summertime profusion of paintbrush, columbine, daisy, and harebell. The trail becomes steeper as you near its junction with the Grand Ditch. After a particularly steep stretch and a series of switchbacks, you arrive at the canal. Note the little triangular trail marker, saying simply "trail" and pointing back down the way that you came.

A four-wheel-drive service road (closed to the public) parallels the canal. If you follow the road and canal to your left for about 0.5 mile, the road dead-ends and you'll find the waterfall along Big Baker Creek that feeds into the canal and marks the beginning of the ditch's waters. Here, in 1936, workers completed the final section of the Grand Ditch. From west to east, Big, Middle, and Little Baker Creek all feed into the waterway. A trickle at first, the canal picks up in flow as each creek feeds into it, creating a substantial stream of crystal clear, wildflower-lined water. At the Big Baker Creek waterfall, a spillway, some timbers, and other pieces of evidence remain of the final water-engineering works along the ditch. On this 0.5-mile stretch, you'll also find a few shady campsites among the trees to the left of the roadway.

At this point, you have three options: Get back on the Baker Gulch Trail and continue uphill about 1.5 miles farther to Parika Lake at the trail's end; follow the Grand Ditch to your right for about 2 miles to the four-wheel-drive road (the continuation of Grand Ditch Rd.) that steeply switchbacks down to the Holzwarth Trout Lodge (see Hike 5) and then walk approximately 1 mile south along Trail Ridge Rd. back to your car; or simply follow the Grand Ditch to your right for as long as you please before turning back and heading down the way you came.

Shadow Mountain Lookout

WATCHING OVER A LAKESIDE EMPIRE

The largest natural lake in Colorado, Grand Lake has a long history as one of the state's most prized resort spots. Big, rustic lodges attest to the lake community's earliest tourism booms, and million-dollar summer homes (some of them as old as those lodges) ring the shoreline. But even as early as 10,000 years ago, the lake was already a seasonal haven for travelers. Ute Indians used the lake and the surrounding forests and mountains as summer fishing and hunting grounds, no doubt basking in the region's natural beauty just as people do today. The Cheyenne and Arapaho also passed through the area, a fact that led to conflict over this treasured destination.

Legend holds that a battle between the Ute and Arapaho led to one of the lake's former names. While camped at the lake, the Ute were attacked by a band of Arapaho. The Ute women and children took refuge on a wooden raft, rowing to the center of the lake for safety. But a sudden storm capsized the raft, drowning all on board. The remaining Ute tribespeople, believing the lake to be haunted by the spirits of those who were killed that day, never returned to the shores of the watery tomb, which they referred to as "Spirit Lake."

With the arrival of settlers and prospectors, the lake again drew people to its shores. Judge Joseph L. Wescott came in 1867 and built a cabin in the lee of Shadow Mountain. He homesteaded, trapped, and fished, catching dozens of trout at a time to sell to area hotels or trade for supplies. Others joined Wescott at his hunting and fishing paradise, building homes and setting up shop along the same stretch of shore at the west side of the lake. Grand Lake City was the result—with cabins, larger homes, and mercantiles such as Mrs. Dickenson's Grocery dotting the newly dubbed Main Street, bisected by First and Second Streets. By the 1880s, after heated battles and much to Judge Wescott's disgust, the rapidly growing town opted to expand along the opposite shore of the lake, where a new main thoroughfare, Grand Avenue, was established along the shoreline.

The Grand Lake Yacht Club was organized in 1902, with the "yachts" at first consisting of rudimentary boats with makeshift sails. (The

Once an important fire tower, the Shadow Mountain Lookout today offers hikers fine panoramic views.

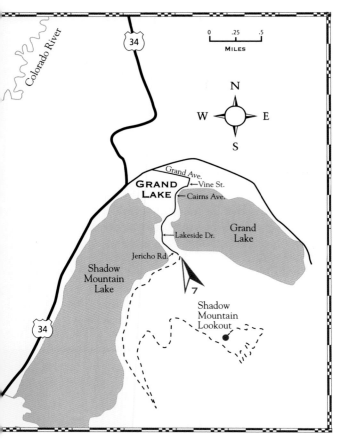

prestigious club is still going strong, holding an annual regatta every August.) With the establishment of Rocky Mountain National Park in 1915, a new generation of auto tourists also discovered the area around Grand Lake.

The 1930s and 1940s brought the Colorado–Big Thompson Project, a massive water-diversion effort that sent the water of the Colorado River drainage eastward through the Continental Divide to the communities and farms of the Front Range. The project also created the shallow reservoir of Shadow Mountain Lake, connected to Grand Lake via a channel cut near the location where Judge Wescott's cabin once stood. The project also created the massive water-storage reservoir of Lake Granby, and thus was born a water-sports mecca along a network of three lakes.

Completed in June 1933 at an elevation of 9,923 feet, the Shadow Mountain Lookout was the last of four fire lookout towers built in Rocky Mountain National Park. The three-year process of establishing a lookout on this remote perch overlooking Grand Lake began in 1930 with the construction of a "fire trail" that climbed up Shadow Mountain. Workers strung 3.5 miles of emergency phone lines from the Grand Lake Ranger Station up to the lookout site.

It was a challenge hauling the building materials to the site of the proposed lookout, no flimsy tower. The Shadow Mountain Lookout's design called for two full stories of rubble stone masonry topped by the observatory, to be surrounded by a balcony built of logs. In a 1938 National Park Service tome on examples of rustic park architecture, Albert H. Good compliments the lookout for its unusually pleasing proportions for a fire tower, crowing that it shows "the happy results where a masonry structure can appear to grow out of a natural rock outcrop." Getting those hefty materials up the trail to the building site required that most reliable of Colorado mountain workers: the mule. Workmen, no doubt glad to have paying jobs in the Great Depression year of 1932, toiled all that year and into the following spring to complete the tower.

Staffed from 1933 through 1968 by seasonal fire rangers who lived inside the tower, Shadow Mountain Lookout's strategic perch offered an unrivaled panorama encompassing hundreds of square miles of forest in every direction. Today's hikers enjoy the full benefit of that panorama, which affords views of Grand Lake, Shadow Mountain Lake, and Lake Granby; the Continental Divide; the peaks and meadows of Rocky Mountain National Park (including the long horizontal band of the Grand Ditch—see Hike 6); and the mountains that flank the park, including the Indian Peaks, Gore, and Vasquez Ranges. The lookout was staffed again during the fire seasons of the early 1990s and was restored in 1992. Sporting a solar panel and serving as an emergency ranger cabin, today the Shadow Mountain Lookout is listed in the National Register of Historic Places.

LOCATION:	Rocky Mountain National Park at Grand Lake
DESCRIPTION:	A gorgeous walk tops out at the last fire tower built in Rocky Mountain National Park.
DISTANCE:	9.6 miles, out and back
HIKING TIME:	5 hours
RATING:	Moderate
TRAILHEAD ELEVATION:	8,400 feet
MAXIMUM ELEVATION:	9,923 feet
MAP:	*Colorado Atlas & Gazetteer*, p. 28, C4
CONTACT:	Sulphur Ranger District and Granby Forest Service, (970) 887-4100; Rocky Mountain National Park, (970) 586-1206, www.nps.gov/romo/; for camping information, call the Arapaho National Recreation Area office, (970) 627-8272, www.fs.fed.us/r2/arnf/recreation/anra/.
GETTING THERE:	From Grand Ave. in the town of Grand Lake, take Vine St. south to Lake Ave., then immediately bear left at the fork onto Cairns Ave. Follow Cairns for about 0.5 mile as it curves south and then west. Turn left (south) on Lakeside Dr. and go over the bridge. (A plaque at the north end of the bridge marks the site of Judge Wescott's cabin, the first home at Grand Lake City.) Just past the bridge, Lakeside Dr. passes CR 695 on the left. To get to the trailhead, stay on Lakeside another 0.25 mile to Jericho Rd. Follow Jericho for a short distance along Shadow Mountain Lake until it ends at the parking area for the East Shore Trailhead.
GOOD TO KNOW:	There are no facilities at the East Shore Trailhead. The trail is a designated National Scenic Trail in the Continental Divide Trail system. By the time you join the Lookout Trail you are within the boundaries of Rocky Mountain National Park, but no fee is required to hike into the park from here. No motorized vehicles or pets are allowed and no bicycles are allowed on park trails or in the backcountry. A backcountry permit is required for fires or camping (there is no camping along the East Shore Trail). Fishing is permitted with a license.

On your way to the trailhead you will pass CR 695, the old Main St. Here, and along First St. and Second St., you'll find many of Grand Lake's original cabins and its first general store. The dock and all of the buildings are now privately owned, so be sure to respect private property and stay on the roadways.

THE WALK

Your hike begins on the East Shore Trail—an easy, level walk through pine and aspen woods along the shore of Shadow Mountain Lake. After about 1 mile, turn left at the Lookout Trail junction. You are now in Rocky Mountain National Park. Watch for deer, geese, and osprey, the latter of which also live in a protected nesting habitat along the East Shore Trail. This is mountain lion habitat, too. The area is home to a profusion of wildflowers and mushrooms.

The Lookout Trail is a narrower and steeper trail, tracing a few ridges up Shadow Mountain with a series of moderate switchbacks. From the junction of the East Shore Trail and the Lookout Trail, it is 3.3 miles to the Shadow Mountain Lookout, according to the sign (although the Trails Illustrated map of this area puts the distance at 3.8 miles).

At the summit of the trail stands the rustic stone structure of the Shadow Mountain Lookout. Just south of the tower and down the hill a bit, a dilapidated privy, with separate stalls for men and women, and the remnants of a log and plank structure remain from the lookout's heyday. You may walk up the two flights of sturdy log stairs to the observation balcony, but the interior is always locked and off-limits. The top of the tower offers a commanding view of Grand Lake, Shadow Mountain Lake, and Lake Granby, with Rocky Mountain National Park beyond.

Hike back down the way you came.

Grand Lake's old Main St. (CR 695) ends at a picturesque stretch of lakeshore.

Ute Trail to Tombstone Ridge

GRISWOLD'S LAST HILL

Gun Griswold, like many Northern Arapaho Indians of his time, believed that people journey through four stages, or "hills," of life: childhood, youth, adulthood, and old age. Each stage, like a season of the year, comes with its own set of responsibilities and trials. Griswold, as a 73-year-old tribal elder living on Wyoming's Wind River Reservation in 1914, thought he had climbed all of his hills. But when Coloradans Harriet Vaille and Edna Hendrie asked him to return to the mountains of his youth for an important job, he accepted one last challenge.

Arapaho Indians Sherman Sage and Gun Griswold with Tom Crispin

Vaille and Hendrie were members of the Colorado Mountain Club, an organization advocating the establishment of Rocky Mountain National Park. The club's president, James Grafton Rogers, had just reviewed a map of the proposed park and had been appalled by the lack of names assigned to its features. USGS geographer Robert Marshall recommended adding names to the unidentified places to increase the park's cultural cachet and chances for congressional approval. Harriet Vaille led a nomenclature committee that decided to draw inspiration from the American Indian groups, including the Arapaho, Ute, and Apache, that had lived in the region before the settlement of white people on their high-plains and mountain homelands forced them onto reservations beyond Colorado's borders (the Southern and Ute Mountain Utes retained small reservations inside of Colorado).

Gun Griswold, his 63-year-old friend Sherman Sage, and a half-Arapaho, half-white interpreter named Tom Crispin agreed to help the Colorado Mountain Club. Escorted by Vaille and Hendrie, the Indians arrived in Longmont by train on July 14, 1914. There they met Vaille's cousin Oliver Toll, who had

The Ute Trail with a distant view of Longs Peak

volunteered to record the Indian names; Shep Husted, their guide; and David Robert Hawkins, a Princeton student. The six men drove to Estes Park, exchanged their automobiles for horses, and set out on a two-week trip through today's Rocky Mountain National Park to Grand Lake.

The party started out from Longs Peak Inn and headed west to Mary's Lake. "What do you remember about this place?" Toll asked along the way. Crispin translated the question into Arapaho for Sage and Griswold. The two aged Indians answered in their musical language, speaking, according to Toll, "in a kind of chant with a hitching sort of rhythm which makes it, in its way, exceptionally beautiful."

After two days on the trail they ascended Windy Gulch to Trail Ridge. According to Toll's report, they crossed Trail Ridge via today's Ute Trail on July 19, "getting many names of mountains." In Griswold's youth, this was a well-traveled path connecting summer and winter hunting grounds.

Continually forced westward from their ancestral lands between the Atlantic Ocean and the Great Lakes, the Arapaho people settled on the northern plains west of the Missouri River in the early 1700s. They acquired horses in about 1730, either through trade with other tribes or by raiding their enemies. Horses enhanced their ability to hunt bison, an animal that increased their economic power by giving them everything they needed for day-to-day living, as well as trade items that bought squash and beans from agricultural tribes living on the upper Missouri. Further pressure from their enemies pushed them onto the plains of Colorado in the early 1800s.

Before Oregon-bound emigrants blazed a trail across the plains and before the Pikes Peak gold rush brought white prospectors, ranchers, farmers, and town builders to Colorado in 1859, the Arapaho hunted bison in the land between the Platte and Arkansas Rivers. Allied with their former Cheyenne enemies, they successfully defended this territory from Kiowa and Comanche incursions from the south and Sioux invasion from the north. Oftentimes, they traveled west into the Rocky Mountains for game, lodgepoles, and other necessities. Battles with the mountain-dwelling Ute Indians were common. That was the Colorado of Gun Griswold's youth.

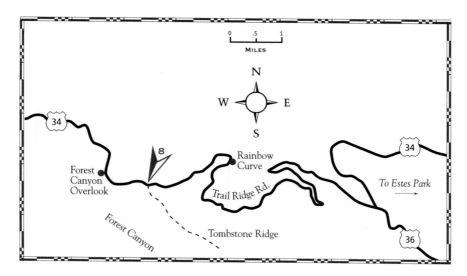

In the mid-1800s, white emigration along the Platte River and settlement along the Front Range in Denver and elsewhere separated the plains bison herds, as well as the entire Arapaho nation, into two parts. The Northern Arapaho moved north to Wyoming and Montana, while the Southern Arapaho stayed southeast of Denver with the Southern Cheyenne. The northern tribe avoided the tragedy of the 1864 Sand Creek Massacre, when Colonel John Chivington's Colorado Volunteers attacked a

Peaks bordering Forest Canyon, from the Ute Trail

peaceful Cheyenne and Arapaho village, killing at least 160 men, women, and children (see Hike 2). But they could not avoid the resulting conflicts with the United States, nor the smallpox and cholera epidemics, nor Griswold's people's ultimate removal and resettlement on a reservation. That was the Colorado he remembered from most of his adult life.

Now, as an old man, Griswold found himself on another kind of reservation, one that the white men were planning to set aside from and for themselves. His back ached as he rode this last hill of his life, giving names to places that had been taken from his people and from the Indian enemies of his people. Griswold called Longs Peak and Mt. Meeker *nesotaieux*, or the Twin Guides. Hallett Peak was *banah ah-netaieux*, or Thunder Peak. Above timberline west of Windy Gulch, the party rode past the lumpy rocks known today as Tombstone Ridge. Griswold called this route *taieonbaa*, or the Child's Trail, because its slopes were so steep that, for safety, children had to dismount their horses and walk.

On the return trip from Grand Lake to Estes Park, Griswold himself dismounted on Flat Top Trail, sat down by a rock, and told his friends that he was an old man, the trip was too hard for him, and he wanted to be left right there. They understood, but took him home instead.

Congress voted to create Rocky Mountain National Park the following year. Geographers adopted many of the names Griswold and Sage supplied while discarding others. Griswold probably didn't mind; the journey itself was more important.

LOCATION:	Rocky Mountain National Park, Trail Ridge Rd.
DESCRIPTION:	This trail traces a section of the route that Ute and Arapaho Indians traveled between their summer and winter hunting grounds. In 1914, an expedition of Arapaho elders and their companions traveled this way while naming geological features in the future Rocky Mountain National Park.
DISTANCE:	5 miles, out and back
HIKING TIME:	3 hours
RATING:	Moderate (because of elevation)
TRAILHEAD ELEVATION:	11,500 feet
MAXIMUM ELEVATION:	11,500 feet
MAP:	*Colorado Atlas & Gazetteer,* p. 29, A5
CONTACT:	Rocky Mountain National Park, (970) 586-1206, www.nps.gov/romo/

GETTING THERE:	From Estes Park take US 34 or US 36 to Rocky Mountain National Park and follow the signs to Trail Ridge Rd. (US 34 is Trail Ridge Rd. inside the park). This scenic alpine byway connects Estes Park to the Kawuneeche Valley on the west. It ascends to a peak elevation of 12,183 feet and offers unparalleled views of glacier-carved mountains. Follow Trail Ridge Rd. past Rainbow Curve, which has a scenic overlook and restrooms, and continue to a pullout on the south side of the road. If you get to the Forest Canyon Overlook, you've gone too far.
GOOD TO KNOW:	Trail Ridge Rd. is usually open from Memorial Day through mid-October. Call ahead for road conditions. Prevent altitude sickness by drinking plenty of water and going slowly. Bring extra layers of clothing, as Trail Ridge is usually windy and cold. Dogs are not allowed on trails inside the park. There are no facilities at the trailhead, but restrooms are available at scenic overlooks east and west of the pullout on Trail Ridge Rd. Stay on the trail to protect the fragile tundra—it takes some alpine plants 100 years to grow an inch—and keep children away from the steep drop-offs.

THE WALK

From the Trail Ridge Rd. pullout, hike southeast up a short rise. As the trail levels out, continue across the tundra past upright rock formations on your left. These distinctive features gave Tombstone Ridge its name. The Continental Divide, conspicuous with several peaks towering above 12,000 feet in elevation, is across Forest Canyon to the south. The Big Thompson River gets its start near here below Forest Canyon Pass. Keep going southeast in the general direction of Longs Peak until the trail descends into Windy Gulch at Timberline Pass. Turn around here or extend the hike by going farther into the gulch.

MacGregor Ranch to Gem Lake

"A Veritable Eden"

In 1877, the Union Pacific Railroad hired journalist Robert Strahorn to travel throughout the West and publicize its potential wealth and natural wonders to would-be settlers and future tourists. Strahorn took the dream job, but insisted on bringing his wife, Carrie, along for the adventure. During the next several years, the couple explored every backroad, byway, and boomtown in Colorado and seven other Western states and territories. Carrie's account of the extended journey, published in book form as *Fifteen Thousand Miles by Stage*, provides a unique personal glimpse of Estes Park's MacGregor Ranch in 1878.

"I have endeavored to give a picture of the Old West," Carrie wrote in her book's introduction, "to tell of the efforts which a Westward marching population made to establish

MacGregor Ranch and Longs Peak seen from the Gem Lake Trail

homes on the border line of civilization and beyond, enduring hardships and privations with the courage of heroes." Alex MacGregor and his wife, Clara, were two such heroes.

Alex MacGregor deserves much of the credit for establishing Estes Park as a haven for tourists. When he claimed his 160-acre homestead on Black Canyon Creek in 1873, the area was not much more than a scenic cow pasture owned by a few reclusive homesteaders and a British aristocrat who wanted to turn the entire valley into a private game preserve. Coloradans knew about the park's abundant wildlife and singular beauty, but unreliable roads kept them away. Alex solved the problem by building a first-class tollway—capitalized by his mother-in-law—between Lyons and Estes Park in 1875. As visitors and homesteaders populated the once-remote area, the Earl of Dunraven gave up his hunting preserve idea and instead built what might have been Colorado's first resort hotel.

After completing the road, Alex enlarged his homestead into a 1,200-acre ranch, built a sawmill to supply lumber for the growing town, and opened a post office and general store. Clara served as the valley's first postmistress, managed the store, helped operate the ranch, and nursed a newborn boy into toddlerhood. In her spare time, she painted landscapes that elicited much praise from tourists who camped on her property in the summer.

Carrie Strahorn was one of those tourists. "We moved along the zigzag road from summit to summit," she wrote, describing a stagecoach trip along Alex's tollway in 1878, "thinking always that the next pinnacle would fairly afford a view of eternity itself, and it was a surprise to look down into a valley for our destination." She called Estes Park "a veritable Eden" sprinkled with ranch homes guarded by Longs Peak. "The crack of the whip sent the tired horses galloping down…to MacGregor ranch, where there were many people on pleasure bent, some in tents or small cottages, and some in the main home building."

The author heaped praise upon the valley but saved some flattering prose for Clara's paintings, too. "Mrs. MacGregor was an artist possessing rare merit," she gushed. "Her decorative work around the house proved her ability with the brush."

Clara developed that ability as a student at the Chicago Academy of Design in 1871. While working under the guidance of renowned landscape painter Henry

Crawford Ford, she became interested in the Western frontier. An 1872 sketching trip took her to Colorado's South Park, where she met Alex. Their shared adoration for the mountains turned into a love affair that lasted a lifetime.

The couple passed on their affection for the property to their children and grandchildren. After Alex died from a lightning strike in 1896, his son Donald took over the operation. Donald expanded the ranch to 3,000 acres and maintained its cabins and outbuildings until 1950. His daughter Muriel continued the legacy of stewardship on her own until her death in 1970. Having no heirs, Muriel left the ranch to a charitable trust. After a 13-year struggle to save the property from development, the trust sold a conservation easement to Rocky Mountain National Park. Today, the Muriel MacGregor Trust operates the ranch as a living history museum. Its cattle herd, horses, chickens, and other animals recall the region's agricultural past, while its still-splendid wilderness, which is accessible to the public by way of the Twin Owls and Gem Lake Trails, remind today's hikers of Carrie Strahorn's veritable Eden.

Gem Lake

LOCATION:	Rocky Mountain National Park, MacGregor Ranch
DESCRIPTION:	This hike skirts the bottom of the Twin Owls rock formation; offers fantastic views of MacGregor Ranch, Estes Park, and 14,259-foot Longs Peak; and ends at Gem Lake.
DISTANCE:	3.6 miles, out and back
HIKING TIME:	3 hours
RATING:	Moderate, with steep sections
TRAILHEAD ELEVATION:	7,750 feet
MAXIMUM ELEVATION:	8,900 feet
MAP:	*Colorado Atlas & Gazetteer*, p. 29, A6
CONTACT:	Rocky Mountain National Park, (970) 586-1206, www.nps.gov/romo/; MacGregor Ranch, (970) 586-3749, www.macgregorranch.org/

GETTING THERE:	At the junction of US 34 and US 36 in Estes Park, take the US 34 Bypass (Wonderview Ave.) north to MacGregor Ave. Turn right and go 0.6 mile to the MacGregor Ranch entrance (at the intersection with Devil's Gulch Rd.). To visit the ranch before going on the hike, turn right at the fork that's marked "MacGregor Ranch Entrance." Or continue 0.5 mile to the Twin Owls/Gem Lake Trailhead. Be aware that the small parking lot fills up early.
GOOD TO KNOW:	MacGregor Ranch hours are 10 a.m. to 4 p.m., Tuesday through Friday, June through August. Museum admission is charged. Day hikers do not need to pay Rocky Mountain National Park entrance fees at this location. Dogs and bikes are not allowed on the trail. Camping is allowed inside the park; call (970) 586-1242 to obtain a backcountry camping permit. Restrooms are available at the trailhead and at Gem Lake.

While you are in the area, go see the Knoll-Willows Preserve in Estes Park. Nestled within earshot of busy downtown shops, the 20-acre getaway features a short creekside trail that bisects an elk calving area on its way to the remains of *Denver Post* reporter and event promoter Albert Birch's stone cabin. Perched atop a hill overlooking downtown Estes Park, the ruins form a picturesque foreground to views of Rocky Mountain National Park's highest peaks. To get there, turn left into a gravel parking lot directly across the road from the Stanley Hotel.

The Stanley, best known for its architecture and association with Stephen King's book and movie *The Shining*, offers daily history and ghost tours. Call ahead, (970) 577-4110, to make reservations.

As of this writing, Rocky Mountain National Park was planning to move the Twin Owls/Gem Lake Trailhead off MacGregor Ranch, just up Devil's Gulch Rd. Call ahead for information. The ranch may still be accessible from the Twin Owls Trail.

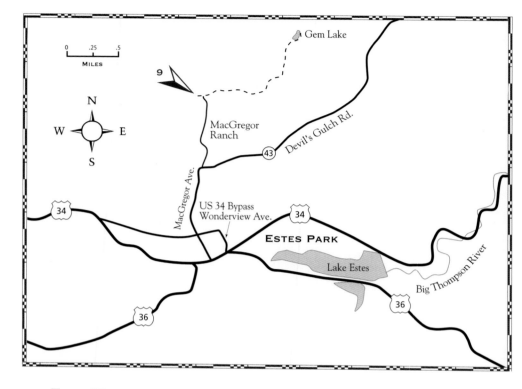

THE WALK

Most of the hikes in this book lead to historic places; this hike begins at one. It is an ideal choice for families with small children or seniors who would rather skip the hiking portion and take a leisurely stroll around a restored and picturesque mountain ranch instead.

Begin at the Twin Owls/Gem Lake Trailhead on the east side of the parking lot. The first section of the trail is fairly steep. The distinctive owl-like rock formations loom above the trail to the north, while the ranch's weathered but recently restored structures can be seen below to the south. Marked side trails offer access to the rocks for climbers. At 0.7 mile, the trail intersects with the alternate Gem Lake Trail that begins on Devil's Gulch Rd. Follow the Gem Lake Trail east as it climbs Lumpy Ridge and then gradually turns north. This section offers more views of Estes Park, Lake Estes, Longs Peak, and Mt. Meeker. Look for interesting rock formations along the trail, including Paul Bunyan's Boot. The final section of the trail is steep enough to elevate the heart rates of even the most experienced hikers. But diminutive Gem Lake, a scenic treasure walled in on three sides by layered granite cliffs, is a nice payoff for the effort. If you have lunch here, be prepared to fend off an army of fat chipmunks. Return by the same route.

Eugenia Mine

A FORTUNATE FAILURE

Carl Norwell never struck it rich while gutting Battle Mountain's belly. Yet, had his search for gold on Longs Peak's northeastern neighbor been more successful, Rocky Mountain National Park might not exist today.

Norwell and his Chicago partner Edward Cudahy staked the Eugenia mine on September 23, 1905, and recorded their find three years later. Sometime during that period, they began to tunnel into the hill using steam-powered tools. No one knows how much gold they found, but it must have been enough to justify their sizable capital investment. Over the next dozen years or so, Norwell pushed the tunnel 1,000 feet into the mountain and installed a rail system to remove the ore. He lived in a log cabin below the mine shaft with his family. Every now and then, the noise from dynamite explosions, drilling, and shoveling was interrupted by music as his two daughters practiced piano in their home.

Four months before Norwell discovered the Eugenia mine, President Theodore Roosevelt enlarged the existing Medicine Bow National Forest southward from Wyoming into north-central Colorado, including the area encompassed by today's national park. This executive decision, which reflected a concern among wilderness lovers about the overuse of our nation's woodlands, did not prohibit logging, mining, or grazing. But it did place limits on those uses.

Inn Brook runs through mine remnants.

About a mile east of the Eugenia mine, the proprietor of the Longs Peak Inn was calling for further federal protection for the area. Enos Mills, a naturalist, writer, and conservationist, wanted to set aside the region around Estes Park as a sort of natural playground for tourists. The idea was popular among locals who hoped to benefit from the tourist trade, with members of the newly formed Colorado Mountain Club, and with a growing middle class with leisure time to hike, fish, hunt, and enjoy the outdoors. The idea took root when Mills, Stanley Hotel owner F.O. Stanley, and others established the Estes Park Protective and Improvement Association in 1906.

But other interests opposed further regulation. Many Westerners, and Coloradans in particular, believed that the creation of forest reserves and other federally protected areas impeded economic development. Loggers, ranchers, and miners wanted unregulated access to public lands and their resources. "My home is on the [forest] reserve,"

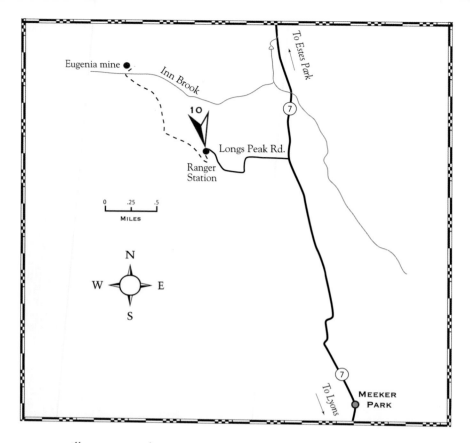

one sawmill operator said at a meeting regarding the extension of Medicine Bow National Forest, "and I earn my bread with a little 10-horsepower sawmill, running the saw myself. If you wonder why I object to the reserve, it is because I love liberty, hate red tape, and believe in progress."

In 1911, the Estes Park Protective and Improvement Association's discussions about the establishment of a natural playground, or game preserve, evolved into a proposal to establish Rocky Mountain National Park. With help from the American Civic Association, the Denver Chamber of Commerce, and powerful Denver attorney James Grafton Rogers, Mills embarked on a four-year campaign to protect his beloved mountains in perpetuity. Initially, he wanted to create a 1,000-square-mile park that extended south from the Longs Peak region all the way to Mt. Evans. However, more practical-minded proponents understood that the larger area included places such as Central City, which had produced a lot of gold in the past. Tasked with drafting legislation to create the park, Rogers advised caution. By downsizing Mills's proposal to a 700-square-mile park that excluded potentially rich mining areas, he minimized opposition from the mining industry.

President Woodrow Wilson signed the Rocky Mountain National Park bill into law on January 26, 1915. Carl Norwell abandoned the Eugenia mine four years later. He never found his bonanza and never started a gold rush to Longs Peak. The remnants of his operation, including the upright boiler, ruined log cabin, and tailings pile, attest to a failure that benefits us all.

LOCATION:	Rocky Mountain National Park
DESCRIPTION:	The short, easy Eugenia Mine Trail—perfect for families with young children—leads from the Longs Peak parking lot to the remnants of an early 20th-century mine.
DISTANCE:	2.8 miles, out and back
HIKING TIME:	2 hours
RATING:	Easy
TRAILHEAD ELEVATION:	9,400 feet
MAXIMUM ELEVATION:	9,840 feet
MAP:	*Colorado Atlas & Gazetteer*, p. 29, B6
CONTACT:	Rocky Mountain National Park, (970) 586-1206, www.nps.gov/romo/
GETTING THERE:	The Eugenia Mine Trail begins at the Longs Peak Trailhead. To get there from the north, go to Estes Park and take CO 7 south to Longs Peak Rd. From the south, go to Lyons and follow CO 7 west and then north past Meeker Park to Longs Peak Rd. Drive 1 mile to the parking lot.
GOOD TO KNOW:	The Longs Peak parking lot fills up early. On weekends, you might have to park on the road below the lot. Restrooms, a ranger station, picnic tables, and a gift shop are available at the trailhead. Dogs and bikes are not allowed on the trail.

THE WALK

Begin at the Longs Peak Trailhead. Follow the trail uphill 0.5 mile and take the right-hand fork at the sign for the Eugenia mine (the left fork goes to the summit of Longs Peak or to Chasm Lake). Hike 0.9 mile over gently rising and falling terrain along the eastern flank of Battle Mountain. Traverse a split-log bridge over a small stream to the Eugenia mine ruins.

Ruins at the Eugenia mine

Just across the creek, called Inn Brook for the Longs Peak Inn that is located downstream, is a deteriorated log structure on a stone foundation. Follow the creek upstream to a tailings pile. Structural timbers, possibly used to support a headframe, protrude directly from the creek. The National Park Service closed the mine entrance for safety reasons. Just above the tailings pile is a boiler that might have powered a hoist.

Return by the same trail.

Agnes Vaille Shelter on Longs Peak

AGNES VAILLE'S TRAGIC SUCCESS

Forest rangers working at the Longs Peak Trailhead keep a log of all accidents that have occurred on what some have called Colorado's favorite mountain. The log

Agnes Vaille

records hundreds of minor misfortunes and dozens of major tragedies. But one such tragedy, the death of Agnes Vaille on January 12, 1925, stands apart from the rest.

Widely known as a devotee of Colorado's alpine wonderlands, Agnes Vaille loved a challenge. She had already climbed all but 16 of the nation's mountains higher than 14,000 feet. Steeped in Longs Peak lore, she knew that no one had ever climbed the mountain's 1,680-foot-high East Face in winter. In late 1924, this nearly impossible feat became her goal and her obsession.

Aware that she could not do it alone, Vaille enlisted her friend Walter Kiener, a Swiss mountaineer and fellow Colorado Mountain Club member. After Vaille died, Kiener told authorities what had happened. He never discussed the matter again until one night in 1931, when he told the whole story to his friend Charles Edwin Hewes while they sat together next to the fire at the Hewes-Kirkwood Inn near the Longs Peak Trailhead. Hewes's journaling of the tale augments the official report with personal details that make the tragedy even more heart wrenching.

Rocky Mountain National Park Superintendent Roger Toll—who also happened to be Vaille's cousin—wrote the official report that went to National Park Service higher-ups and appeared in local newspapers and the Colorado Mountain Club's monthly magazine. According to the report, Vaille and Kiener left the Longs Peak Inn and headed for the 14,259-foot-high summit at 9 a.m. on Sunday, January 11. Already tired after getting little rest the night before, the determined pair endured temperatures that dipped far below zero. They reached their goal at 4 a.m. the next day, but severe weather and exhaustion denied them the opportunity to celebrate.

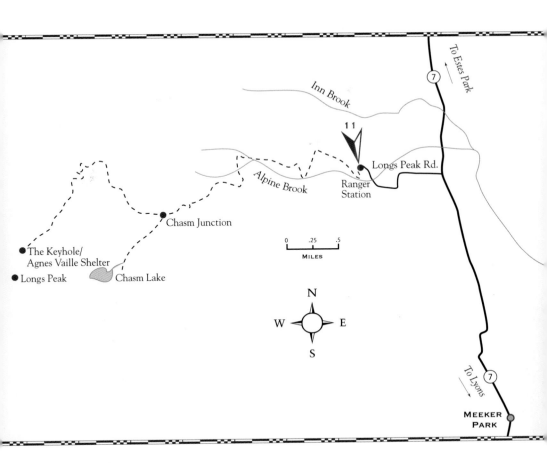

On their way down via the mountain's north side, wrote Toll:

> Agnes lost her footing and slid a distance of about 150 feet over a steep face of
> rock and across a snow bank at the bottom. When Kiener reached her, he asked if
> she was hurt, but Agnes assured him repeatedly that she had received no injury.
> On account of her nearly exhausted condition, and perhaps on account of shock
> and possible bruises from her fall, it was now impossible for her to make further
> progress. She admitted to Kiener that her hands and feet had been partially frozen
> most of the night. She mentioned this only because of her inability to loosen a
> strap, and apologized for asking for help. Her courage and pluck never failed her
> from the first moment of the trip to the last.

Kiener tried without success to help Vaille get moving again. Unable to carry his
companion, he left her in the snow bank and went for help. Two and a half hours later,
he reached Timberline Cabin, a little wood shack nestled among the wind-whipped
flag trees and stunted shrubbery east of the summit. Here he found a relief party that
consisted of three men who had come up from the Longs Peak Inn after Vaille and
Kiener failed to return on time. Three of them accompanied Kiener on his rescue

East Face of Longs Peak at sunrise

mission, while the fourth stayed in the cabin to keep a fire going. But fierce winds and whiteout conditions forced two of the rescuers to turn back. One of them, Longs Peak Inn caretaker Hubert Sortland, got lost and died in the storm.

Kiener and Jacob Christian found Agnes at 4:00 that afternoon. She was lying facedown in the snow with an ice axe attached to her left wrist. According to Toll, "It is doubtful that she had lived an hour after Kiener had gone for help."

Though Kiener's personal story does not contradict Toll's official report, its details do shed light on Vaille's obsession and the manner of her death. "Our inclination to climb the East Face of Longs Peak came when [we] had just ascended Mt. Evans early in the fall of 1924," Kiener told Hewes in 1931, "and while resting on the summit…we looked off north and beholding the grand appearance of Longs, we resolved to climb its East Face in the near future." Proving that the climb was no amateur lark, he added, "With the reputation Agnes enjoyed in the Colo. Mt. Club as the equal of any member, man or woman, for daring endurance and my own experience in both Switzerland and America, we felt that we could make a successful winter climb." But after their third attempt failed, "Agnes became the object of considerable adverse criticism" from friends and family. Told that their quest was impossible, Vaille and Kiener set out to prove them wrong. "A regrettable but definite challenge arose…which we proposed to meet."

Kiener went on to discuss their final, successful ascent to the summit. "I was greatly perturbed and grieved to note that my companion's strength was about spent. For some time I had noticed that she was far from being in wonderful form." They reached the top, took a temperature reading of –14 F, and began their descent. After the sun came up and the clouds cleared a little, Kiener was able to see Vaille's face for the first time in many hours. "The light of dawn revealed the features of my brave companion….[A]ppalling lines of suffering, anguish, pain, haggard and deep drawn had developed in the countenance of that heroic woman." Then she fell.

> [S]he fell and skidded a long ways down over the smooth, snowy slope, and lay there until I could descend. It was broad daylight now with the wind steadily rising …and as the sun rose over the distant plains, we discussed the situation….She was insisting, in that supernatural voice that smote and terrified me, that a half hour's sleep would restore her. Assisting her to some rocks that seemed to offer some protection from the wind, I put her knapsack under her head as a pillow, placed her axe in her hand, for she seemed to cling to it as a treasured thing; and with all the speed at my command I started across the Boulder Field for help.

Walter Kiener lost more than a friend that day. He lost the tips of most of his fingers and most of his toes to frostbite. He also lost his reputation. Some blamed him for the disaster, while others blamed Vaille for her reckless ambition. Everyone agreed that the quest was foolhardy.

Today, winter ascents on Longs are common, but never routine. The Agnes Vaille Shelter helps remind hikers and climbers that the mountain must be approached with humility and respect in all seasons.

Alpine Brook along the Longs Peak Trail

LOCATION:	Rocky Mountain National Park
DESCRIPTION:	Hiking Longs Peak, whether your destination is the Agnes Vaille Shelter or the summit, will be a rewarding and unforgettable experience. The trail leads directly to the shelter and continues to the summit via the nontechnical (in summer) Keyhole Route.
DISTANCE:	12 miles to the Agnes Vaille Shelter and back; 15 miles to the summit and back
HIKING TIME:	12 hours
RATING:	Difficult
TRAILHEAD ELEVATION:	9,405 feet
MAXIMUM ELEVATION:	Vaille Shelter, 13,160 feet; summit, 14,259 feet
MAP:	*Colorado Atlas & Gazetteer*, p. 29, B6
CONTACT:	Rocky Mountain National Park general information, (970) 586-1206, www.nps.gov/romo/; backcountry camping permits, (970) 586-1242

GETTING THERE:	From Estes Park, drive 9 miles south on CO 7 to Longs Peak Rd. Turn right and drive 1 mile to the parking lot. The Longs Peak parking lot fills up early, but this should not be a problem if you arrive well before sunrise on a weekday.
GOOD TO KNOW:	Restrooms, a ranger station, picnic tables, and a giftshop are available at the trailhead. Dogs are not allowed on the trail. Get a backcountry permit, available from area ranger stations, for overnight stays at the Boulderfield, Battle Mountain, and Goblins Forest sites.

Plan to hike Longs between mid-June and mid-September, when the Keyhole Route (that portion of the hike between the Keyhole and the summit) is usually free of snow and ice. Call ahead for current conditions.

This trail is recommended for experienced and physically fit hikers only. If you plan to summit, begin your hike at 3 a.m. in order to be off the mountaintop by noon (remember to bring a flashlight or headlamp and extra batteries). Several layers of clothing are a must, even when it is warm at the trailhead. Wear good hiking boots, long pants, and a wind- and water-resistant jacket. Bring gloves, a hat, spare socks, food, and plenty of water. Being unprepared can lead to altitude sickness or hypothermia. Keep a slow, steady pace and know your limits.

Be aware of natural hazards, including sudden and drastic weather changes, rockslides, and avalanches. Be especially wary of afternoon storms. If lightning occurs, get off summits and ridges. Turn back at the first sign of a storm.

It might be tempting to try for the summit despite a late start or adverse conditions. Be smart and don't succumb to summit fever.

Before you begin your hike, sign in at the trail register and check with the ranger on duty for the latest conditions on the mountain.

Hikers starting in the early morning hours will complete the first few miles in darkness. The trail's popularity guarantees that you will have company.

Hike through the lodgepole pine forest for 0.5 mile and go left at the junction with the Eugenia Mine Trail. Continue south to Alpine Brook, which you might hear but not see in the dark, and then head west after a northerly switchback. Cross over Larkspur Creek and Alpine Brook where they converge, and then switchback and once again cross a bridge over Alpine Brook.

The forest starts to thin out shortly after Alpine Brook. Chances are good that the wind will pick up, too. As the trail turns west again, head up Mills Moraine over a rocky trail that is bordered

Agnes Vaille Shelter and the Keyhole formation

by krummholz (German for "twisted wood"). Keep going west past a side trail that leads to the Battle Mountain campsites and continue on the main trail west to Chasm Junction. A backcountry privy, which boasts the best view of any toilet in the nation, is available off the trail. Take the main Longs Peak trail 0.5 mile north across Mt. Lady Washington's eastern shoulder to Granite Pass (12,080 feet).

On the far side of the pass, follow the trail up a few switchbacks to the Boulderfield campsites. This was the site of the Boulderfield Inn, which catered to hikers from 1925 to 1936. The trail disappears here, and hikers must pick their way west over the rocks to the Keyhole formation.

The Agnes Vaille Shelter, the highest building in the National Park System, was built at the foot of the Keyhole between 1925 and 1927. Donated by Agnes's father, F.P. Vaille, it serves as a memorial to his daughter and a refuge for hikers in need.

The Keyhole Route, which is usually nontechnical in the summer but requires some scrambling over sometimes-narrow ledges that are exposed to steep drop-offs, begins here. Climb through the Keyhole and follow painted bull's-eyes, popularly called "fried eggs," across the Ledges on the west face of Longs. Watch out for verglas, an almost invisible layer of ice. Continue only if the route is dry.

Past the Ledges, descend a little to the Trough and then hike up a talus slope to another exposed ledge system appropriately called the Narrows. At the end of this section, scramble up the Homestretch to the summit. Don't forget to sign the register.

Return by the same route.

REGION 3
Boulder

Top: *Chautauqua Auditorium in 1902*
Bottom: *Boulder foothills from the Marshall Mesa Trail*

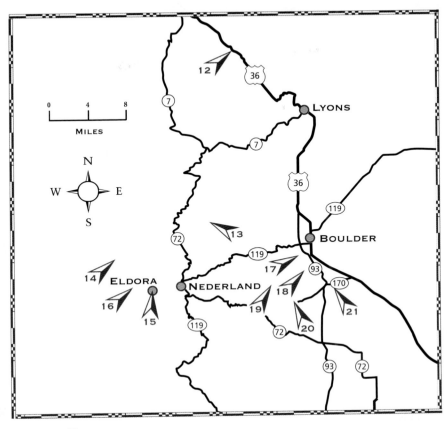

CONTENTS

Lion Gulch Trail to Homestead Meadows

PROVING UP

Sarah Walker, known to her friends as "Grandma," lived alone in a small mountain cabin 13 miles west of Lyons. She moved to the remote and beautiful upland park after separating from her husband shortly after 1908. Her land, obtained from the federal government through the Homestead Act, provided the necessities: fresh water from a spring and grassy pasture for a milk cow. She planted a garden, raised chickens, and even worked at a nearby sawmill. The English immigrant supplemented her meager income by selling eggs and cream in faraway Lyons. Lacking a horse, she hiked 3 miles to the road—today's US 36—and hitched a ride to town from there. Walker lived this way for 15 years.

This single woman's fortitude is praiseworthy, but not unique. Her early 20th-century neighbors, especially the women, matched her determination measure for measure. Together they defined the last chapter of the Front Range homesteading era.

Passed by Congress in 1862, the Homestead Act meant one thing for the nation's westering masses: free land. The government surveyed the public domain,

Irvin Homestead

Brown Homestead

divided it into quarter sections (160-acre parcels), and offered them to settlers for a nominal filing fee. Though Congress amended its land distribution scheme several times in subsequent years, the act's purpose never changed. America was determined to settle its Western frontier through a democratic system of agricultural development. And despite problems—such as the displacement of native peoples and widespread cheating and speculation—the system worked. Through the Homestead Act, the nation granted 270 million acres (10 percent of its total area) to citizens.

Of course, every good deal has a catch. Settlers were required to "prove up" their claims before they were given titles. That is, they had to live on their homesteads for at least six months per year for five years, build a house, improve the land through cultivation and other means, and provide evidence of income related to those improvements. As Sarah Walker and her neighbors discovered, proving up on mountain land could test the limits of even the hardiest of pioneers.

Mrs. Charles Engert knew the ins and outs of proving up better than most. She and her husband had their eyes on a 320-acre spread located about a mile south of Sarah Walker's place. But as the postmaster for Lyons, Charles couldn't get away from work long enough to satisfy the Homestead Act's residency requirement. So, for five years in a row, his wife spent six long months in their remote mountain cabin alone. Her courage and diligence paid off when they received title to the land in 1921.

Unfortunately, the 4,413-acre Big Elk Fire destroyed the Engerts' cabin in 2002. But the public hardly noticed this minor tragedy after a slurry bomber broke apart and caught fire in midair. Three people died in the accident. These heroes were part of an army of 749 firefighters who protected residents of Pinewood Springs, Big Elk Meadows, and Estes Park. No other lives or homes were lost.

Today, the blackened forest of scorched aspen and ponderosa is on the mend. In the summer, wildflowers contrast with charred stumps, demonstrating how fire rejuvenates mountain ecosystems. And though the Engert cabin is gone, pieces of melted glass and bits of ceramic dishes lying around in the dirt still remind visitors of the pioneer homesteaders and their hardships. But spending just one day at any of the existing historic sites will convince anyone that the rewards for proving up were well worth the trouble.

LOCATION:	Arapaho and Roosevelt National Forests
DESCRIPTION:	The Lion Gulch Trail offers something for everyone: historic structures and artifacts, idyllic mountain streams, and lovely meadows with abundant wildflowers.
DISTANCE:	8.3 miles, out and back (side trails lead you to additional homesteads)
HIKING TIME:	4 to 5 hours
RATING:	Difficult
TRAILHEAD ELEVATION:	7,360 feet
MAXIMUM ELEVATION:	8,660 feet
MAP:	*Colorado Atlas & Gazetteer*, p. 29, B7
CONTACT:	Canyon Lakes Ranger District, (970) 295-6700, www.fs.fed.us/r2/arnf/
GETTING THERE:	From Boulder, drive north on US 36 to Lyons. Follow the same highway through town and drive 13 miles northwest to the trailhead. There is a gravel parking lot on the south side of the road.
GOOD TO KNOW:	A restroom, but no water, is available at the trailhead. Hikers, horseback riders, and mountain bikers are welcome. Camping is allowed, but the Forest Service asks that you do not camp in or near any of the historic structures.

THE WALK

The Lion Gulch Trail follows a small creek 2 miles to a relatively open and flat area with grassy meadows and additional short trails leading to several homesteads. This description leads to four of the area's eight homesteads, plus the site of an old sawmill.

From the trailhead, follow the path down to the creek and then cross over on a wooden bridge. On the opposite side, a map indicates the location of eight separate homesteads. The trail continues west and gains 1,300 feet in elevation before reaching the meadows. This section is a real treat for hikers searching for some stress relief. You cross the stream 10 times on wooden bridges, split logs, and rocks. Blue columbine and wild rose line the shady path. Dappled sun filters through ponderosa and spruce trees in splotchy patches that sparkle on mossy stones, little pools, and miniature waterfalls.

After the tenth crossing the trail leads to an open meadow. Continue north to a sign interpreting the Homestead Act. Keep an eye to the left for the rusted remains of an old truck by the creek. Curious hikers will find several other autos permanently parked nearby in the brush.

A little farther west, the trail splits left and right. Signs posted at the junction indicate mileage to the Walker, Griffith, Brown, and Irvin Homesteads; the Meadow Loop Trail; and a sawmill to the right. The other sign points to the Engert, Laycock, Boren, and Hill Homesteads, as well as Pierson Park. Note that the Engert place burned to the ground during the 2002 Big Elk Fire.

The most accessible structures and artifacts are just over the rise to the right. Walk about 0.25 mile to Sarah Walker's homestead, which consists today of a foundation and a few scattered domestic artifacts, and then continue another 0.25 mile to the Griffith Homestead. This site offers a little more to see, including part of a log cabin, a collapsed bunkhouse, and a chicken coop.

At the ruined cabin, look for a sign marked "trail" and then go north 0.3 mile to the Meadow Loop–Sawmill Trail junction, passing a private road along the way. Turn left (west) at the sign and continue 0.5 mile down a hill, across a meadow, and through a pine grove to another meadow and a remarkably intact house, which was part of Harry and Susan Brown's Hereford cattle ranch.

Go north past the house and follow the Meadow Loop for 1 mile as it turns east and returns to the Sawmill Trail. Walk 0.5 mile east to the Irvin Homestead and the site of a ruined sawmill. Plan on spending some time here; there's plenty to explore, including the Irvin house, remnants of R.J. Nettleton's sawmill, a three-hole outhouse, a chicken coop and rabbit hutch, a bunkhouse, and other outbuildings. Be sure to check out the spring-fed bathhouse, which features a sunken tub.

Return to the Lion Gulch Trail by way of the Griffith Homestead, minus the Meadow Loop. Additional trails (not described here) lead to the Laycock, Engert, Hill, and Boren Homesteads, adding about 5 miles to the hike.

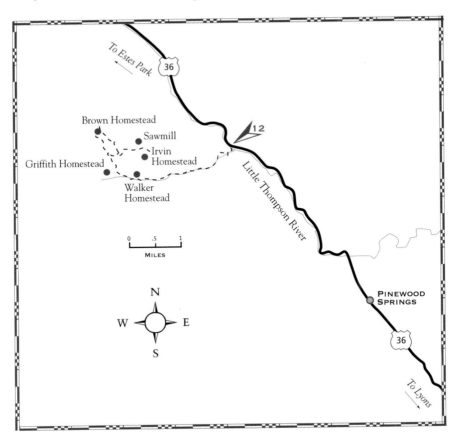

Switzerland Trail

RIDING THE WHIPLASH ROUTE

In October 1858, a little mining party made its way into the untapped hillsides near the mouth of Boulder Canyon. Expecting a long, hard Colorado winter, what they enjoyed was an unseasonably mild one, and after a few months of prospecting they found gold in a streambed in early 1859. What followed was one of the state's first gold rushes, and the Gold Hill Mining District was organized by July.

Mont Alto once buzzed with life as a partying and picnicking destination along the "Switzerland Trail" scenic rail line.

"By the fall of 1859," wrote artist and author Muriel Sibell Wolle, "a small quartz stamp mill had been hauled by oxteam across the plains and up Left Hand creek, where it was set up at the base of Gold Hill." By the next spring ore was being processed at the mill, said to be one of a kind in Colorado. The gold soon played out, and some 1,500 miners moved on. But new discoveries a decade later brought miners in again, and the region was alive with activity once more. More than 1,000 people had returned to live in the valley at the Gold Hill camp by 1880. The gold mines at the nearby town of Ward—where another mill busily processed ore—proved even richer. But only a wagon road connected Ward with the rest of the valley and the important center of Boulder farther beyond.

So in 1897, the newly organized Colorado & Northwestern Railway started surveying roads and laying tracks up the valley into the vicinity of the region's gold mines, much of whose ore was sitting, piled and waiting to be transported down to Boulder. Two other railroads had made a go of it in past years, getting only as far as Sunset. The Colorado & Northwestern was determined to succeed, and part of its strategy was that the railroad would not be just a freight line. It would be one of the world's most scenic excursion lines, and the company would build the amenities to bring the tourists in.

Getting to Ward meant a climb of more than 4,000 feet, and that meant a series of horseshoe and hairpin turns over the course of the 26-mile line up and around the hillsides of the valley. The road's scenery earned it the nickname "Switzerland Trail," but some felt that the name "Whiplash Route" better captured it. The Colorado & Northwestern first laid its tracks up Fourmile Canyon to the camp of Sunset, then turned right to climb to Ward and the vicinity of Gold Hill. The company built a

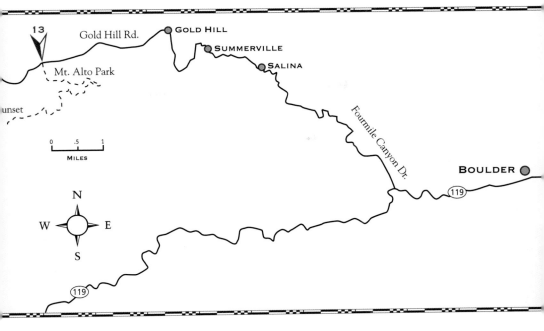

station at the end of the line, where wagons carried tourists into the welcoming town of Gold Hill with its restaurants and hotels. Later, it added a line turning left from Sunset and climbing over to Sugarloaf and Eldora.

To attract excursionists, the company erected a rustic lodge at a promontory near Gold Hill, with a dance pavilion, picnic tables, cabins, and an outdoor fountain made from chunks of white quartz. The scenic overlook amid tall ponderosa pines made for an attractive resort spot where summer tourists could spend the day before catching another train back to Boulder. The site was named Mont Alto Park (the spelling became "Mount" in ensuing years).

In June 1898, the festivities for the "Formal Opening of the Whiplash Route from the Verdant Valley of Boulder to the Cloud Kissed Camp of Ward" centered at Mont Alto. That first day, "Every train leaving Boulder, and there were four of them, was crowded to utmost capacity," the Boulder *Daily Camera* reported. The paper commended the Colorado & Northwestern for its "get up and hustle" in pulling off the all-day dance-and-picnic celebration. For years thereafter, a few hundred tourists rode the Switzerland Trail every day, and the railroad offered popular "moonlight rides" that ran past midnight. Historian Forrest Crossen writes, "Excursion trains pulled out of Boulder in sections for Mont Alto, one baggage car usually filled with beer on ice."

The mining camp of Sunset saw its own heyday thanks to the tourist line. Located at the all-important junction where rail lines branched off for Eldora and Ward, Sunset was the site of booming mines such as the Free Coinage, Poor Woman, and Scandia. In addition to its rail station and water tank, Sunset offered freighters and tourists a saloon, a general store, and a hotel called the Columbine. "After the railroad came through," recalled one old-timer, the Columbine "had fifty people for every meal and tourists were thick as bees all summer."

The gold boom raged through the first few years of the 20th century, with Ward growing into the county's biggest mining camp. When in 1904 the line was extended from Sunset to Eldora, the railroad dismantled the lodge at Mont Alto and reassembled it section by section at Glacier Lake, about 2 miles southwest of Sunset. With the demise of the gold boom a few years later, tourists were left with only memories of rides on the Whiplash Route and days spent dancing at Mont Alto.

LOCATION:	A few miles from Gold Hill, just northwest of Boulder
DESCRIPTION:	A 4.7-mile walk along an old railroad grade takes you to the remnants of a lodge at a scenic overlook, then down to the mining town of Sunset on the floor of Fourmile Canyon.
DISTANCE:	9.4 miles, out and back
HIKING TIME:	5 hours
RATING:	Moderate
TRAILHEAD ELEVATION:	8,600 feet
MAXIMUM ELEVATION:	8,600 feet (with a low elevation of 7,800 feet at Sunset)
MAP:	*Colorado Atlas & Gazetteer*, p. 29, D7
CONTACT:	Roosevelt National Forest, Boulder Ranger District, (303) 541-2500, www.fs.fed.us/r2/arnf/

GETTING THERE:	From Boulder, drive west on CO 119. Just past town, turn right onto Fourmile Canyon Dr. at the sign for Gold Hill. Keep following the signs to Gold Hill for about 8 miles along this winding road; Gold Hill is just past Salina and Summerville. At Gold Hill, bear west (left) on Gold Hill Rd. About 2.5 miles past Gold Hill you'll see a sign for Switzerland Trail/Gold Hill Site. Turn off to the left side of the road and park in the parking area by the sign.
GOOD TO KNOW:	Popular among Boulder-area railroad-hiking buffs, this walk combines scenery and history, with the gradual inclines you'd expect from an old railroad grade. The level, 1.2-mile jaunt to the picnic area makes for a nice hike with kids. If you want to hike down the canyon to the historic mining town of Sunset, though, the resulting 9.4-mile round-trip and 800-foot drop in elevation is too much of a challenge for little ones.
	The Switzerland Trail is a gorgeous year-round trail for hiking, biking, and snowshoeing. The road is open to four-wheel-drive traffic, so you'll likely have motorized company, but the length, beauty, and relative ease of this wide track makes it a favorite for hikers and especially cyclists. Because it sees a lot of ATV use, the best time to hike or bike it is the off-season. This is a great, easy-to-follow snowshoeing route. Horseback riding is allowed.
	At the Mount Alto Picnic Area are many picnic tables, as well as campsites and cooking grills.

The old mining town of Sunset

THE WALK

From the parking area, walk south on the Switzerland Trail (CR 109/FR 327) about 1.2 miles to Mount Alto Picnic Area. Along the way you'll pass through some cuts in the road, blasted out to make room for the railroad grade. At the picnic area, a massive fireplace and its lone standing chimney mark the site of the old lodge that once stood alongside the rail line. You can also see the humble remains of the stone fountain.

Another 3.5 miles down the winding, gradually sloping railroad grade takes you through ponderosa pine forest and wildflowers to the town of Sunset. Along the way, stretches of the rail line rise on the opposite side of the canyon. The occasional tailings heap, headframe, stone bridge foundation, and other remnants serve as evidence of the area's mining and railroading past.

Turn back at Sunset. If you want to keep going past Sunset, it's another 4.0 miles of gradual uphill to a cul-de-sac on Sugarloaf Rd. (From Sunset, be sure to stay on the Switzerland Trail, CR 109/FR 327, rather than the more substantial Fourmile Canyon Dr.) This was once a railroad line with grades that were never more than 4 percent, so all of the hills are nice and gradual. But because it's a long road and it gets rocky in spots, it's a fairly challenging mountain-bike ride or hike to do the whole route at once.

The Fourth of July Mine

GREAT EXPECTATIONS

Some dispute the tale, but in September 1872 the *Rocky Mountain News* reported that C.C. Alvord had discovered his silver lode on July 4 of that year, hence its name: the Fourth of July. And the *News* fairly screamed about its prospects: "It appears to be the outcropping of an enormous silver ledge, literally bursting from the mountain." This "great freak of Nature," the *News* crowed, "will afford room and material—judging from the surface indications—for a hundred thousand men to mine for generations to come."

Sadly, those were little more than "surface indications," and exaggerated ones at that. Alvord staked the mine above the North Fork of Middle Boulder Creek, in a relatively flat spot along the steep and boulder-strewn flank of South Arapaho Peak. Alvord sank a shaft 200 feet deep, erecting a sturdy log shafthouse around it. Beside the shaft he built a log bunkhouse for the mine crew and a blacksmith shop. A stable sheltered the horse that spent its days turning the "whim" to crank the mine's hoist.

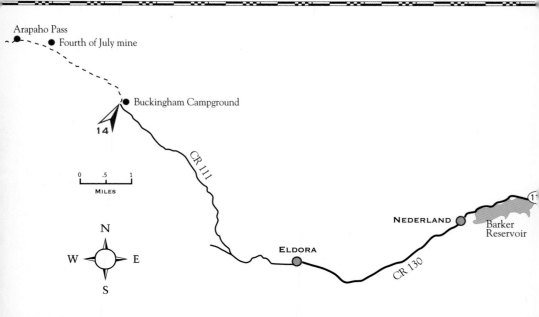

And for a while, the mine proved a serviceable one. The crew pulled a fair amount of silver and even some gold from the shaft. They dug a tunnel downslope from it, where a mill, another blacksmith shop, a steam power plant, and more boardinghouses and stables went up during a five-year flurry of activity. But to complicate matters, the Fourth of July sat right beside a stream that fed into the North Fork of the Middle Boulder. Water from the stream constantly seeped into the mine, and drainage proved an ongoing struggle. The cost of extracting the ore quickly outweighed the profits, and the whole operation all but shut down by 1880. Alvord had found two other veins along the North Fork of the Middle Boulder, but he left those behind as well.

Twenty years later the mine still sat idle. But, as mining historian Donald Kemp relates, a last-ditch ploy made up for a little bit of the mine's inactivity. As might be expected, the ore had contained an appreciable amount of copper. The mine's new promoters launched a publicity campaign—complete with 32-page embossed brochure—to fire up interest in a mine that they touted as one of the highest potential sources of copper the region had ever seen. They sold 3 million shares of stock at $1 a share. With the promoters showing only casual interest in the mine's day-to-day workings, and with no engineer on staff, the crew had only their best estimates to guide them. They set blast after blast, drilling the tunnel farther toward the presumed source of the copper. On the day they expected to reach it, they set a final, much-anticipated charge—only to blow a hole right back out of the mountainside a few feet from the portal where they had entered. Having driven the tunnel in U-shaped fashion and wasted a lot of dynamite in the process, the crew renewed its efforts. But those efforts proved no more lucrative, and the Fourth of July shut down for good.

By the time artist and writer Muriel Sibell Wolle visited the mine in 1944, the shafthouse on Arapaho Trail had long since begun its inevitable fall to ruin. "One could look through the building and see up through the broken, sway-backed roof large patches of blue sky," she wrote. "Some rusty machinery stood inside amid debris of rocks and fallen timbers, and the wind whistled through the ribs of the broken building." Today, only the rusted machinery and a few vestiges of those timbers remain.

Muriel Sibell Wolle shot this photo of the Fourth of July shafthouse and boiler in 1944.

LOCATION:	Indian Peaks Wilderness, 26 miles west of Boulder
DESCRIPTION:	A beautiful 2-mile hike takes you steadily uphill through an alpine landscape to the remnants of the Fourth of July silver mine.
DISTANCE:	4 miles, out and back
HIKING TIME:	3 hours
RATING:	Moderate
TRAILHEAD ELEVATION:	10,100 feet
MAXIMUM ELEVATION:	11,300 feet
MAP:	*Colorado Atlas & Gazetteer*, p. 29, D5
CONTACT:	Boulder Ranger District, (303) 541-2500, www.fs.fed.us/r2/arnf/

GETTING THERE:	Drive 17 miles west of Boulder on CO 119 to Nederland. Keep going through Nederland and just beyond, then turn right at the sign for Eldora (this is CR 130, known as Eldora Rd.). At about 3.5 miles past Nederland you'll arrive at the center of Eldora. Keep going through Eldora; the pavement gives way to a narrow, unmaintained dirt road just past town. (The next stretch can be driven in a passenger car with decent clearance, but four-wheel drive is preferable.) At about 0.75 mile along the dirt road, bear right at the signs for Hessie. You are now on CR 111; keep going another 4 miles to the end of the road, where you will find Buckingham Campground and a large parking area.
	Note that you'll pass a few private cabins along the way, so please stay off drives. At about 1.5 mile past the Hessie junction is the site of the long-vanished old mining town of Grand Island. This is private property and there are cabins in the immediate area, so please stay on the main road all the way to the trailhead.
GOOD TO KNOW:	This trail is extremely popular in the summer, especially in July, as is the Lost Lake Trail, which begins at Hessie (see Hike 16). The road from Eldora to both trailheads is narrow, and in peak season the traffic can be a challenge, with drivers jockeying for position and parking all along the road by midmorning when the parking areas fill. If that's a concern, you might want to hike these trails in the off-season. However, the wildflowers are at their absolute peak that same time—around mid-July—and the trail to the Fourth of July mine offers some of the finest wildflower viewing in all of the Indian Peaks Wilderness.
	A permit is required for camping between June 1 and September 15; no groups of more than 12 people (or people and pack animals combined) are allowed. A permit is also required for organized tour groups. No campfires are allowed east of the Continental Divide, which includes all of the trail to the Fourth of July mine. Bikes and motor vehicles are prohibited. Leashed dogs are welcome.
	The campground and parking area offer ample parking and separate men's and women's toilets. Watch for mosquitoes and biting flies in the hottest weeks of summer, but remember too that snow can blanket the trail into July. Signs posted at the trailhead remind you that this is bear country.

Remnants of the Fourth of July mine lie exposed to the elements.

THE WALK

At the parking area, find the trailhead for Arapaho Pass Trail (National Forest Trail 904), also known as the Fourth of July Trail. Set out from here and hike uphill, following the route that miners and their burros and horses once packed up and down.

The hike takes you through woods of lodgepole pine, fir, and spruce, with the occasional aspen grove. The trail parallels a high, steep ridge to the right. The ridge falls off to the left to a rushing creek; across the valley, a facing ridge gives way to steep cliffs. At about 0.5 mile a dramatic series of waterfalls across the valley feeds straight down into the creek below. Enjoy a great view of the falls from a spot where a marker lists wilderness regulations.

Along the first mile of the hike, stretches of wooden planks take you over the marshier areas, and timbers shore up the trail and provide steps. At the 1-mile point and beyond you'll step over gentle, rocky waterfalls that cross the trail, and encounter meadows and pine groves. The profusion of midsummer flowers includes Indian paintbrush, columbine, yarrow, yellow daisies, harebell, larkspur, and even the rare Parry's primrose, which blooms a spectacular deep purple along marshes for only a few weeks of the year. Flowers cover entire hillsides in peak season, roughly mid- to late July.

Follow the signs for the Arapaho Pass Trail. At the 2-mile point, the trail begins to level off as it nears treeline and tundra. Just beyond the marked junction with the trail to Arapaho Glacier is the old Fourth of July mine. Small mine pits remain here and there, and piles of tailings are left as reminders of all the diggings. A shafthouse once covered the boiler, compressor, and other equipment you see. Only a few scattered timbers remain—the others, like the bricks that once supported the equipment, have all been scavenged. Scraps of metal lie about, as do other clues of mining activity long past.

If you feel like going beyond the mine, you have a few options. Walking past the mine for 1 mile to the summit of Arapaho Pass takes you to the Continental Divide at 11,905 feet. A fantastic view of the Winter Park area awaits you at the top, as does Lake Dorothy, a beautiful little alpine lake. Or, from the mine, you can follow the signs for the Arapaho Glacier Trail, which takes you high up to the glacier on the other side of the ridgeline.

Caribou

FACING DOWN THE ELEMENTS AT 10,000 FEET

Late in the summer of 1869, Samuel Conger and a group of his fellow prospectors climbed and bushwhacked their way up through a roadless stretch of dense woods in highest Boulder County. Their destination: the round, bald promontory where Conger had found an intriguing sample of silver ore. Having crept northward all the way from Central City, the men finally found the bare mountaintop, and near it, they quickly found more silver. The partners each staked out claims. Then, they braced themselves for a fall and winter to be spent mining in a secluded, high-altitude wilderness of weather extremes and wind.

Caribou townsite

With the days of the gold rush waning, news of the miners' silver discoveries spread fast and made headlines. Soon, one of Colorado's first and biggest silver rushes was on; it was also the most northerly. Hundreds of prospectors, many of them Cornish, staked hundreds of claims in the mountainsides surrounding the camp dubbed Caribou. They and their families founded a settlement whose fast-growing population of hardy souls was willing to withstand fierce winds, brutal weather, deep snows, and isolation at 10,000 feet in order to extract the mountains' riches. Mines covered Caribou Hill, the landmark promontory at the foot of which the community settled. Stage roads were fast in coming, one from Central City and the other from Nederland and Boulder. As the mines boomed—living up to their promise and then some—so did the town of Caribou.

By 1879, Caribou boasted more than 100 houses, a bakery, a brewery, grocery stores, a church, and a school. Dogs, too: One resident wryly estimated their number at three dogs to every human. The town had both a brass band and a string band and, like nearly all big mining camps, it had saloons and a red-light district.

Whenever possible, residents reinforced buildings to withstand winds that reached 100 miles per hour. Because of the weather, the children's school "year" lasted May through October. The rest of the time, families hunkered down for the long winter season.

Miners tend a hoist bucket atop Caribou Hill in 1883.

In 1879, a diphtheria epidemic claimed lives, including three young children from one family alone. And just as the camp's residents faced exposure to illness, winds, and snow, another potential danger loomed: wildfire. The fall of 1879 was drier than most, and grass fires ignited on nearby Arapaho Peak. Foreshadowing so many of today's fires, this one was most likely set by "careless campers," writes historian Duane Smith. For two weeks in September the fires smoldered, filling the sky over town with a smoky haze. On a mid-September Sunday afternoon, winds gathered into a "perfect gale," suddenly sweeping the fire up Caribou Hill—where it devastated the mines as miners waged a futile battle against it. Then, it just as suddenly turned north and raced into town.

"The fire ran from dwelling to dwelling with such rapidity that women and children had to flee for their lives, many leaving every thing of value in their houses to be destroyed," a news account related. "Some went as far as Nederland, four miles below, not knowing where the fire would stop." The damage was fast and extreme—and it caught residents by surprise. Thanks to a new water system (built in response to two smaller fires in town), they managed to save Caribou's central district. Still, when the fire burned itself out that night, up to 60 houses and mine structures lay in ruins.

Not a single person died in the blaze. The next day, the stunned residents of Caribou began the long process of rebuilding. And, for a while, the mines kept running. But the 1880s brought a decline, and the Silver Crash of 1893 sealed the district's fate.

Fire struck the town again in December 1899, and again in 1905. By the time of that third, barely noted fire, little was left of a camp where mines once buzzed with life, where parents raised children, and where for more than a decade Colorado and the nation extracted a great deal of their silver riches.

LOCATION:	Roosevelt National Forest, 21 miles west of Boulder
DESCRIPTION:	A high-clearance four-wheel-drive road marks a gradual uphill hike from the historic gold-mining town of Eldora to the legendary silver mines of the Caribou district.
DISTANCE:	6 miles, out and back
HIKING TIME:	5 hours
RATING:	Moderate
TRAILHEAD ELEVATION:	9,000 feet
MAXIMUM ELEVATION:	10,300 feet
MAP:	*Colorado Atlas & Gazetteer,* p. 39, A6
CONTACT:	Boulder Ranger District, (303) 541-2500, www.fs.fed.us/r2/arnf/

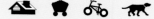

GETTING THERE: The thriving town of Nederland is 17 miles west of Boulder up Boulder Canyon Rd. (CO 119). Keep going through and just beyond Nederland, then turn right at the sign for Eldora (this is CR 130, Eldora Rd.). At just over 3 miles you come into Eldora; watch for Sixth St., a dirt road. Turn right and park beside the road in the general area of the historic Goldminer Hotel. From the hotel, walk north on Sixth up the hill a few dozen yards to a dead end. Go right, then take the first left, then immediately take another right. You're at the trailhead when you see a gate, a wooden sign, and a brown U.S. Forest Service marker for FR 505.

GOOD TO KNOW: Posted at the trailhead are a map, forest regulations, and other information. If the gate is closed, hikers and snowshoers may still access the road. FR 505 is open to high-clearance four-wheel-drives, ATVs, and bicycles; in busy summer months you might see a lot of motorized traffic. But this is still a popular, moderately challenging route for mountain bikers and hikers looking to get into rugged terrain and see some of Colorado's earliest silver mines. You might encounter some mosquitoes, but you may also see hawks, hummingbirds, and other bird life. Camping is permitted at designated sites.

The town of Eldora is a historic district with log homes dating from the 1870s and 1880s alongside newer seasonal cabins. Like Caribou, the town still supports active mining. Just minutes from Nederland, Eldora allows you to avoid the often crowded, narrow roads you must navigate to reach other trailheads in this region.

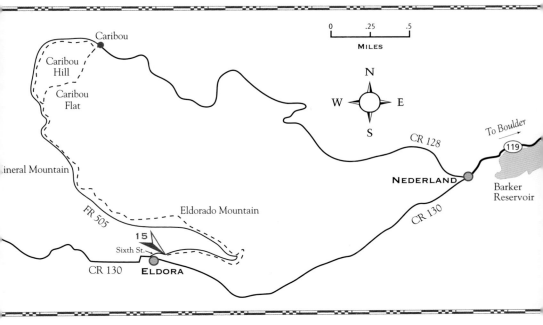

THE WALK

The route for this hike is FR 505, with a few side-trail opportunities near Caribou Hill and the Caribou townsite. When you're not exploring side trails, simply keep following the brown U.S. Forest Service markers for FR 505.

From Eldora, the road climbs alongside Eldorado Mountain. It goes east for about 0.5 mile, then switchbacks to the northwest. A straight, gradual uphill stretch along Mineral Mountain takes you generally north, passing through pine and spruce forest, aspen groves, and fields of wildflowers such as Indian paintbrush and columbine. After about 1 mile are the first remnants of mining operations, and on the hillsides are smaller mine pits here and there. As you approach tree-line and a more alpine landscape, you crest a few hills before a particularly beautiful stretch takes you over Caribou Flat. Past Caribou Flat is the obvious landmark of Caribou Hill.

Overlooking the old townsite, Caribou Hill offers spectacular views of the surrounding valleys. The hill—once a bustling center of mining activity—is dotted with mines, foundations, stone walls, and collapsed structures. An unmarked side trail (505.1M) takes you on a stroll atop the hill and through its history. From here, you may opt to scramble down a steep zigzag trail (still 505.1M) directly to the Caribou townsite. Or, continuing on FR 505 takes you about 1 mile along a gradual downhill past more mine pits, the Seven Thirty Tunnel, and the Caribou Shaft before looping around to Caribou; there are a few designated campsites along this stretch. The site of Caribou marks the end of the hike.

The remains of a home at the foot of Caribou Hill

At Caribou, several roads meet and the partial walls of two huge stone structures prominently stand watch. A picturesque cabin lies collapsed beside the parking area. High-clearance roads and trails lead out from Caribou like spokes on a wheel. At their junction is a parking area with maps showing designated campsites within roughly a mile. The roads are open to hikers, horses, ATVs, four-wheel-drives, skiers, snowmobiles, and bicycles. The Caribou silver mine operates nearby and owns much of the surrounding land; please respect private property.

For a nice extra hike where you can see more of Caribou's history, take FR 128J.1, the smallest road at the far right (east) side of the parking area. The road is much less used and more hiker-friendly than the others. You'll pass the Silver Point Mine and then, on the left, the old Caribou cemetery. The cemetery is on private property, so please stay off. (Just past it, a left-hand side trail leads through dozens of mine pits, reminders of the frenzied days when miners dug holes and abandoned them just as fast.) A few hundred yards more takes you to a prominent headframe, where you can enjoy a great view of the valley leading back toward Eldora. The hike continues down to a view of Nederland at about 1.5 miles from the parking area and passes the St. Louis and Eagle Bird mines, East St. Louis mine, Jackpot mine, and Boulder County mine before hooking back up with the road from Nederland to Caribou.

Hessie to Lost Lake

HESSIE WAS MURDER

About 20 miles southwest of Boulder in the valley of Middle Boulder Creek, the town of Eldora enjoyed a brisk, albeit brief, mining boom a good two decades after Caribou's (see Hike 15). Prospectors began combing these hills around 1889 and 1890, and the pace quickened with the discovery of gold along the flanks of the peaks forming the valley, which the eager prospectors dubbed "Happy Valley." A town mushroomed, drawing 1,000 residents and earning the name of Eldorado. When the post office cited a conflict with a California mining camp claiming the same name, the town's founders shortened it to Eldora. But those first streaks of high-grade gold quickly played out in all of the mines, and within about three years Eldora's boom was over.

Three miles west of town, and 1,000 feet higher, is tiny Lost Lake. Clinging to the talus-covered slopes overlooking the lake were some of the area's busiest mines during those few years, with names like the Lost Lake, the Ma W., the Shirley, and the Norway. Of them, the Revenge held on the longest. Prospector F.M. Strawhun staked the Revenge in August 1897. The mine showed great promise, but too many factors held it back: its rocky terrain, its barely accessible perch at the end of a steep road from Eldora, and the same drainage problem that plagued the nearby Fourth of July mine (see Hike 14). As water filled the shafts, crews pumped it out. In the end, the Revenge's downfall was like that of so many other mines: The high-grade gold vanished, leaving only ore that was too expensive to extract. In July 1907, a new owner reopened the Revenge. But finding the same water problems and, again, only traces of high-grade gold, he, too, moved on. The Revenge has sat idle ever since.

Midway between Lost Lake and Eldora sat the camp of Hessie, at the junction of two forks of Boulder Creek. Captain J.H. Davis founded the streamside settlement in a lush meadow with high peaks all around. He named Hessie after his wife, who came to town and served as its postmistress. The camp grew to include one or two stores, a busy sawmill, and a school. The post office operated (out of the Davises' cabin) for four years, beginning in 1898, and a wagon road led up to the Fourth of July. The settlement of Hessie was the bustling focal point of mines like that one and the Lost Lake diggings. But the most intriguing story from the town's storied

Hessie in 1920—six years after foul play violently claimed the life of one of the town's last remaining residents

Historic mines cling to talus slopes above Lost Lake.

past involves a murder—the perpetrator of which was never caught.

By 1914, only a few stalwarts still called Hessie home. "In a small slab cabin, under the spreading branches of a tall spruce," writes mining historian Donald Kemp, "lived Champ Smith, a tall, gray-haired, blue-eyed bachelor in his early fifties, who had prospected and mined in the region since 1897." In 1914 the veteran miner was extending a tunnel, the Caledonia, about a half-mile below town. On a June afternoon, his 70-year-old neighbor, G.W. Orear, paid a visit to the tunnel, bringing Smith his mail from Eldora. Expecting to see his friend working the tunnel, Orear instead found a sight so horrifying that he turned and ran the 2 miles back to Eldora without stopping. Just inside the tunnel lay the remains of his friend, blown apart by an explosion so massive it had left a crater inside the mine. Fragments of Smith's body—his head included—were scattered everywhere. "Champ's watch," Kemp adds, "was found in three pieces, one of them being the dial, undamaged, with the hands pointing to 7:30."

Thanks to some sleuthing by a Boulder coroner, sheriff's investigators, and Smith's brother John (who rushed to the scene from Denver), what appeared to be a tragic accident proved not to be so accidental. In reassembling Smith's skull they found a bullet hole, and in investigating the mine tunnel they discovered blood on an ore car and a 200-foot trail of blood leading to the site of the blast. Further probing of the tunnel uncovered the .22-caliber bullet.

Smith had been shot well inside the tunnel and his body carried via ore car closer to the portal, where his killer or killers had set his corpse on a charge of dynamite in an effort to destroy all evidence of the shooting. It turned out, too, that Smith's recent appointment to the post of deputy game warden had led to open hostility from his

neighbors when Smith vowed his intent to uphold laws requiring hunting licenses. Smith had lost friends over the matter, and three of those former friends were taken in for his murder. Wilson Davis and two brothers named Smalley, all miners with family in Hessie, awaited trial at the Boulder County jail. But lacking evidence to tie the three to the murder, investigators dropped the case. The men went free and the murder was never solved.

An old mine overlooks Lost Lake.

LOCATION:	Indian Peaks Wilderness, 22 miles west of Boulder
DESCRIPTION:	A short, strenuous hike along a rushing stream leads to a beautiful mountain lake and the remnants of mines on talus-covered mountainsides.
DISTANCE:	3 miles, out and back
HIKING TIME:	4 hours
RATING:	Moderate
TRAILHEAD ELEVATION:	9,000 feet
MAXIMUM ELEVATION:	9,800 feet
MAP:	*Colorado Atlas & Gazetteer*, p. 39, A6
CONTACT:	Boulder Ranger District, (303) 541-2500, www.fs.fed.us/r2/arnf/

GETTING THERE: Drive 17 miles west of Boulder on CO 119 through Nederland. Just beyond Nederland, turn right at the sign for Eldora (this is CR 130, or Eldora Rd.). About 3.5 miles up the road you'll arrive at the center of Eldora. Keep going through Eldora; the pavement gives way to an unmaintained dirt road just past town. (The next stretch can be driven in a passenger car with decent clearance, but four-wheel drive is preferable.) At about 0.75 mile along the dirt road you'll see signs for Hessie.

At this point, you can either park along the road or continue left 0.25 mile farther to a parking area at the Hessie townsite. You'll likely want to park at the fork if you're driving a passenger vehicle or low-clearance four-wheel-drive. The last stretch includes a section of road that, for much of the year, is submerged under a rushing stream. A sign claims that passenger vehicles can pass if "carefully driven," but it's not recommended. The stream has done its work over the years, and there's at least one truly wicked snag along the underwater roadway. If you park along the road, please watch for fire lanes.

GOOD TO KNOW: This trail is very popular in the summer, especially in July, as is the nearby Fourth of July Trail (see Hike 14). The road from Eldora to both trailheads is narrow, and in peak season the traffic can be a challenge, with drivers jockeying for position and parking all along the road by midmorning when the parking areas fill. If that's a concern, you might want to hike these trails in the off-season. However, the wildflowers are at their absolute peak around mid-July. Deer frequent these grassy hillsides, too, especially around the lake.

A permit is required for camping between June 1 and September 15; no groups of more than 12 people (or people and pack animals combined) are allowed. A permit is also required for organized tour groups. Bikes and motor vehicles are prohibited. Leashed dogs are welcome. There are nine campsites around the lake. Because of high impact at the lake, a system of designated, numbered campsites is in use. Watch for mosquitoes in summer.

You can also fish for trout at the lake. On a mid-June afternoon, 8- and 9-inch brookies were biting. This is a great snowshoeing and cross-country skiing trail, although you never know how far up you can get, as the drifts pile high in winter and spring. The wet month of June is a beautiful time for flowers as the snowdrifts recede from the trails, and July is peak blooming season. One recreational map sneers that Lost Lake has "been found"—and it's true that you will have human and canine trail companions no matter what the season. But the area's natural beauty and much of its history are intact and well worth exploring, especially because the trail is so accessible from Boulder.

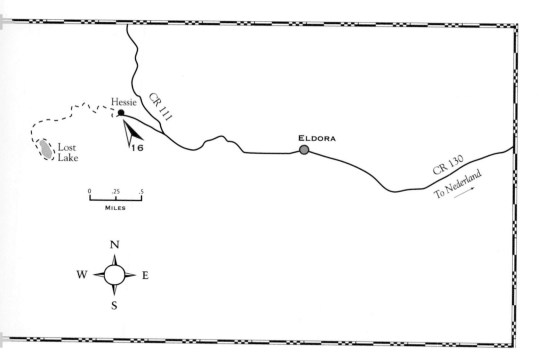

THE WALK

If you parked along the road, wooden walkways take you around the water and to the trailhead. A sign marks the Hessie townsite at 9,000 feet in elevation. Cross the bridge over the stream. You'll see several posted trails leaving from this spot; follow Devil's Thumb Trail (*not* Devil's Thumb Bypass) for Lost Lake.

As you round the first big right-hand bend in the trail, keep an eye out to the left for the remains of a grand home and its decaying front porch. After about 0.5 mile of uphill—just past the first steep section of rocky trail—are some rolling waterfalls. Plentiful boulders make perfect spots for a picnic or sitting and taking in the falls. The falls run heavily in the spring and are a near-frozen trickle in snowshoe season.

About 0.25 mile past the falls, bear left at the sign for Lost Lake Trail. (Other trails lead to Jasper Lake, Devil's Thumb Lake, and Devil's Thumb Pass; these are beautiful, moderately strenuous hikes of 4 to 6 miles. Woodland Lake and King Lake are great hikes if you want to go farther after your Lost Lake jaunt.) After 0.5 mile of steeper uphill through dense forest, you arrive at the lake. You can follow the trail to the right or left as it circles the lake, passing all nine campsites. On the rocky mountainsides around the lake you can spot the mines. The best view of them is to the left, but you can access side trails up the steep slopes to the mines from either direction. As you explore the mine areas, be sure to use the footpaths to avoid causing erosion. They can be tricky to find and easy to lose; watch for cairns, as well.

After you explore the mine areas and circle the lake, come back down the same way you came up.

Chautauqua Trail

A CENTURY OF GATHERINGS

In 1874, a group of New York educators rented the lakeside site of a Methodist camp to hold a series of teaching sessions for Sunday school instructors. The lake was Lake Chautauqua (from an Iroquois word describing the lake's shape and pronounced cha-TAHK-wa), and they called their organization the Chautauqua Institution. When the program proved popular, the institution expanded its offerings to provide other kinds of secular adult education and a "Chautauqua Literary and Scientific Circle" that brought ordinary people together to explore literature, the arts, and public policy. They held concerts and sponsored lectures, and thousands came to listen.

Their idea caught on, and soon a Chautauqua movement was afoot all across America. Colorado's own Chautauqua came into being in 1898 when officials from the City of Boulder, the University of Texas, and the Gulf and Southern Railroad organized a Fourth of July event in the midst of a series of gatherings in Boulder. The event grew out of a $20,000 bond issue approved by Boulder's voters. The city bought 25 acres of the Bachelder Ranch at the southwest edge of town, erecting a dining hall and a grand auditorium in the weeks before the Fourth of July opening ceremony. Housing and classrooms took shape in the form of 150 tents, which were replaced over the following years by cottages brought in from Boulder or built on-site—some 80 of them by 1915, when the last tents were removed. The year 1900 saw the construction of an academic hall, and participants over the coming Chautauqua seasons witnessed the district flourish as offices, lodges, gardens, and a community house joined the growing numbers of residential cottages.

The auditorium played host to a wealth of speakers and performers, providing a higher-profile edge to the quieter, more reflective educational programs that thrived in the Chautauqua district over the decades. Such luminaries as politician and orator William Jennings Bryan, fiery evangelist Billy Sunday, the Kansas City Symphony, and bandleader John Philip Sousa were among the early performers at the auditorium. In homage to the district's historic past, audiences can still sometimes enjoy silent films there.

Top: *The 1900 Academic Hall houses offices for today's Colorado Chautauqua.* **Bottom:** *The Chautauqua art gallery in 1900*

The nationwide Chautauqua movement faded after 1929. But the Colorado Chautauqua, according to the association, "survived the end of the Chautauqua movement, the depression, and World War II largely because of the friendships among the cottage owners and longtime renters who returned each summer during these trying times. Indeed, today 31 of the cottage owners are 3rd, 4th, and 5th generation Chautauquans."

The Colorado Chautauqua is now listed in the National Register of Historic Places, has been designated a National Historic Landmark (the first in the Denver metro area), and the district is a Landmarked Historic District of the City of Boulder. Continuing its historic tradition, today's Colorado Chautauqua still serves as a gathering place and offers lodging, meeting spaces, and a year-round menu of concerts, films, and other cultural attractions. And just as Boulder's Chautauqua is there to educate and entertain, the mountains and trails are there to inspire.

LOCATION:	Chautauqua Park, at the western edge of Boulder
DESCRIPTION:	Chautauqua Trail takes you to the foot of the Flatirons—the uplifted slabs of red sedimentary stone that have served as backdrop and mountain playground for more than a century's worth of Chautauqua fans. The hike ends with a stroll alongside the historic Chautauqua district.
DISTANCE:	2.5-mile loop
HIKING TIME:	2 hours
RATING:	Easy
TRAILHEAD ELEVATION:	5,700 feet
MAXIMUM ELEVATION:	6,100 feet
MAP:	*Colorado Atlas & Gazetteer,* p. 40, A1
CONTACT:	City of Boulder Open Space and Mountain Parks, (303) 441-3440, www.ci.boulder.co.us/openspace/
GETTING THERE:	From Broadway (CO 93) in Boulder, turn west on Baseline Rd. Go 1.1 miles to the signs for the left-hand turn into Chautauqua Park. Ample parking is available at the Ranger Cottage. If there are no vacant parking spaces, keep driving into the district, where you'll find parking throughout.
GOOD TO KNOW:	This is one of the most popular trails around, for good reason. Right at the edge of Boulder, it offers breathtaking beauty beside a historic cultural district. This is a fantastic running trail, and leashed dogs are welcome. (This is one of the best places to view the beautiful dogs of Boulder.) The hike takes you through fields of tall grasses and wildflowers, then along the stunning red Flatirons and the ponderosa pine and Douglas fir woods at their base. The walk is fine in running or walking shoes unless you plan to take any of the side trails up into the Flatirons. All trails are well marked; please stay on designated trails. Horses are allowed, but bikes are prohibited. No camping is allowed. Despite all the human activity along the many trails, this is deer, bear, and mountain lion country.
	The Ranger Cottage at the parking area has historic artifacts and exhibits on the Chautauqua movement and the early days of the Rocky Mountain Climbers Club. Other exhibits discuss the Open Space and Mountain Parks program and the region's flora and fauna. Be sure to set aside some time before or after your hike to explore the Chautauqua district and see its auditorium, dining hall, lodges, teachers' cottages, and other historic buildings. In the district is a popular and beautifully landscaped park, and the venerable dining hall serves breakfast, lunch, and dinner, plus a Sunday brunch. The dining hall is closed on Mondays.

The Chautauqua Trail offers great views of the Flatirons, a famous Boulder landmark.

THE WALK

Chautauqua Trail heads right up to the classic, often-photographed and often-painted view of the Flatirons. From the well-marked trailhead, walk west along Chautauqua Trail 0.6 mile to the Bluebell-Baird Trail. (When you reach Ski Jump Trail 0.25 mile up Chautauqua Trail, you might want to take it for an extra little detour into the woods; just follow the signs back to the Bluebell-Baird Trail.) Take a left onto the Bluebell-Baird Trail. On Bluebell-Baird, you'll first pass Royal Arch Trail on the right, then Mesa Trail, also on the right. There is a stone picnic shelter at the junction with Royal Arch and restrooms at the junction with Mesa. Stay on Bluebell-Baird, which becomes Bluebell Rd. as it curves its way back north toward the trailhead. Follow the road about 1 mile alongside the historic district and its cabins, all the way back to the trailhead. If you'd like to start wandering through the historic cultural district, you can break off from the road at any number of places.

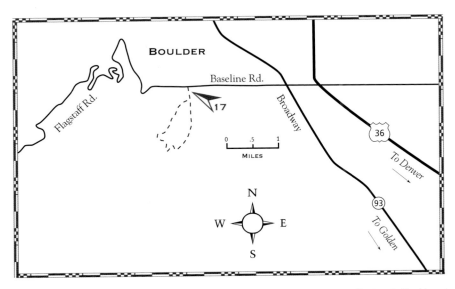

NCAR to the Doudy-DeBacker-Dunn Homestead

UP FROM THE STONES

The late 1850s brought a stream of wanderers and settlers into the Southern Arapaho Indian country of the Rocky Mountain foothills, some of them looking for minerals, some looking for farm- and ranchland. In 1857 or 1858, just as gold seekers and others were coming together to form the town of Boulder, Sylvester Doudy settled on a piece of land between that new community and the hot springs that gave rise to the resort of Eldorado Springs. He built a wooden house, sawmill, and gristmill in the valley and raised cattle there. When a flood swept through the valley in 1864, the house was the only one of the three buildings left standing.

Five years later, Belgian-born farmers John and Marie DeBacker bought the house and Doudy's land for $500. John DeBacker, who had been working the land

The Doudy-DeBacker-Dunn Homestead

just east of the Doudy house, had made a good living by hauling his produce, beef, and dairy products (including eggs packed in sawdust) to the booming mining towns of Black Hawk and Central City. Tragically, Marie died in 1865 after suffering a miscarriage, the result of chasing some cattle from their wheat field. But DeBacker determined to stay at the homestead, and in 1874 he built a two-story stone addition to the wooden house he had bought from Doudy. To make the structure, he interlocked stones of widely varying lengths and dimensions—an amazing accomplishment that draws wonder even today. He ran an irrigation ditch through his homestead, diverting part of it right through the sturdy stone addition to provide running water. The water fed into a washing machine and a cream separator run by a waterwheel.

When DeBacker retired in 1901, his daughter, Emma Dunn, took over the property along with her husband, John. Dairy farmers, the Dunns raised a family

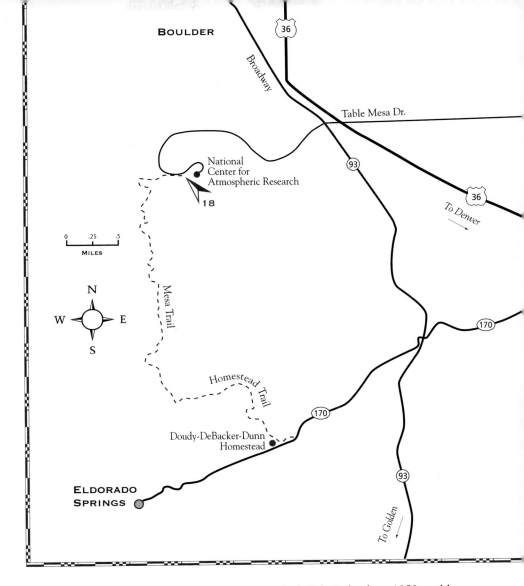

and stayed in the house for more than 50 years. Only John's death in 1953 could convince Emma to move on.

About 5 miles north of the homestead, another impressive stone structure took shape just a few years later. A prominent little plateau of 28 acres overlooking the plains and the city of Boulder was the site that the National Science Foundation chose for a facility to house the National Center for Atmospheric Research (NCAR). Built between 1961 and 1967, the facility was to house some 500 scientists and other workers in spaces for offices, laboratories, and public exhibits. True to its mission as an environmental research center, the facility also needed to make a minimal impact on its natural setting—a mesa top with the dramatic red slabs of the Flatirons rising behind it.

The foundation chose architect I.M. Pei to design the research center. Born in Canton, China, in 1917, Pei had come to the United States to study architecture at MIT and Harvard. After teaching and then working at a New York architectural firm, he founded his own architectural office in New York in 1960, just a year before the NCAR project. Ecological studies were gaining new stature in 1960, and Pei's mission included this challenge: "to create a national symbol of atmospheric research, confirming its legitimacy as an exact science."

For the research center's design, Pei was inspired in part by ancient Puebloan structures like those at Mesa Verde. "You just cannot compete with the scale of the Rockies," he explains. "So we tried to make a building that was without the conventional scale you get from recognizable floor heights—as in those monolithic structures that still survive from the cliff-dwelling Indians." Built of stone and clay, those structures took shape in tall, geometrical forms that fit snugly and organically into their cliffside settings. For NCAR, Pei designed a tight cluster of buildings made of a hammered concrete that incorporated native stone to match the reddish color of the Flatirons. The result was monumental, yet quietly reflective of the natural surroundings.

Explaining the thinking that goes into his designs, Pei says, "In the Middle Ages the focus was the cathedral; one hundred years ago, the city hall; today, anything and everything!" Both the NCAR facility and the Doudy-DeBacker-Dunn Homestead stand as ingenious accomplishments of their times, incorporating the very stones from which they rise and reflecting the Rocky Mountain landscapes around them.

The National Center for Atmospheric Research, designed by architect I.M. Pei, sits atop Table Mesa at the edge of Boulder.

LOCATION:	The southwestern edge of Boulder
DESCRIPTION:	Offering a continuous view of the Flatirons, this hike takes you from the postmodern architectural gem of NCAR to the 19th-century homestead of the Doudy, DeBacker, and Dunn families.
DISTANCE:	11 miles, out and back
HIKING TIME:	5 hours
RATING:	Moderate
TRAILHEAD ELEVATION:	6,300 feet
MAXIMUM ELEVATION:	6,500 feet
MAP:	*Colorado Atlas & Gazetteer*, p. 40, A1
CONTACT:	City of Boulder Open Space and Mountain Parks, (303) 441-3440, www.ci.boulder.co.us/openspace

GETTING THERE:	From Broadway (CO 93) in Boulder, take Table Mesa Dr. west. Go 2.5 miles, and up to the top of the mesa, to the National Center for Atmospheric Research at the end of Table Mesa. Park in the NCAR parking lot.
	To do this hike in the reverse order, from the intersection of Broadway and Table Mesa Dr./South Boulder Rd. in Boulder, take Broadway 2.6 miles south to Eldorado Springs Dr. (CO 170). Turn right and drive 1.7 miles to the Mesa Trailhead. There are two parking areas, one on either side of the road.
GOOD TO KNOW:	Like the Chautauqua hike (see Hike 17), this walk is fine in running or walking shoes unless you plan to take any of the side trails up into the Flatirons. All trails are well marked; please stay on designated trails. Horses and dogs (on leash or under voice control) are allowed, but bikes are prohibited. No camping is allowed. Despite all the human activity along the many trails, this is deer, bear, and mountain lion country.
	Restrooms are available at the Doudy-DeBacker-Dunn Trailhead (Homestead Trail) and in the NCAR building when it is open. There are picnic tables at the Homestead Trailhead, which is just past the homestead and across a bridge over South Boulder Creek. This hike passes alternately through pine woods, meadows, and cactus-strewn mesas. This is a spectacular trail for viewing wildflowers in the spring and summer. Overall the trail is easy, but the hike's length and the occasional switchback make for a somewhat strenuous walk.

THE WALK

From the parking area, follow the path to the back side of NCAR and the Walter Orr Roberts Nature Trail, named for the center's first director. At 11 viewpoints along the nature loop are markers exploring weather and climate phenomena and the park's plant and animal life. The entire nature loop is accessible by wheelchair. Hike to the western end of the loop, where you'll see a trail marker and access to the Mesa Trail.

Follow the signs down the side of the mesa to the Mesa Trail (avoiding any trails that are closed for revegetation), then up a few switchbacks to another rise at the big water tank. From here, keep hiking south on the Mesa Trail.

After about 3 miles, in a stretch of forest you will arrive at the ruins of a wooden cabin and a few stone paths, along with sections of crumbling stone walls. At the cabin are a rusty old cot and set of bedsprings; you can even see the remains of some flowerbeds. A second little structure lies across the trail. From the vicinity of these cabins and just before a series of gentle downward switchbacks, look off at the plains in the distance to the south. There, beside a wind farm, you can see what remains of the now-shuttered Rocky Flats weapons plant, where plutonium triggers for atomic bombs were fabricated during the Cold War.

At about 4 miles from NCAR you reach the junction of the Mesa Trail and Homestead Trail. Take Homestead and stay on it for another 1.5 miles. The last stretch is a steady downhill to broad, grassy meadows—the farm- and ranchlands of early settlers. Soon, the impressive stone homestead stands before you. At the homestead is a marker detailing the history of the three families who lived, farmed, and ranched here. The remains of a stone fence zigzag throughout the grounds. According to the marker, the walls extend for miles and were built by drifters who arrived with the mining boom. These out-of-work miners "would clear the fields and construct the walls in return for lodging and meals."

From the homestead, go back to NCAR the way you came; just keep bearing generally north at the Mesa Trail markers to stay on the Mesa Trail. For your return hike, you might want to explore a number of well-marked alternate loops to add some variety on the way back.

Meyers Homestead

A VALLEY EMPIRE

Following his doctor's advice, James Walker trekked to Colorado from Missouri in 1869. He arrived in Boulder County ill and carrying only a few dollars. A band of Arapaho Indians took him in, and he lived with them until better health allowed him to move on. Work as a farmhand earned him enough money to buy a small parcel of land west of Eldorado Canyon, where a spring provided year-round water and open meadows promised good farming and grazing land.

Walker married Phoebe Skinner, a Boulder schoolteacher, in 1876, and Phoebe gave birth to their only child, a son named William. In 1882 the Walkers filed a claim on a 160-acre homestead. The family lived in an older log cabin on the ranch during the warm season and spent winters in Boulder, where Phoebe taught school and James found work as a carpenter. He invested in some livestock to raise at the homestead, and thus began life on what would grow to be one of the biggest ranching operations ever assembled in the Boulder area. The 1880s proved to be lean years because of Phoebe's ill health and frequent medical expenses. Having experienced complications while giving birth to William, she never enjoyed truly good health afterward. But by taking on odd jobs and gradually making a success of his ranch, James helped the family weather tough times. Fall hunting brought in wild game, and he tended a large garden; using water from the farm's spring, he raised enough produce to feed his family and still have plenty to share with neighboring homesteaders.

James Walker's solitary sawmill commands a lush meadow at the Meyers Homestead.

"Walker did not agree with open range practices popular at that time," writes local historian Joanna Sampson, in which "cattle were turned loose to survive as best they could without supplemental feed during winter." Sure enough, when the winter of 1886 to 1887 proved particularly brutal, the Walkers' cattle were some of the only ones in Colorado to survive because James had kept them contained and provided them with hay from the previous summer. The Walkers' cattle were Galloways, a black-coated Scottish variety of hardy, incorrigible bovines bred to withstand Scotland's rough climate. Selling the cattle meant two-day cattle drives to Denver's stockyards—a wearying part of the operation that son Will took over once he was old enough. The Walkers hired a neighbor, young Veronica Kossler, to help care for Phoebe in her ill health. Veronica married 25-year-old Will in 1902.

As his operations grew successful, James Walker bought parcels from neighboring homesteaders when they moved on. One of those properties was a lush, wooded tract known as Meyers Gulch, named for Andrew Meyers, the first homesteader to settle and log the land. James used the Meyers Gulch land for logging and for pasturing his livestock, building a sawmill on the property to process the trees as they were felled. Throughout his ranch, James over the years built a blacksmith shop, a granary, a smokehouse, a wagon barn, a root cellar, chicken and turkey houses, and a barn for corn storage and pigs. He and Phoebe had moved into a new, larger house on the ranch in 1883. As the Walkers added to the property, new corrals and fences went up; eventually, there were 13 barns on a spread that included up to 450 cattle at a time.

An opportunity appeared in the 1890s that enabled the Walkers to shed their remaining debt. When gold was discovered nearby in 1894, an Englishman—Lord Bertie Langridge—paid James $50,000 to mine on his land. A few years later, David Moffat's Denver, Northwestern & Pacific Railroad came through South Boulder Canyon on its way to the Continental Divide at Rollins Pass. Like other area ranchers, James sold the railroad the right-of-way through his property—another financial windfall.

In all, the Walker Ranch grew to some 6,000 acres around Boulder Creek. Today, Boulder County manages 3,778 of those acres as open space. The property earned National Register of Historic Places status as a historic cultural landscape in 1984, with the boundaries extended in 1988 to include the Meyers Homestead. The ranch is the largest designated historic cultural landscape in Colorado.

Sawmill at the Meyers Homestead

LOCATION:	West of Boulder
DESCRIPTION:	Wildflowers and bird life abound along this stroll through the woods and meadows of an old homestead.
DISTANCE:	5.2 miles, out and back
HIKING TIME:	3 hours
RATING:	Moderate
TRAILHEAD ELEVATION:	7,300 feet
MAXIMUM ELEVATION:	8,080 feet
MAP:	*Colorado Atlas & Gazetteer*, p. 39, A7
CONTACT:	Boulder County Parks and Open Space, (303) 441-3950, www.co.boulder.co.us/openspace/

GETTING THERE: From Boulder, take Baseline Rd. west. Stay on it as it becomes Flagstaff Rd., then continue for 7 miles. When you see the "Walker Ranch, Meyers Gulch" sign on the right, turn in and follow the signs to "Trailhead and Picnic Parking."

GOOD TO KNOW: The Meyers Homestead Trail is within the well-maintained Walker Ranch, an open space listed on the National Register of Historic Places. Trailhead facilities include toilets, ample parking, picnic tables, and a large covered picnic area. Information about the park and its facilities, wildlife, and plant life is available at the trailhead. The group shelter at nearby Meyers Gulch can accommodate 75 people; call ahead for reservations.

This is mule deer, mountain lion, and bear habitat, and the park is home to migrating herds of elk in winter. Ninety species of birds have been spotted here. The trailhead is stocked with a checklist for birdwatchers; a wildflower guide would also come in handy. The Meyers Homestead Trail is a wide, smooth path all the way, so hiking boots aren't necessary unless you plan to explore side trails.

This trail is a superb choice for mountain biking or snow-shoeing. Horseback riding is allowed, as are leashed dogs. The park is open from sunset to sundown and no camping is permitted. No motor vehicles are allowed on the trails. Mountain bikers are welcome to enjoy any designated trail at Meyers Homestead, and hikers can explore the entire homestead (although rangers ask that you keep your impact minimal). Past the trail's endpoint is private property, so please don't trespass.

THE WALK

As you start down the Meyers Homestead Trail, note the burn area to the left. A wildfire in September 2000 scorched several acres near the trailhead, but most of the ranch escaped fire damage. The trail immediately dips down into an expansive grassy meadow —which, if you catch it at the right time, is dazzling with wildflowers. Also in the

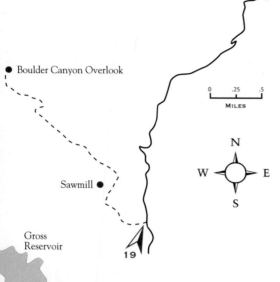

Baseline Rd.

Flagstaff Rd.

• Boulder Canyon Overlook

```
0      .25      .5
|---|---|---|
   MILES
```

```
      N

W ──◯── E

      S
```

Sawmill •

Gross
Reservoir

19

meadow is the enormous skeleton of rancher James Walker's sawmill. A side trail leads to the mill and into the hills beyond it, but cyclists, please take note: This is not a designated trail, so you'll need to leave the bike behind if you want a closer look at the mill.

The hike is easy at first, sloping down into the meadow, then it levels out and emerges from the meadow into a gradual uphill the rest of the way. Along the remainder of the trail, open fields alternate with stretches of pine and spruce woods and small groves of shimmering aspens alongside a meandering stream. All the while, you might spot lupine, wallflower, paintbrush, sticky geranium, horsetail, black-eyed Susan, mullein, wild rose, and more. The occasional rabbit or chipmunk might scurry past. Some hikes have nice *sounds*, and this is one of them: the many species of birds, the rippling stream hidden beside the trail, breezes drifting through the aspen leaves. Here and there you'll also spot bits of evidence that this was once a thriving ranch.

At the end of the 2.6-mile trail, the Boulder Canyon Overlook rewards you with a magnificent view of Boulder Canyon, Sugarloaf Mountain, and the peaks beyond.

Crags Mountain Resort and Moffat Road

ELDORADO'S HOT SPOT

One evening in the fall of 1912, residents of Marshall, Superior, and other communities and ranches south of Boulder noticed an eerie glow emanating from Eldorado Canyon's walls. In Spanish, Eldorado means "the golden one," and the canyon was earning its name. The closest witnesses could see flames as the Crags Mountain Resort, once advertised as having "the most beautiful scenery on the whole Moffat Road," burned to the ground.

A.D. Stencel bought the Crags in 1907 and remodeled it into a first-class hotel with rustic cabins and furnished tents for rent. The two-level hostelry featured first-story rooms with private baths and second-story rooms with screened sleeping porches and views of the canyon's 1,500-foot cliffs and South Boulder Creek below. The resort offered free dancing and a restaurant that served "all the delicacies of the Denver market at popular prices."

Crags Mountain Resort overlooking Eldorado Canyon, circa 1910

Stencel counted on steady business from city dwellers who arrived via daily Denver, Northwestern & Pacific trains traveling the Moffat Road. Passengers boarded at Fifteenth and Bassett Streets in Denver and disembarked at the Scenic siding on the north side of Eldorado Mountain, where they walked or rode burros down a half-mile trail to the hotel. The round-trip cost $1 and a 50-ride booklet could be bought for $22.50.

Other guests rode a funicular rail system to the hotel from the canyon floor. This ingenious mountain tramway consisted of counterbalanced cars on parallel sets of rails connected by a system of cables and pulleys. As one passenger-filled car advanced up the hill, another went down. Engineers filled a water tank on empty downward-moving cars to equalize the weight. Guests who preferred the strenuous life could walk to the resort along the Rattlesnake Gulch Trail, then called Crags Boulevard.

Stencel also capitalized on Colorado's reputation as a healthy haven for tuberculosis patients. Tuberculosis was commonly called "consumption" or "the white plague" in the late 19th and early 20th centuries. Before the discovery and use of effective drugs in the 1940s, doctors prescribed a variety of "cures." Dr. Samuel Edwin Solly, a recovered consumptive living in Colorado Springs, recommended fresh, dry mountain air in his widely read booklet *The Health Resorts of Colorado Springs and Manitou*.

Fireplace at the Crags Mountain Resort ruins

Thousands of so-called lungers abandoned their homes and rushed to the nation's highest state. Denver drew the lion's share of patients, and many of the wealthier ones lived in mountain hotels for extended periods. The Crags Mountain Resort's crisp climate, pure mineral water, easy access to a 76-degree artesian pool in Eldorado Springs, and healthy activities such as burro riding and gold prospecting appealed to many of the recent arrivals.

By 1912, visitation from out-of-state TB patients and Denver tourists had declined. Stencel's free dances, pure spring water, and promises of "choice specimens of mineral ore" that could be picked up off the ground no longer filled his rooms, cabins, and tents. The air was still fresh and clean, but the business climate had turned sour.

According to historian Joanna Sampson, locals saw a mysterious couple get off the train at the Scenic siding and hike down to the resort in November of that year. They departed by train hours later. That evening, a fire consumed the resort. Local historians suspect that the unprofitable hotel was burned for insurance money.

LOCATION:	Eldorado Canyon State Park
DESCRIPTION:	This sometimes-steep trail leads to the ruins of the Crags Mountain Resort, an early 20th-century hotel, and continues to views of the still-in-use Moffat Road grade and tunnels.
DISTANCE:	3.8 miles, out and back
HIKING TIME:	3 hours
RATING:	Moderate
TRAILHEAD ELEVATION:	5,800 feet
MAXIMUM ELEVATION:	7,000 feet
MAP:	*Colorado Atlas & Gazetteer*, p. 40, A1
CONTACT:	Eldorado Canyon State Park, (303) 494-3943, www.parks.state.co.us/

GETTING THERE:	From Boulder, take CO 93 south 3 miles to CO 170 and turn right (west) to Eldorado Springs. The highway ends in town and becomes a dirt road (Eldorado Springs Dr.). Go slowly through the residential area to Eldorado Springs State Park. Drive about 0.5 mile along South Boulder Creek to the Fowler–Rattlesnake Gulch Trailhead, which is on the left. If the small parking lot is full, look for spaces in designated pullouts along the road or near the entrance station.
GOOD TO KNOW:	A daily or annual Colorado State Parks pass is required. The parking lots fill early. Pets must be on a leash and camping is prohibited. The park is open from dawn to dusk year-round. Restrooms are near the east-entrance parking lot.

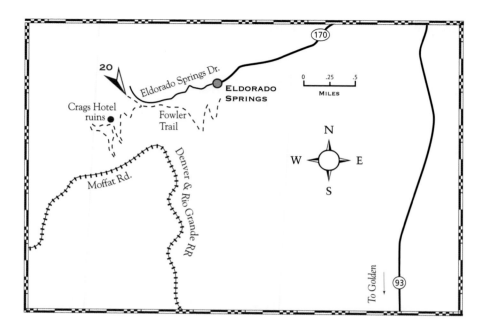

THE WALK

From the Fowler–Rattlesnake Gulch Trailhead, follow the level Fowler Trail 0.1 mile east to the Rattlesnake Gulch sign and turn right. The trail gets steeper and passes talus slopes as it goes west and south into the gulch. Follow it around the end of the gulch and up the opposite slope, go up a couple of switchbacks, and stop at the sign for the Crags Hotel ruins, which are 1.5 miles from the trailhead. Explore the cement fountain basin, a standing brick and stone fireplace, and foundation walls. The entire site is littered with nails, brick fragments, and pieces of ceramic dinnerware.

For an unobstructed view of Eldorado Canyon's walls and its cliff-hanging rock climbers, take the Rattlesnake Gulch loop about 0.2 mile westward to the Continental Divide overlook. A sign points the way. After resting at the bench, continue southward along the loop. At its southernmost point, the trail stops within 50 yards of the Moffat Road's tracks, which cling to Eldorado Mountain's steep northern slope. This was the Scenic siding, where passengers got off the train before hiking or riding burros down to the hotel. Two tunnels, both exhibiting the road's signature neoclassical cement pedimented entrances, bore into the mountain nearby. Do not leave the trail to investigate the tracks or tunnels; the slopes and tunnels could be dangerous and are outside of the park's boundaries.

The loop trail descends a steep grade and ends back at the hotel site. Return to the trailhead by the same route.

Marshall Mesa Trail

THE COAL MINER'S SON

On July 9, 1910, police officers apprehended 10-year-old Tony Gabriella and some of his friends for throwing rocks at strikebreakers near the Gorham coal mine on Marshall Mesa. Reported in the Boulder *Daily Camera*, the incident reminded people that labor strikes in Colorado's northern coalfield—a 6,800-square-mile area that surrounded the eastern Boulder County and southwestern Weld County towns of Lafayette, Louisville, Erie, Marshall, and Superior—affected everybody, including kids. Miners and their families went without pay, and sometimes without food. Residents paid higher prices for the coal they used to heat their homes. Mine superintendents tried to maintain production by bringing in scab laborers. Union toughs fought agents hired by the mine owners in the streets with fists, knives, and guns. And police officers found themselves in the middle of it all, trying to keep the peace.

When William Kitchens found an outcropping of coal near present-day Marshall in 1859, he could not have predicted the upheaval the discovery would eventually cause. Miners were flooding Kansas Territory at the time, but they weren't lured by coal. They wanted gold. Still, the treasure seekers and the merchants, ranchers, and farmers that followed would need coal for fuel. An enterprising fellow could make a buck or two selling the unglamorous stuff. Kitchens dug a hole, named it the Washington Lode, and hauled wagonloads of its black bounty to Denver, where he sold it by the bushel (25 bushels equaled one ton).

Gorham mine on Marshall Mesa, 1914

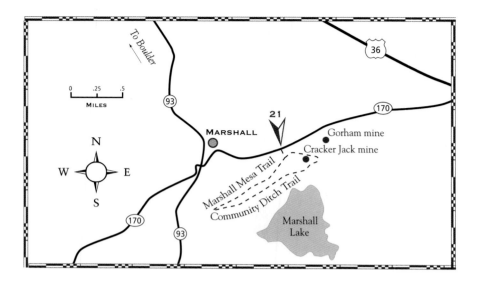

By the mid-1860s, Kitchens had grown tired of mining and decided to sell the Washington Lode to Joseph Marshall, an entrepreneur with ambition and big plans. Marshall expanded his domain by obtaining a land grant for an additional 1,480 acres. A community of miners, their families, and shopkeepers formed northwest of the mesa as Marshall and other investors developed mines and unearthed new coal seams.

The Golden, Boulder & Caribou Railway brought the Industrial Age to Marshall Mesa in 1878. An immediate reduction in transportation costs allowed mine owners to increase production by 100 percent in a single year. In 1879, freight trains shipped 50,000 tons of Joseph Marshall's coal to smelters, rail yards, and home furnaces across the state and beyond.

Large-scale coal mining made a lasting mark on Marshall Mesa's physical and social landscapes. A massive conveyor system, called a "tipple," moved coal from the Gorham mine to freight cars lined up at the foot of the mesa's northern slope. Boarding houses, administrative offices, and other facilities surrounded this structure. Demographics shifted rapidly in the late 1800s and early 1900s as southern and eastern European immigrants joined Americans and northern Europeans in the mines.

Interethnic relations sometimes turned violent. In 1891, a group of Marshall miners went on strike, citing threats to their jobs from immigrants who were willing to work for lower pay. Wives joined their husbands in the fight to drive foreigners from the mines.

Though divided by ethnicity, the miners sometimes joined together to fight for better working conditions and wages. Coal mining was dangerous, dirty, low-paying work. Underground rooms could collapse, killing workers. Coal dust could ignite, causing massive explosions and fires. A miner could die slowly from black lung, a cardiopulmonary disease caused by prolonged exposure to coal dust. For this, miners received about $1 per ton of coal mined—often paid in company scrip —and were forced to give it back when they bought groceries in company stores and rented company houses. These hardships hurt people of all nationalities, including Tony Gabriella, the rock-throwing youngster who was reprimanded at the Gorham mine in 1910.

Gabriella's outburst occurred during the so-called long strike, a period of labor unrest that lasted from 1910 to 1914. Miners demanded fair wages, better working conditions, and the right to unionize. The owners, refusing to recognize their employees' collective pleas, imported replacements and hired Baldwin-Felts detectives to guard their properties. Church and town leaders begged the adversaries to resolve their differences before people got killed. Most of the miners and guards remained peaceful, but a violent minority kept tensions high. Reports of street brawls and gunfights filled local newspapers. Boulder County sheriffs maintained order but feared a spark that would blow the powder keg sky high.

The Ludlow Massacre provided that spark (see Hike 48). On April 20, 1914, striking miners clashed with Colorado National Guard militiamen at the Ludlow tent colony in Colorado's southern coalfield near Trinidad. Five miners and one child died from bullet wounds, while two women and 11 children suffocated in a cellar trying to escape a fire that leveled the colony.

Bear Peak and Green Mountain from Marshall Mesa

The news shocked strikers in the northern coalfield. Three days after the tragedy, Sheriff Sanford Buster confronted a group of Marshall miners holed up in a cottage. "We are going to protect ourselves and our families," they said, clutching rifles. "And not allow anything to happen like happened at Ludlow."

Violent altercations, including a bloody gunfight at the Hecla mine near Louisville, continued for several months before President Wilson called in federal mediators. The miners had gained nothing when the longest strike in Colorado history ended on December 10, 1914.

Coal mining continued at Marshall Mesa and throughout the northern coalfield for the next three decades. Production spiked during World War I but declined steadily until the Gorham mine closed in 1939. Today, cement foundations, a few timbers, and coal dumps mark its location. But underground seams still burn with old fires consuming what is left of the coal.

LOCATION:	Marshall Mesa Open Space and Historic Mining Area
DESCRIPTION:	This easy loop through Boulder County's coal-mining past combines the Marshall Mesa and Community Ditch Trails. Near the Marshall Mesa Trailhead and within sight of the abandoned Colorado & Southern railroad grade, a sign interprets the area's transportation history.
DISTANCE:	2.3-mile loop
HIKING TIME:	1 hour
RATING:	Easy
TRAILHEAD ELEVATION:	5,520 feet
MAXIMUM ELEVATION:	5,740 feet
MAP:	*Colorado Atlas & Gazetteer,* p. 40, A1
CONTACT:	City of Boulder Open Space and Mountain Parks, (303) 441-3440, www.ci.boulder.us/openspace/

🐾 👫 🚲 🐕

GETTING THERE:	From Boulder, take CO 93 south to CO 170 and turn left (east). Follow CO 170 as it winds northeast into the small town of Marshall. Stay on CO 170 when it turns right (east) and then continue 0.7 mile to the Marshall Mesa Trailhead. Park in the small, unpaved lot. This is a popular destination for people with dogs, and the lot fills early.
GOOD TO KNOW:	Dogs must be on a leash or meet the Boulder Open Space voice and sight control standard. There are no public restrooms. If you have extra time, consider combining this short hike with a trip to nearby Eldorado Canyon and the Crags Mountain Resort ruins (see Hike 20). Mountain bikers can extend the ride by starting at the Doudy Draw Trailhead, which is across CO 170 from the Mesa Trailhead, and following the Community Ditch Trail northeast to Marshall Mesa. To reach the Mesa Trailhead, see "Getting There" on p. 91.

The Walk

Marshall Mesa Trail leads south to the base of the mesa, where it crosses a ditch and meets the Community Ditch Trail. The loop begins and ends here. Veer southwest on the Marshall Mesa Trail along and gradually up the mesa's north face through ponderosa pines. Cutting through the grove, the trail passes an outcropping of white sedimentary rock that was formed on the bottom of an ancient sea. A sign explains the geology. A little farther west, another sign tells hikers about underground coal fires, some of which might still be burning.

The trail continues westward through a gate and offers a tremendous view of Boulder and the Flatirons. Just north of the mesa, big mounds of dirt mark the locations of old coal dumps. At 0.9 mile, Marshall Mesa Trail meets the Community

Gorham mine foundations

Ditch Trail. Take the Community Ditch Trail east to double back along the top of the mesa (although you may take the Community Ditch Trail farther west for more great views of Marshall, Boulder, and the Flatirons to the northwest, and Eldorado Canyon to the west). Follow Community Ditch about a mile east. The trail leaves the ditch and descends where the ditch empties into Marshall Reservoir (the reservoir is private property). The concrete foundations that once supported the Gorham mine tramway, ore chute, and related loading machinery are visible northeast of the trail. As the trail bends northwest toward the trailhead it passes the Cracker Jack mine. The trailhead and parking lot will be within sight.

REGION 4
Denver

Top: *A scene along the Argentine Central rail line above Waldorf, with Argentine Pass in the distance*

Bottom: *Sandstone formations in Red Rocks Park*

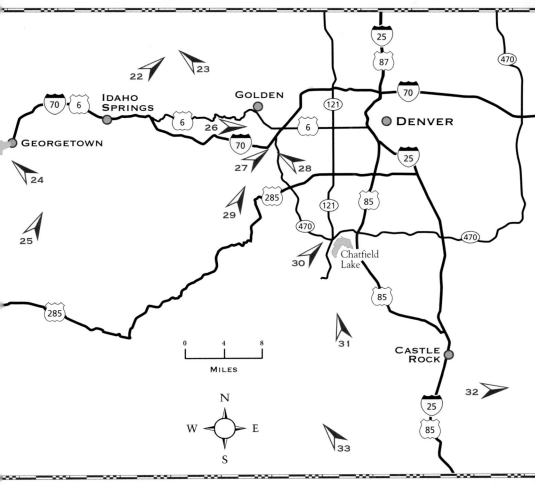

CONTENTS

Frazer Meadow Barn

LUMBERMAN FELLED BY A TREE

Unable to make his fortune as a miner in Black Hawk, John Frazer decided to try his luck in the timber trade. The decision cost him his life.

Frazer didn't have to move very far. In 1868, he went down Golden Gate Canyon Road a few miles and then built a new road up a hill to a relatively level spot amid a forest of mature pine trees south of Tremont Mountain. He cleared about 25 acres for a hayfield, built a single-room log cabin and a barn, and put in a small garden of root crops. He didn't need much more than that. As a bachelor, he needed only to provide for his horses, his cows, and himself.

Frazer picked a good time to start his new career as a logger. The Gilpin County gold mining industry had just broken through a major technological barrier, thanks

Frazer Meadow Barn

to Nathaniel P. Hill, a Brown University chemistry professor who perfected a workable smelting method. The industry needed extra timber for its expanding mines, mills, and towns. With Hill's Boston and Company smelter going full blast and the hills surrounding Black Hawk and Central City stripped bare of trees, Frazer should have had a ready market for his timber up and down North Clear Creek. Still, he had trouble finding the money to file a claim when an influx of homesteaders prompted him to prove up on his land (see Hike 23). As a squatter, he did not have legal title to property he had worked for 15 years. Taking advantage of Pre-emption Act provisions and a $200 loan from his friend Hugh McCannon, he filed for 160 acres that included his cabin, barn, and hay meadow in 1883. Samuel Parker, an African American who worked with Frazer, signed the document as a witness.

By that time the bachelor was no longer alone. Besides Parker, he had his brother Rufus to help him out and keep him company. In 1889, he claimed an additional

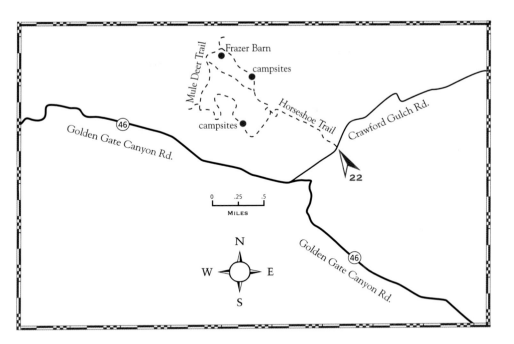

quarter section north and northwest of the original spread while Rufus took up an adjacent parcel. Between the two of them they owned three-quarters of a square mile. Twenty-one years after giving up on his Black Hawk get-rich-quick scheme, he had found a permanent home and stable employment on the side of a mountain where summers are short and the winters severe.

Frazer accomplished all this despite a serious handicap. Records show that he was "peglegged" or had a "game leg." Whatever his problem, it did not stop him from doing hard labor. With help from Samuel and Rufus, he cut trees, loaded them on horse-drawn wagons, and hauled them over miles of rutted dirt roads to his customers. And his logs were not of the Christmas tree variety. A cross section of the "Independence Tree," which is on display in the Golden Gate Canyon State Park visitor center, shows how big they can get: It has one ring for every year between 1776 and the time it was cut.

Frazer lumbered along, bad leg and all, until 1894. Then, one winter day while he was hauling timber to Central City, a chain holding his cargo broke. The heavy logs rolled off the wagon and onto him, fracturing his skull.

Because Frazer died without a will and because his debts exceeded the value of his assets, his property did not go to his brother. Tom Belcher, a neighbor, bought the land. He farmed Frazer's meadow and ran a few head of cattle. His family never lived in Frazer's cabin (which burned down in the 1980s), but they did use his barn to store hay. The mower is still visible in the grass near the dilapidated structure.

LOCATION:	Golden Gate Canyon State Park
DESCRIPTION:	The Horseshoe and Mule Deer Trails lead to a picturesque 1880s barn built by logger John Frazer.
DISTANCE:	4 miles, out and back
HIKING TIME:	2 to 3 hours
RATING:	Moderate
TRAILHEAD ELEVATION:	8,140 feet
MAXIMUM ELEVATION:	9,050 feet
MAP:	*Colorado Atlas & Gazetteer,* p. 39, B7
CONTACT:	Golden Gate Canyon State Park Visitor Center, (303) 582-3707, www.parks.state.co.us/

GETTING THERE:	From Golden, take CO 93 north 1 mile to Golden Gate Canyon Rd. (CO 46). Drive 13 miles west to Golden Gate Canyon State Park. Follow signs to the fee area. Then take the next right, Crawford Gulch Rd., to the visitor center. Go 0.5 mile down Crawford Gulch Rd. to the Frazer Meadow Trailhead.
GOOD TO KNOW:	All vehicles entering the park must purchase and display a Colorado State Parks pass. Mountain bikes and horses are allowed in the park, but not on Horseshoe Trail. Dogs must be leashed. The visitor center has restrooms, historical and wildlife exhibits, and a trout demonstration pond (no fishing), The Frazer Meadow Trailhead has restrooms. The park's camping facilities include cabins, yurts, backcountry shelters, and tent sites. Call (800) 678-2267 or (303) 470-1144 to make reservations.

THE WALK

From the Frazer Meadow Trailhead, pick up the hiker-only Horseshoe Trail at the western edge of the parking lot and head west along a small stream. All trails in Golden Gate Canyon State Park are named after local animals and are well marked with posts depicting footprints. Though the trail is never steep, it gains elevation consistently as it passes through pine forest, aspen groves, and small meadows. It parallels a stream and is mostly shady, even in midday.

At 1.1 miles, the Coyote Trail branches right and leads to the Greenfield Meadow campsites. A little farther on, another trail branches off to the left and leads to the Rim Meadow campsites. Stay on Horseshoe Trail until it ends at Mule Deer Trail. Head right (northeast) on Mule Deer 0.2 mile to the Frazer Meadow Barn. Tremont Mountain, at 10,388 feet, dominates the view to the northwest. Look for a hay mower along the meadow's northern edge. Return the way you came.

Tallman Ranch

THE FORGOTTEN VALLEY

In 1870, Anders Tallman left Sweden aboard a transatlantic ship bound for America. His wife and three children followed a year later. Their motives for emigration are unclear, but the emergence of a united and belligerent Germany under Otto von Bismarck might have had something to do with the decision. So, the Tallmans left Scandinavia just as nationalistic fervor embroiled Europe in war. Tallman's wife anticipated making a new start in a country that had recently ended its own war and was looking westward to a frontier filled with promise. But her American dream ended almost before it started.

Tallman's wife never saw the American shore, let alone the frontier. She died aboard the ship, leaving her husband with the children. Anders spent the next six years searching for a place to raise his son, Nils, and daughter, Anna (the third and

possibly older child, John, might have gone his own way and cared for himself). He found what he was looking for in Colorado—which gained statehood that year—several miles from the mining towns of Black Hawk and Central City. The mountains in this region made Anders think of Sweden, but he didn't spend too much time reminiscing about the past: Within the year he married Steena Bengson, another Swedish immigrant. His chosen home, so full of reminders of his native country, became known as Forgotten Valley.

The landscape was not the only thing that reminded Tallman of his homeland. Fellow Swedes filled every gully and gulch for miles around, and Steena's family lived 2 miles north of Forgotten Valley. Some of Tallman's Swedish friends came to Colorado to claim a piece of the state's famed mineral wealth, while others came for the land. Tallman chose the latter. He and his family lived in a converted

Tallman Ranch, Forgotten Valley

one-room schoolhouse that he moved to the property in the late 1870s. In time, they added outbuildings, including a barn, stable, and workshop. Their milk house was especially ingenious. During the summer, they routed Nott Creek's frigid water over its floor to keep the milk, butter, and other perishables cool.

The Tallmans survived on homegrown staples and traded surplus food for other necessities—such as flour and sugar—in the nearest towns. Steena did the shopping. Her trip to the Black Hawk markets took seven hours by ox-drawn wagon, each way.

After a stroke left Anders crippled in 1890, most of the bartering and farming fell to Steena. But Anders, confined to a chair on his front porch, still contributed by shooting elk or deer that strayed into his large potato field.

Anders continued to do his part despite his poor health because he understood that the unforgiving mountain environment would not abide slackers. Everyone pulled their own weight, including the grandchildren. Legend has it that one day while Steena was away, her grandson Rudolph tried to milk the cows. But the cows, who were comfortable with Steena and no one else, refused to stand still. Unfazed, Rudolph went inside the house, put on Steena's apron and bonnet, and went back outside to finish the chore without further trouble.

Rudolph inherited his grandparents' ranch from his mother, Anna, in 1913. After his death in 1927, Ruth (his widow) and daughter remained on the land. Ruth eventually remarried and kept the property until 1955. Ultimately, the State of Colorado acquired the land and incorporated it into Golden Gate Canyon State Park. By preserving the Tallman Ranch and the story of its stewardship, the park has ensured that Anders' Forgotten Valley will always be remembered.

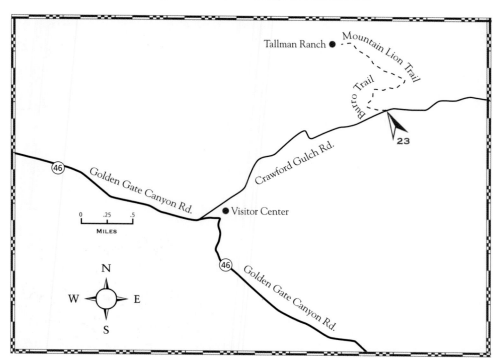

LOCATION:	Golden Gate Canyon State Park
DESCRIPTION:	The Burro and Mountain Lion Trails lead to the 1870s Tallman Ranch and a picturesque pond in Forgotten Valley.
DISTANCE:	2.4 miles, out and back
HIKING TIME:	2 to 3 hours
RATING:	Moderate
TRAILHEAD ELEVATION:	7,800 feet
MAXIMUM ELEVATION:	8,300 feet
MAP:	*Colorado Atlas & Gazetteer,* p. 39, B7
CONTACT:	Golden Gate Canyon State Park Visitor Center, (303) 582-7707, www.parks.state.co.us/
GETTING THERE:	From Golden, take CO 93 north 1 mile to Golden Gate Canyon Rd. Drive 13 miles west to Golden Gate Canyon State Park. Follow signs to the fee area, and then take the next right, Crawford Gulch Rd., to the visitor center. Go 2.2 miles down Crawford Gulch Rd. to the Bridge Creek Trailhead.
GOOD TO KNOW:	A Colorado State Park pass is required for all vehicles entering the park. Mountain bikes and horses are allowed on selected trails, including the Burro and Mountain Lion Trails to Tallman Ranch. Dogs must be leashed. The visitor center has restrooms, a gift shop, and historical and wildlife exhibits. The Bridge Creek Trailhead has restrooms and picnic areas. The park offers many camping options, including yurts, cabins, tent sites, and open, three-sided Appalachian Trail–style huts.

THE WALK

Starting at the Bridge Creek Trailhead, take the Burro Trail and head up the hillside about 0.5 mile. The first section is fairly steep but levels out a bit once it reaches a junction with the Mountain Lion Trail. Keep left and follow the con-joined trails for about 100 yards through a pine grove. When the trails separate, stay left again and follow the Mountain Lion Trail north-west for 0.6 mile to a small

Tallman Ranch house

lake. The Tallman Ranch house and two deteriorating outbuildings are on a hillside on the opposite side of the lake. Return by the same route.

Waldorf and the Argentine Central Railroad

BOOM AND BUST ON McCLELLAN MOUNTAIN

The 1868 discovery of the Stevens silver lode south of Silver Plume brought prospectors flocking to the rocky slopes of McClellan Mountain. Soon the Waldorf Mining and Milling Company of Edward John Wilcox owned some 80 veins of silver and a little gold throughout the district. Many of these "argentine" (or silver) lodes didn't pan out, but about nine flourished through the 1870s. At the base of Argentine Pass, the mining town that would later earn the name Waldorf grew to include a boarding house, a hotel, homes, stores, stables, and an assay office, all spread along one main road below the behemoth milling operation that clung to the tundra at the tunnel above town.

The Wilcox Tunnel, driven through the mountain in 1903, bisected all of Edward Wilcox's main ore veins over its 4 miles' worth of underground workings. The ore from the Stevens Mine, the earliest producer and one of the biggest, exited the tunnel at Waldorf. "Shortly after the mine was discovered, its owners hired two men to take out

Inside a Waldorf eating house in 1910

ore at thirty dollars a ton," wrote artist and historian Muriel Sibell Wolle. "As the men had no means of hauling the ore from the mine to the trail which they had cut through the trees, they filled rawhide sacks with the ore and rolled them down to the trail. For those that did not burst they received full pay; but so many of them broke open on the rocks that the system proved unprofitable."

Argentine Pass became the main supply route for wagons and stages hauling freight over the divide from Silver Plume and into the mining districts of Summit County. And the road sufficed, at first, for hauling ore down to Silver Plume from Waldorf. But the trek was a long one, and it grew increasingly arduous as the mines continued to produce. The solution was a railroad.

In 1905, on an August morning, Wilcox oversaw the groundbreaking at Silver Plume of a new rail line that would connect that town to his mines, 8 miles south. Silver Plume mayor Charles H. Dyer broke ground, and Wilcox's wife threw the first shovelful of dirt onto the grade. Other civic leaders did likewise, then 50 workers posted 15 feet apart along a staked path

The Santiago mine on McClellan Mountain

drove their picks into the ground in unison. Over the next two months, laborers finished the grade to the mines. Then they laid the first tracks of the Argentine Central Railroad. They worked through the brutal winter season, completing the task in four long months of labor.

They drove a golden spike into the rails at the mine tunnel, and the town was christened Wilcox, the name later changing to Waldorf. At an elevation of 11,666 feet, the new town's post office was rumored to be the country's highest.

Wilcox continued the line all the way to the summit of McClellan, another 8 miles of track away. That final 8 miles, built solely as a scenic attraction, drew thousands of riders and was touted as the tourist line to the "top of the world." ("A lifetime in a day!" its ads crowed.) Indeed, it was the highest narrow-gauge steam railroad line ever. Due to the extreme weather at the summit, the line's operators could only run it for three months out of the year. And it only ran six days a week: Wilcox, a former Methodist minister and still a good Christian, refused to operate it on Sundays. The scenic portion of the line was soon earning Wilcox 10 times the revenue he was getting from his ore.

Wilcox built those first 8 miles of track to ease the expense of getting his ore into Silver Plume. The task completed, he stood to save a lot of money. But just as he had declined a British syndicate's offer of $3 million for the railroad and his mines, the price of silver crashed, bringing the panic of 1907. By 1908, Wilcox was out of money. The next year, having spent $300,000 building his railroad, he sold it for $44,000. Three years later it went for $5,000. In 1918 it was abandoned, and in 1919 the last train rode the tracks downhill, its crews pulling out the rails behind them as the train inched its way back to Silver Plume.

In the 1950s, a fire destroyed nearly every building left standing in Waldorf. Refusing to give up, a lone miner who was working the area built as his home the Quonset hut that still stands today, as do the impressive mill, water tower, and outbuildings at the mine above the townsite.

LOCATION:	Arapaho National Forest
DESCRIPTION:	It's uphill all the way, but the sprawling remnants of a historic mining center make the climb worthwhile.
DISTANCE:	13 miles, out and back
HIKING TIME:	7 hours
RATING:	Difficult
TRAILHEAD ELEVATION:	9,900 feet
MAXIMUM ELEVATION:	13,132 feet
MAP:	*Colorado Atlas & Gazetteer*, p. 39, C5
CONTACT:	Clear Creek Ranger District, (303) 567-2901, www.fs.fed.us/r2/arnf/

🏕️ 🛒 ⚔️ 🚲 🐕

GETTING THERE:	From the Georgetown National Historic Landmark District, follow the signs to Guanella Pass Rd. at the south end of town. Drive 2.5 miles south on Guanella Pass Rd. to Waldorf Junction, a well-marked right-hand turnoff with a small parking area. Park here.
GOOD TO KNOW:	Guanella Pass Rd. is paved all the way to Waldorf Junction, a fancy name for the fork onto FR 248. The hike follows the high-clearance four-wheel-drive FR 248 all the way to the townsite of Waldorf and its mine, which sits high on the slopes of the formidable McClellan Mountain. Hikers and mountain bikers take note: The road gets a lot of use by ATVs, motorcycles, and sundry four-wheel-drives. But it is also a scenic, challenging, and popular mountain-biking route. Campsites along the way and around the Waldorf site make this a great route for a two-day bike trek or hiking outing.
	A longer alternate route (18 miles round-trip) begins from CR 330 at the town of Silver Plume and follows the Argentine Central Railroad grade to Waldorf and beyond, nearly to the summit of 13,587-foot McClellan Mountain. It joins the hike described here just above the first set of switchbacks on FR 248, then follows the same route thereafter.

THE WALK

Follow the dirt road all the way to Waldorf. Roughly the first 1.5 miles is a series of switchbacks. After the switchbacks, it is about 5 miles to Waldorf.

The road—which just beyond the switchbacks is the grade of the old Argentine Central Railroad—climbs steadily along the flank of McClellan Mountain. It parallels Leavenworth Creek, which meanders through woods and meadows to the left of the road. Wide and flat for long stretches at a time (true to its past as a railroad bed), the road passes through aspen groves and dense pine woods that in summer bloom with yellow and red Indian paintbrush, blue harebell, pink fireweed, and wild strawberries. Sections of the road are rocky and make for challenging biking. Otherwise, the path is only moderately difficult and a gradual uphill all the way. Side trails lead down to the creek and into meadows. You can find campsites along these or up higher, closer to the mine.

The road opens onto Waldorf at about timberline. You'll know you are getting close when you see the occasional structure and tailings heap on the hillsides across the valley to the left (east). Some of these are the remnants of the Vidler mine, a contemporary of Waldorf. You'll also see, in the distance straight ahead to the south, the winding road up Argentine Pass. The site of Waldorf is unmistakable: an expansive flat with crumbling stone foundations, deteriorating wooden structures, and scattered timbers strewn across yellowed tailings. A shack still houses the gears that once ran cables up and down the mountainside.

Behind these remnants, a 0.25-mile trail climbs straight up the mountainside to a rocky basin that holds the sprawling remains of the massive Santiago mine and mill structures, sheltered by the steep slopes of McClellan Mountain. A set of rails loops out from the mill and into the mine tunnel's portal in the mountainside. In one of the shacks, electric floor heaters, insulation, and asphalt roofing attest to more recent use, and preservation efforts have stabilized the mill thanks to funding in part from the

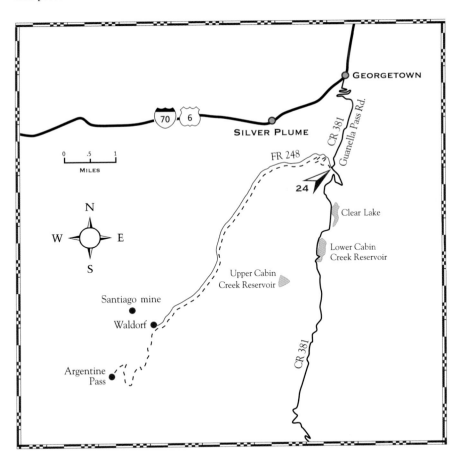

The old townsite of Waldorf

State Historical Fund. The site offers a magnificent view of the surrounding peaks, including 13,738-foot Argentine Peak and 13,408-foot Mount Wilcox (named for Edward Wilcox) across the valley.

All around Waldorf is a network of interconnecting roads and trails, each good for hiking and a few of them offering alternate routes back down to the main road you walked up on. From Waldorf you'll hike back down the way you came.

For even more of a hike, before you head back down go about 1.5 miles farther south up a series of switchbacks to the 13,132-foot summit of Argentine Pass. (The route up the pass is the road that clearly climbs up to the summit; the 0.5-mile spur to the left leads to the tailings of the old Vidler mine.) The Argentine Pass road is passable to four-wheel-drives but not quite all the way to the summit. From that point on, it's hikers only; large sections of the road to the summit and beyond have long since washed out.

If you'd rather see more of the Argentine Central Railroad grade, hike or bike the road that leads to the right of the Quonset hut at Waldorf. The road switchbacks and then steadily climbs for about 4 miles before ending just below the summit of McClellan Mountain. Because of all the side roads and trails, however, knowing which route is the railroad grade can be tricky; a map is a good idea. This is an often rocky but very scenic route for a hike or bike trek and an especially attractive option if you're camping overnight.

Mount Evans

A PEAK WITH A PAST

The opening of a road to the summit of Pikes Peak near Colorado Springs in 1888 succeeded not only in getting tourists up the peak, but in pulling their tourism dollars away from Denver. So in 1917, Denver mayor Robert W. Speer secured state funding for a similar project—another, higher highway, this one to the summit of Mount Evans, one of the fourteeners nearest the city. Upon its completion in 1930, the Mount Evans Highway became the highest paved road in the United States. (Rocky Mountain National Park's Trail Ridge Road is the highest *continuous* paved road in the United States—a tricky distinction.) The Mount Evans Highway was also the first highway in Colorado whose sole purpose was to provide a scenic drive.

The highway caught the attention of astronomer A. Compton of the University of Chicago, who realized the value of a paved road for the purpose of getting up where cosmic rays were more easily observed. The highway, Compton surmised, would also make it a lot easier to lug the necessary equipment up to that altitude. Cosmic rays, writes astronomy professor Robert Stencel, "are charged atoms boiling off the sun and stars, filling space." Scientists of the 1930s were busily studying these rays in conjunction with their new research into nuclear theory. So in 1935, Burnham Hoyt, famed architect of Red Rocks Amphitheatre, designed an A-frame building at the summit of Mount Evans to house the University of Denver's cosmic ray study facility. The year 1972 brought the first summit telescope to the site, and a 1996 upgrade resulted in the Meyer-Womble Observatory that stands today. Until the year 2000, the 2,100-square-foot facility was the highest observatory on Earth.

The Crest House atop Mount Evans, elevation 14,264 feet

Meanwhile, for both better and worse, the scenic Mount Evans Highway also brought millions of casual visitors to the beautifully fragile, weather-beaten, and often dangerous ecosystem at the summit of Colorado's 14th-highest peak. With all those people driving to the top and lingering, civic leaders of the 1930s soon decided that a welcoming and sheltering structure was needed.

Denver Mountain Parks, the brainchild of John Brisben Walker (see Mount Falcon Park, Hike 29), built the Crest House in the good-weather months of 1940 and 1941. They called it the "Castle in the Sky," and indeed it was. Standing at 14,260 feet in elevation, the star-shaped house built of native boulders and stone was once touted as the highest structure in the world—a claim that never fails to generate arguments over what the definition of "structure" is. Nevertheless, it was a remarkable architectural achievement.

Meyer-Womble Observatory and Mount Evans summit

Modernist Denver architect Edwin Francis designed Crest House with what the State Historic Preservation Office describes as a mix of "organic, futuristic, and art modern elements that reflect not only its time period but illustrate an adaptation to its western, mountaintop setting." And, according to the *Canyon Courier*, Francis considered it his best design. The paper added that he "had been inspired by 'the moon, stars and heavens.'" Its huge windows took advantage of the expansive vistas all around and provided a dizzying view of Denver. Inside, spherical light fixtures resembled the moon, completing the night-sky theme.

A restaurant and tourist stop, the Crest House welcomed visitors for three decades and earned National Historic Landmark status. "Crest House employees assisted hundreds of lost, stranded, injured or ailing visitors to a summit where the atmospheric pressure is 60 percent that of sea level," the *Courier* reported.

On September 1, 1979, a propane tank exploded at the house. The explosion and ensuing fire demolished the structure, leaving only the star-shaped foundation and some arched walls dramatically rising from their rocky perch beside the high-altitude lab. The Forest Service received more than $500,000 in insurance claims and damages, but in the end made the controversial decision not to rebuild the landmark structure. Emphasizing that people who trek into the high country must ultimately take responsibility for their own safety, even if they get there via highway, the Forest Service explained that it had "no requirement or obligation…to ensure the presence of people on a relatively continuous basis at the summit of Mt. Evans for safety related purposes."

Thus, the ruins remain at the site, providing shelter for tourists, hikers, and bikers who can also take advantage of the small pay telescopes installed in 1992 on an observation platform at the building's terrace. Ramps and stairs inside the structure allow anyone to explore, and interpretive panels provide history about the house, the highway, and other facets of this mountain with a rich past.

LOCATION:	Mount Evans Wilderness, southwest of Idaho Springs
DESCRIPTION:	A challenging walk along the country's highest paved auto road summits atop 14,264-foot Mount Evans, the site of the University of Denver's High Altitude Research Station and the remains of a lodge once touted as the "Castle in the Sky."
DISTANCE:	11.5 miles, out and back
HIKING TIME:	7 hours
RATING:	Difficult
TRAILHEAD ELEVATION:	12,830 feet
MAXIMUM ELEVATION:	14,264 feet
MAP:	*Colorado Atlas & Gazetteer*, p. 39, D5
CONTACT:	Clear Creek Ranger District, (303) 567-3000, www.fs.fed.us/r2/arnf/about/organization/ccrd

GETTING THERE:	From Idaho Springs, drive south on the well-marked Mount Evans Hwy. (CO 103) 13 miles to Echo Lake. Just after Echo Lake, turn right (south) on CO 5 and proceed another 9 miles to Summit Lake. Park in the large parking area.
GOOD TO KNOW:	You must pay a fee (currently $3 per person or $10 per car) to drive the Mount Evans Hwy. It opens in late May and stays open as long as snowfall allows, usually through mid-September. The University of Denver's high-altitude laboratory is open to the public with reservations only. The highway is a popular, often crowded roadway; expect a lot of traffic during summer. This is an extremely popular cycling route, too, so watch for bikes. There is ample parking at Summit Lake, which is a beautiful alpine lake above timberline with footpaths along its shore. Outhouses are available, and rangers might be on hand at the stone shelter (built in the 1920s while the road was under construction) to offer history and nature talks and to share information about the peak's wildlife. Because of adverse weather conditions, the road is often closed beyond Summit Lake.

At the summit is a large parking lot beside the remnants of the Crest House. Ramps, steps, and sidewalks meander through the site, which contains plentiful interpretation about the history of the house and highway. Pay telescopes help you take advantage of the spectacular views, and several restrooms are on-site. There is a gate at a short roadway to the observatory. Even if the gate is closed, it is OK to walk the hundred yards or so to the observatory.

This is one of the highest spots in Colorado. When hiking or biking, be prepared: Weather conditions are unpredictable, and you must be in good shape to tackle such a trek. Bring plenty of water and remember that the sun's rays are fierce at this altitude. Get an early start to avoid early afternoon thunderstorms, lightning, and sleet. And be prepared for high winds anytime, and cold and snow even in summer.

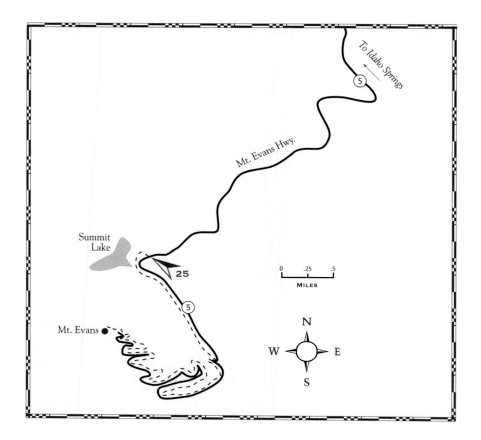

THE WALK

For the easiest and safest walk, and to make the least impact on this well-visited mountain, the road is the preferable route. After parking at Summit Lake, simply get back on the road and walk up alongside it, sharing the path with cyclists and following its winding route as it switchbacks up the mountainside 5.5 miles to the summit parking area. To reach the summit proper, hike up the little 0.25-mile path from the parking area.

Long considered a less safe and more environmentally damaging route, the hiking trail from Summit Lake has been improved by the Forest Service and is now, the rangers say, quite safe all the way. The trailhead is at the north end of the lake, just past the stone shelter. The trail leads a few hundred yards to an overlook of the Chicago Lakes, which lie 1,000 feet down to the north. The trail then bears west onto the steep ridge overlooking Summit Lake, and then follows the ridge southward to the summit. For the most part, the trail is visible all the way; follow cairns whenever it isn't. This route is much more challenging and is only for experienced high-altitude hikers. It is also much more direct and steeper than the road and shaves a few full miles off the hike.

Lookout Mountain and Buffalo Bill Trails

OLD WEST MEETS NEW WEST

William F. "Buffalo Bill" Cody died on January 10, 1917. That same day, just 1 mile from Cody's proposed burial spot on Lookout Mountain above the city of Golden, craftsmen were building a grand lodge for business tycoon Charles Boettcher. Today, a short trail connects Cody's final resting place to Boettcher's summer home. But these two sites, and the historical figures they help us remember, are joined by more than proximity.

About 90 years after Buffalo Bill's death, his name is still synonymous with our popular perception of the Old West. As a young man, Cody trapped beaver in the Rocky Mountains, searched for gold in Colorado, rode for the Pony Express, scouted for the U.S. Army, fought the Plains tribes during the Indian wars, and earned his nom de guerre by hunting 4,280 buffalo for work crews building the Kansas Pacific Railroad to Denver. Journalists, dime novelists, and play-wrights, sensing in Cody the makings of an authentic American hero, spun these experiences into legend. In 1883, Cody dramatized his iconic life in an arena show called *Buffalo Bill's Wild West*. Seen by millions of people around the world—including Great Britain's Queen Victoria—the show featured real-life cowboys, American Indians,

COLONEL W. F. CODY,
" Buffalo Bill "

William F. "Buffalo Bill" Cody

horses, and buffalo. Audiences came for the gunfights, rodeo tricks, and specialty acts, but they left with a new chapter of American history called "How the West Was Won."

Anticipating our modern fixation with creating enjoyable learning opportunities in classrooms and museums, Cody called his act "an educational exposition on a grand and entertaining scale." He taught watered-down (some would say one-sided) Western history to a nationwide audience in an age preceding mass-communication

Charles Boettcher's summer home

vehicles such as television or movies. Consulted by every U.S. president from Ulysses S. Grant to Woodrow Wilson and honored by European royalty, Cody became the most famous American in the world. In the process, he made "the Wild West"—the fuzzy frontier between the conquered and unconquered—as much a part of the 20th-century national consciousness as apple pie. And if perception sometimes masquerades as reality, one could argue that Cody helped create the real West, too.

Like the showman, Charles Boettcher lived center stage. When the transcontinental railroad came through Wyoming in 1869, he emigrated from Germany to work in his brother's Cheyenne hardware store. As visionaries like Nathan Meeker and Robert Cameron planted successful farm colonies in northeastern Colorado in the 1870s, he relocated his business to serve a growing agricultural empire. Then Leadville boomed and Boettcher filled his till by selling picks and shovels to miners.

The money bought him a permanent home in Denver and also seeded one of Colorado's most important industries. He must have learned a thing or two about irrigated agriculture from his Greeley customers because he knew enough to convince investors to build the South Platte Valley's first sugar beet factory in 1901. Other factories followed; in time, the Great Western Sugar Company became so big and influential that its labor requirements permanently altered Colorado's ethnic composition.

But he was just getting started. Lacking quality cement for the factories, he built the first Portland cement plant in the Rocky Mountain region. The Ideal Cement Company became one of the largest producers of Portland cement in the world.

By the time Boettcher decided to build a summer home, he could stand on top of Lookout Mountain and gaze upon the land, knowing he—as much as any other person in Colorado—had driven its agricultural and industrial development. But Colorado lost something when it exchanged its Old West duds for New West attire. It needed a symbol to remind citizens and visitors of its roughrider past. It needed Buffalo Bill.

Harry Tammen, co-owner of the *Denver Post* and one of Colorado's best boosters, co-opted Buffalo Bill as one might buy a corporate trademark. By 1912, Cody was flat broke. Tammen agreed to lend him money but wanted control of the Buffalo Bill show's assets as collateral. Tammen auctioned off mustangs, wagons, cattle, a train, and even Cody's favorite horse, Isham. Contractually beholden to Tammen, Cody appeared in his debtor's own arena show, the Sells-Floto Circus. At the end of his career, the once-great showman had become a parody of himself.

After Buffalo Bill died, Tammen arranged to bury him on Lookout Mountain. Never mind that the deceased showman had drawn up a will in 1907 stating his wish to be buried on Cedar Mountain, above the town of Cody, Wyoming. Bill's widow Louisa contradicted the will, saying that her husband had changed his mind. Persistent stories assert that Tammen paid Louisa $10,000 to pick the Lookout Mountain spot. Rumors aside, the funeral procession—attended by some 18,000 mourners—became Buffalo Bill's last show. A *Denver Post* eulogy noted the "passing of the great West."

Craftsmen finished Boettcher's summer lodge just after Buffalo Bill was laid to rest. Its native rock foundation, rustic fieldstone walls, and exposed interior roof beams evoke an Arts and Crafts nostalgia for preindustrial times. The house, like Cody's nearby grave, reminds visitors that Buffalo Bill's Wild West and Charles Boettcher's New West are one and the same.

LOCATION:	Lookout Mountain Nature Center and Preserve
DESCRIPTION:	This easy hike connects business tycoon Charles Boettcher's summer mansion to the Buffalo Bill Memorial Museum and Grave.
DISTANCE:	1.8 miles, out and back
HIKING TIME:	1 hour
RATING:	Easy
TRAILHEAD ELEVATION:	7,580 feet
MAXIMUM ELEVATION:	7,580 feet
MAP:	*Colorado Atlas and Gazetteer*, p. 40, C1
CONTACT:	Lookout Mountain Nature Center, (303) 526-0594, http://openspace.jeffco.us/; Boettcher Mansion, (303) 526-0855; Buffalo Bill Memorial Museum and Grave, (303) 526-0747, http://www.buffalobill.org/
GETTING THERE:	From Denver, take I-70 west to Exit 256. Then turn right on Grapevine Rd. and take an immediate left on US 40. Go west on US 40 to Lookout Mountain Rd. Proceed up the mountain, turn left on Colorow Rd., and follow it to the Lookout Mountain Nature Center.
GOOD TO KNOW:	The Boettcher Mansion is open for self-guided tours on many Saturdays throughout the summer, except when closed for an event. Call ahead. The Buffalo Bill Memorial Museum and Grave is open daily 9 a.m. to 5 p.m. May through October, and 9 a.m. to 4 p.m. November through April.

THE WALK

After touring the Boettcher home and the Lookout Mountain Nature Center, exit the parking lot and cross Colorow Rd. to the Lookout Mountain Trailhead. The trail descends 0.4 mile southeast to the Buffalo Bill Trail through ponderosa pines and colorful wildflowers, including foothills bluebell, white field chickweed, and purple larkspur. Take the Buffalo Bill Trail and continue southeast. The 0.5-mile trail reaches its lowest elevation and then turns east, passing picnic areas designed for the Denver Mountain Parks system in the 1930s by world-renowned landscape architect Frederick Law Olmsted, designer of New York City's Central Park.

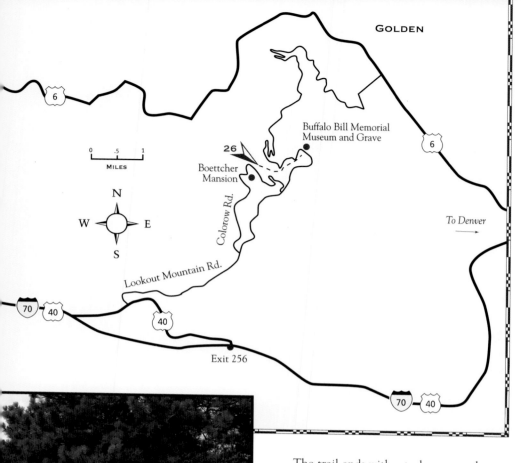

GOLDEN

6

Buffalo Bill Memorial
Museum and Grave

6

26

Boettcher
Mansion

Colorow Rd.

To Denver

0   .5   1
MILES

N
W   E
S

Lookout Mountain Rd.

70 40

40

Exit 256

70 40

The trail ends with a truly spectacular view of Golden and Denver at the Buffalo Bill Memorial Museum and Grave parking lot. The great view is even better from the museum's observation patio. Spend some time in the museum (admission charged), visit the gravesite (free), get a bite to eat at the snack bar (try the fudge), and peruse the Pahaska Tepee gift shop. Restrooms are in the gift shop.

Return by the same route. The Lookout Mountain Trail section will be more difficult going back.

William F. Cody's grave

Mount Vernon Village Walk and Red Rocks Trail

MOUNT VERNON, JEFFERSON TERRITORY

"We have no protection for life or property but the code of Lynch Law," complained a committee of concerned citizens in the October 20, 1859, edition of the weekly *Rocky Mountain News*. The committee's statement reflected a growing concern among the 8,000 or so newly arrived fortune seekers living in Denver City and the gold camps to the west. Although ad hoc "people's courts" and mining district laws

Reverend J.R. Dean's headstone is one of the few remnants of Mount Vernon, the once-thriving provisional capital of Jefferson Territory.

maintained a semblance of order amid the gold rush's excitement and confusion, the region's inhabitants were living in a jurisdictional no-man's-land. Lacking a unified formal government, the *News* editorialized, "We have been dependent solely upon ourselves for laws and [the] strength to restrain the vicious, punish the guilty, and protect the just."

Technically, this area—before this time inhabited only by American Indians and a few traders—was part of Kansas Territory. But territorial legislators, seated 700 miles away in Leavenworth, exercised authority in name only. Recognizing "an inherent right…to govern themselves in the absence of regular government," the newcomers created a temporary provisional authority that would operate pending the hoped-for establishment of their own separate and legitimate U.S. territory.

In August 1859, delegates representing Denver and the various mining districts met in convention and passed the Organic Act of the Territory of Jefferson. Two months later, the pseudo-territory's voters elected Robert W. Steele as governor.

Steele conducted much of the public's business from his home in Mount Vernon, lending credence to the oft-made claim that the small village was, for a short time, Jefferson Territory's de facto capital. The truth is more complicated, and much more interesting.

Dr. Joseph Casto, a lay minister from Illinois, founded Mount Vernon in late 1859 after taking part in one of the most important events in Colorado history. One year earlier, he joined the multitudes heading west toward a "New Eldorado" where gold had been discovered by William Green Russell and his party of Georgians. Casto's traveling companion was *Rocky Mountain News* founder William N. Byers.

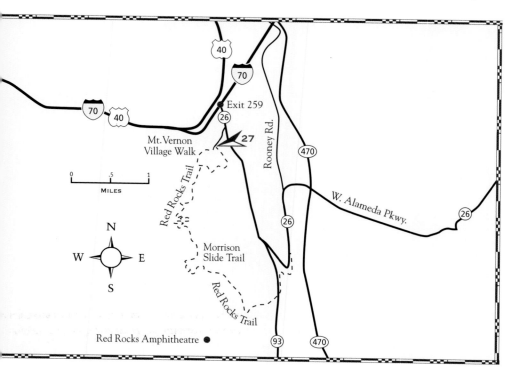

Upon arrival, many fortune seekers were disappointed with the paltry flecks of placer gold they were able to pan out of the South Platte River's tributaries and headed back to civilization. As one prospector quipped, these so-called go-backers "did not find gold ready washed out, sacked up and labeled to their address where they formerly resided." Casto stayed.

In the spring of 1859, a group of intrepid fortune hunters, including Casto, rode into the mountains to find the placer gold's source. One of them was John H. Gregory, who discovered the fantastically rich lode claim that reinvigorated the Pikes Peak Gold Rush and led to the establishment of Central City, Black Hawk, and other prosperous North Clear

Mount Vernon cemetery

Creek mining towns. Some sources place Casto with Gregory at the discovery. Others insist that Gregory left him behind that day. Whatever happened, the result was the same.

While Byers told the world about Gregory's Diggings through his newspaper, Casto thought about ways to capitalize on the coming surge of humanity. He came up with two ideas. First, he established the town of Mount Vernon at a strategic location between Denver and a canyon leading to the mountain mining camps. Then, on December 7, 1859, he and three other men organized the Denver, Auraria, and Colorado Wagon Road Company. This outfit built a toll road through Mount Vernon to Mountain City, near Gregory's Diggings. He hoped that his town would profit from heavy traffic going to and from the prosperous mining camps.

His scheme worked, at first. By mid-1860, the town boasted 44 adult residents, two hotels, a blacksmith shop, a grocery store, a saloon, Governor Steele's private home, and a feed and livery stable. A newspaper correspondent described it as "a beautiful and romantic village…[with] a number of neat and tidy residences."

Reverend J.R. Dean, a 30-year-old minister, taught in the town's first school. Born in Vermont, Dean attended a theological seminary in Michigan and then found work at a Baptist church in Iowa. A severe case of tuberculosis forced him to quit preaching and continue his westward odyssey. He found a home in Mount Vernon, hoping that the dry, cool mountain air would restore his health. However, the lung disease was too much for him and he died in August 1860.

Dean's gradual death foreshadowed his town's decline. Just after Congress invalidated Robert Steele's provisional government by establishing Colorado Territory on February 28, 1861, citizens became concerned that new toll roads would reduce traffic through Mount Vernon and affect business at the hotels. "We found the citizens...very much excited," one reporter wrote about one company's plan to "build a new road into the mountains following Amos Gulch" near Golden, thereby shortening the route to the mines. These folks became enraged upon learning that their beloved former governor was bankrolling the new route.

Casto tried to save his town by denigrating alternate roads in local newspapers, but no amount of purple prose could forestall the end of his Rocky Mountain dream. Within a few years, trains made all of the wagon roads obsolete and Mount Vernon crumbled into obscurity. Reverend Dean's gravestone, standing amid a few other markers in the town's cemetery, became the only lasting memorial to this remarkable chapter of Colorado history.

LOCATION:	Matthews/Winters Park, near Morrison
DESCRIPTION:	The Mount Vernon Village Walk is an easy 0.9-mile loop around the site of an abandoned 1860s town. Like the nearby Dinosaur Ridge Trail, this hike may be extended to include scenic Red Rocks Park and Dakota Ridge.
DISTANCE:	0.9 to 6.2 miles*
HIKING TIME:	1 to 4 hours*
RATING:	Easy to difficult*
TRAILHEAD ELEVATION:	6,300 feet
MAXIMUM ELEVATION:	6,800 feet*
	*Varies according to the trail or combination of trails hiked. See walk description for details.
MAP:	*Colorado Atlas & Gazetteer*, p. 40, C1
CONTACT:	Jefferson County Open Space, (303) 271-5925, http://openspace.jeffco.us/

GETTING THERE:	From Denver, take I-70 west past C-470 to the Morrison exit (259). Follow CO 26 south 0.1 mile and turn right into the Matthews/Winters Park parking lot.
GOOD TO KNOW:	The Mount Vernon Village Walk Trailhead area features ample parking, restrooms, and a shaded picnic area with grills. Matthews/Winters Park opens one hour before sunrise and closes one hour after sunset. Dogs must be leashed at all times. Bikes are welcome but must yield to all other trail users. Fires are prohibited except in designated areas; use charcoal only.

THE WALK

One of Colorado's earliest cemeteries and a few rubble foundations are all that remain of this once-proud pseudo-capital of Jefferson Territory.

Mount Vernon Village Walk

To do the Village Walk without extensions, take a short path south past the restrooms and picnic area. Cross Mount Vernon Creek to the trailhead and bear right. As you go uphill, Mount Vernon Canyon—which once served as a corridor for wagon roads to some of Colorado Territory's earliest hard rock mines—is on the right, and an open vista of rolling hills where the village of Mount Vernon once stood is on the left. Veer south, go up another slight rise, and watch for a side trail leading to the Mount Vernon cemetery. Look for Reverend Dean's headstone, placed here in 1860.

Return to the main trail and continue south to the Red Rocks Trail junction. Stay on the Village Walk Trail as it turns east. Round the hill as you head north and watch for remnants of sandstone and concrete foundations along the way. These might be the remains of a structure associated with a small mine or quarry. Continue to circle north and west until you reach the trailhead.

Mount Vernon Village–Red Rocks–Dakota Ridge Loop

For a moderately difficult but scenic 6.2-mile tour of Mount Vernon Village, Red Rocks Park, and Dakota Ridge, begin by following the Mount Vernon Village Walk directions (in the previous section) south to the Red Rocks Trail junction. The Village Walk continues around the hill to the east. Instead, take the Red Rocks Trail south 0.8 mile over open meadows and ravines. After crossing a shallow, or possibly dry, creekbed in Cherry Gulch, go up the hill a few yards to another trail junction. For a good view of Mount Vernon and Red Rocks Park from above, bear right and take the 1.2-mile Morrison Slide Trail. This detour goes up and over a flat shoulder of Mount Morrison before rejoining Red Rocks Trail to the south (this is a good spot to turn back if you do not want to add the Dakota Ridge Trail to the hike).

Back on Red Rocks Trail, go south past sandstone formations to W. Alameda Pkwy. Cross the street, pick up the trail again, and then continue south until you reach Red Rocks Trail Rd. A side trail leads to Red Rocks Amphitheatre's lower north parking lot and provides access to the amphitheatre. We recommend taking some time to check it out if you have not seen it before.

Pick up the trail on the east side of Red Rocks Trail Rd. and follow it east until you meet the road again. Turn left and stay on the shoulder. Cross a bridge over Mount Vernon Creek and then watch for traffic and cross CR 93 to reach the Dakota Ridge Trail. Follow this 0.5-mile path to the top of the hogback, noting the dramatic change from the Fountain formation's red sandstone to the buff-colored Dakota sandstone. On the hogback's east side, hook up with W. Alameda Pkwy. and follow the right shoulder north a few yards until you reach a crosswalk and the main Dakota Ridge Trailhead. The dinosaur footprint site is about 100 yards to the north. After you check out the footprints, return to the trailhead and follow the directions for the Dakota Ridge Trail on p. 136 of Hike 28. Upon reaching the Jurassic Park and Ride parking lot on the west side of the hogback, cross CO 26 and return to the Matthews/Winters Park parking lot.

Dinosaur Ridge and Dakota Ridge Trails

COLORADO'S FOSSIL FEUD

"It was evident," Arthur Lakes scribbled in his 1877 field journal, "that there had been the skeleton of a monster here." He was right. While exploring a "Cretaceous hogback" just north of Morrison with his friend Henry Beckwith, the Oxford-educated Episcopal minister and self-taught geologist found "the cast of a very large bone belonging to some gigantic animal." Before then, fossil fragments from dinosaurs had been unearthed in western Europe and in the eastern United States, but no one had ever stumbled upon anything quite as big as this. His discovery excited paleontologists working in prestigious museums and universities everywhere and initiated the scientific equivalent of Colorado's 1859 gold rush.

Lakes eventually became known in textbooks as the "father of Colorado geology," but from 1877 to 1879 he enjoyed his role as a leading dinosaur hunter in the West. He kept careful notes and painted accurate vignettes of his work throughout the period. These sources, some of them only recently found and published, illuminate one of the most exciting eras of American scientific inquiry.

Two wealthy, openly competitive, and occasionally unethical men dominated U.S. paleontology at that time. Othniel Charles Marsh of Yale University and Edward Drinker Cope, who worked on federal geological and geographical surveys, hired independent—and sometimes amateur—fossil hunters to conduct fieldwork in the West's remote locales. Just as gold and silver seekers panned streams, dug mines, and jumped each other's claims while they pulled as much wealth from the rocks as they could, the fossil hunters scrambled to find new species from an age of immense and wonderful creatures that scientists like Marsh and Cope were only beginning to understand. And in late March 1877, Lakes hit the mother lode.

Volunteer T. Caneer cleans dinosaur tracks on Dinosaur Ridge. These are from an iguanodon.

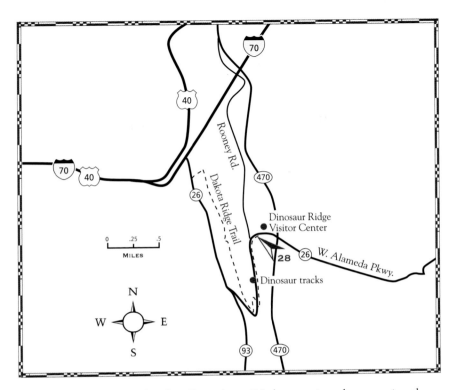

After discovering that first "large bone," Lakes continued to examine the hogback's stratified spine for other parts of the animal. To his eyes, this uplifted ridge resembled a huge Cretaceous-period book revealing 80 million years of biological bounty. Lakes speculated that the area was once "a shore line of angry waves beating against the foot of the Rockies…[which] could hardly be called mountains at all." This inland sea did cover parts of today's High Plains from the Arctic Ocean to the Gulf of Mexico between 145 and 65 million years ago. Lakes jumped to a stone ledge and, looking around, saw:

> …a vertebra, carved, as it were, in bas relief on a flat slab of sandstone. It was so monstrous, however, thirty-three inches circumference so utterly beyond anything I had ever read or conceived possible that I could hardly believe my eyes and called to my friend Captain B [Beckwith] to confirm the vision. We stood for a moment without speaking gazing in astonishment at this prodigy and threw our hats in the air and hurrahed: and then began to look for more.

Soon after, they located two more huge fossils, "apparently the butt ends and part of the shaft of some limb bones….They reminded one more of the broken columns of some old temple than anything else." When the elated pair brought the specimens to Morrison, some of the townspeople guessed that the entire hogback "might be the remains of some petrified monster."

Lakes described his discovery to Othniel Marsh in a letter dated April 2. After waiting in vain for a reply, he decided to play upon the professor's well-known rivalry with Edward Cope. He sent specimens to both men, asking them if they could identify them and perhaps offer a financial deal for further excavations. The strategy worked and both men offered him a job. Lakes signed on with Marsh at $100 per month.

Lakes spent the summer camped out on the hogback known today as Dinosaur Ridge. He sent Marsh "very nearly a tons weight of bones," including dinosaurs later identified as *Apatosaurus ajax* and *Stegosaurus armatus*. That winter, he joined Marsh in New Haven, Connecticut, for laboratory work. He returned to the Morrison-area quarries in 1879 and then went north to Como Bluff, Wyoming, where he supervised the excavation of dinosaur specimens that still delight visitors at Yale's Peabody Museum and the National Museum of Natural History at the Smithsonian Institution. And though Lakes left paleontology to become a respected geologist, his dinosaur discoveries add a welcome scientific twist to Colorado's early reputation as a mining state populated by diggers of another kind.

LOCATION:	Jefferson County Open Space, near Morrison
DESCRIPTION:	Dinosaur Ridge Trail is an easy 2-mile out-and-back walk along W. Alameda Pkwy. to interpreted historical, geological, and paleontological sites. The Dakota Ridge Trail is a moderately difficult 4.4-mile out-and-back hike that follows the hogback's crest and offers good views of Red Rocks Park to the west and Denver's southern suburbs to the east. Ambitious trekkers should consider doing a 6.2-mile loop that includes both trails plus the Mount Vernon Village Walk and Red Rocks Trail.
DISTANCE:	2 to 6.2 miles*
HIKING TIME:	1 to 4 hours*
RATING:	Easy to difficult*
TRAILHEAD ELEVATION:	6,200 feet
MAXIMUM ELEVATION:	6,800 feet* *Varies according to the trail or combination of trails hiked. See walk description for details.
MAP:	*Colorado Atlas & Gazetteer*, p. 40, C1
CONTACT:	Friends of Dinosaur Ridge, (303) 697-DINO, www.dinoridge.org/
GETTING THERE:	From Denver, take I-70 west past C-470 to the Morrison exit (259). Follow CO 26 south to Dinosaur Ridge. At the first intersection, stay on CO 26 as it winds around the south end of Dinosaur Ridge and turns north (do not continue straight to Morrison). The visitor center is northeast of the ridge just past Rooney Rd.
GOOD TO KNOW:	Restrooms, information, and a gift shop are located at the Dinosaur Ridge visitor center (open 9 a.m. to 4 p.m.). Dogs must be leashed at all times. Mountain bikes are welcome and common along the Dakota Ridge Trail. Rock climbing is prohibited in Red Rocks Park.

THE WALK

Hikers may choose to do either of the hikes separately or combine the two with the Mount Vernon Village Walk and the Red Rocks Trail.

Dinosaur Ridge Trail

Dinosaur Ridge Trail begins at the Dinosaur Ridge visitor center parking lot. Follow the green dinosaur footprints painted on the pavement along W. Alameda Pkwy. Walk on the right-hand shoulder and watch for traffic. Parents should keep an eye on their children to make sure they don't stray onto the road. For those who would rather drive, there are three roadside parking areas along the route.

The trail leads past 17 sites marked with interpretive signs. Together, they tell the region's story from 150 million years ago to the present. About 0.25 mile up the road, visitors will reach the most impressive of the sites: a slab of rock showing more than 300 dinosaur footprints. Signs help visitors visualize giant three-toed iguanodons and smaller carnivorous theropods roaming mangrove swamps near the edge of the Western Interior Seaway.

Follow the road south around a hairpin turn to the other points of interest, including sites where Lakes discovered *Stegosaurus*, *Diplodocus*, *Apatosaurus*, *Allosaurus*, and *Camarasaurus* fossils in 1877. Return to the visitor center by the same route.

Red Rocks Park

Dakota Ridge Trail

From the Dinosaur Ridge visitor center, follow W. Alameda Pkwy. south about 100 yards past the dinosaur footprint site to the trailhead. Walk up several steep switchbacks over powdery and somewhat slippery sandstone to the top of Dakota Ridge. C-470 and several active and abandoned clay and coal mines are visible to the east, while Red Rocks Park and the Mount Vernon townsite lie to the west. There are several exposed sections with steep drop-offs, so keep an eye on children. Follow the trail along the ridge's crest about a mile to a saddle. Zorro Trail veers downhill to the right. Continue north for another 0.7 mile and stay on the trail as it heads down the hogback's west side. If you are not doing the Mount Vernon Village–Red Rocks–Dakota Ridge Loop, turn back before heading downhill. The trail ends at the base of the hogback near the Jurassic Park and Ride parking lot. If you would like to continue on the 6.2-mile loop hike from the Park and Ride lot, cross CO 26 to the Matthews/Winters Park parking lot. From here, follow the directions for the Mount Vernon Village Walk on p. 131 of Hike 27.

Mount Vernon Village–Red Rocks–Dakota Ridge Loop

Fit hikers should consider linking the short Mount Vernon Village Walk and the Dakota Ridge Trail with the scenic Red Rocks Trail to create a wonderfully diverse and challenging 6.2-mile loop that features one of Colorado's oldest cemeteries, spectacular views of Red Rocks Park and its famous natural amphitheatre, and some of the dinosaur-related sites mentioned previously. You may begin the hike on any of the three trails, but we recommend starting at the Village Walk Trailhead, which has plenty of parking, restrooms, and a picnic area shaded by cottonwoods.

From the Dinosaur Ridge visitor center, drive south on W. Alameda Pkwy. and follow it west around the Dakota hogback to its junction with CR 93. Continue north on CO 26 a little over a mile to the Matthews/Winters Park parking lot (located on the west side of the road).

Begin your hike by following the Mount Vernon Village Walk directions on p. 131 of Hike 27 until you reach the Red Rocks Trail junction. From here, take the Red Rocks Trail as described in the Mount Vernon Village–Red Rocks–Dakota Ridge Loop section on p. 131 of Hike 27. This route will eventually return you to the Matthews/Winters Park parking lot.

Mount Falcon Park

DREAMING BIG

Born in Pennsylvania, John Brisben Walker came to Denver via West Virginia in 1879. A newspaperman with a Ph.D. from Georgetown and an adventurous past that included a stint with the Chinese army, Walker made his start in Colorado by farming alfalfa. But he kept his eye on the future, scheming real estate developments and dreaming of a grand home in the mountains.

In 1887, Walker opened Denver's very first amusement park—Riverfront Park—in the heart of the city, where Cherry Creek flows into the South Platte River. Walker built a "Castle of Commerce" that housed amusements alongside exhibits about agriculture and manufacturing (thus making it Denver's first museum), and the adjacent land was a rowdy fairground. "The park had a racetrack and baseball diamond," the *Rocky Mountain News* reminisced in 1940, and on at least one occasion Walker, a baseball fan, awarded each player on the winning team "a whole pie from a recently installed bakery exhibit." At the park, spectators watched chariot races and fireworks spectacles with "painted iron scenery, hundreds of performers and scores of ballet dancers," the *News* wrote. "Tons of explosives were used and the grandstand literally rocked."

Walker Would Make of Mt. Morrison Greatest Show Place of the World

Architect J.J.B. Benedict envisioned a towering, fanciful Summer White House —but it would never be.

Following his Riverfront Park venture, Walker moved back east and made a new investment: He took over a struggling magazine—*Cosmopolitan*—and got it back on its feet by publishing the works of burgeoning literary talents such as Mark Twain, H.G. Wells, and Leo Tolstoy. He sold the magazine to William Randolph Hearst for a fortune, some say $1 million. He returned to Colorado and bought 4,000 acres near Morrison, developing the land's focal point into what is today Red Rocks Amphitheatre. All around Red Rocks, he envisioned a system of lands set aside to remain forever wild adjacent to the city. That vision gave rise to the spaces now known as the Denver Mountain Parks.

Walker and his family had moved onto Mount Morrison, but he dreamed of living in a grander home on nearby Mount Falcon. In 1909, he oversaw a crew of immigrant laborers as they built his next castle: a mansion of native stone that sported a tower, observation deck, library, music room, servants' quarters, and eight fireplaces. He designed a set of winding roads that served as racetracks for the

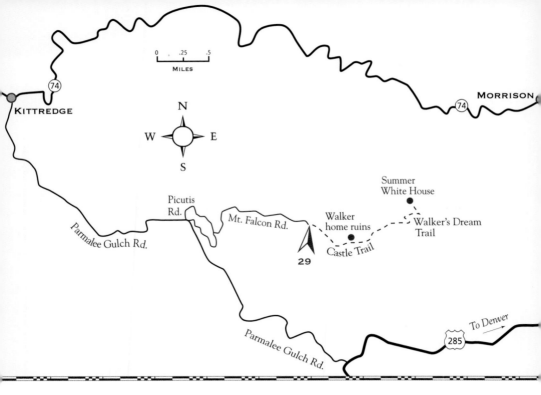

automobiles he had been making as owner of the Stanley Steamer Company. The steam-powered cars raced along today's Castle Trail, drawing spectators up from the city and into Walker's beloved mountain lair.

Soon, Walker had plans for bringing a new breed of visitor up to his mountain getaway. He schemed a "Summer White House" so future presidents of the United States could vacation in Colorado, where raptors soared and where neighboring Red Rocks Park offered the dignitaries a place to gather with the best minds of their generation. He even sold the idea to America's schoolchildren, many of whom contributed dimes to the cause. Less than a mile from Walker's stone mansion, the presidents' summer home was designed as a 22-room feudal castle, complete with battlements, buttresses, and towers on all four corners.

But it only began to take shape, never getting further than a foundation and a cornerstone of Colorado marble, laid in a 1919 ceremony that featured a parade of Stanley Steamers all the way from Morrison to the top of Mount Falcon. Foreshadowing the summer castle's gloomy fate, at the endpoint of the parade sat the scorched and ominous ruins of Walker's mansion, which had been struck by lightning just the year before and burned to the ground. Before that, the tragic death of Walker's wife, Ethel, and the onset of World War I had brought Walker's other ventures to a standstill. And so his dream of a summer White House vanished along with them.

Still, Walker's legacy lives on in the form of the Denver Mountain Parks, Red Rocks Amphitheatre, and even today's Highlands neighborhood and Regis University —both founded on developments of Walker's. And Mount Falcon Park continues to draw visitors to the trail where Stanley Steamers once raced to a stone mansion and through a beloved mountain paradise.

LOCATION:	Just north of Indian Hills
DESCRIPTION:	A leisurely walk along trails that once served as racetracks for Stanley Steamers arrives at the remains of John Brisben Walker's stone mansion and the site of his never-built summer home for U.S. presidents.
DISTANCE:	3.2 miles, out and back
HIKING TIME:	2 hours
RATING:	Easy
TRAILHEAD ELEVATION:	7,500 feet
MAXIMUM ELEVATION:	7,600 feet
MAP:	*Colorado Atlas & Gazetteer*, p. 40, C1
CONTACT:	Jefferson County Open Space, (303) 271-5925, http://openspace.jeffco.us/

GETTING THERE: Drive west from Denver on US 285 South. When you cross the junction with C-470, keep going another 4.3 miles on US 285 to Parmalee Gulch Rd., the road to Indian Hills (there's also a sign for Mount Falcon Park). Turn right and go 2.7 miles to Picutis Rd. Turn right and keep following the brown Mount Falcon Park signs another 2 miles to the park. Park in either of the two large parking areas.

GOOD TO KNOW: Mount Falcon Park is the ultimate hiking spot near Denver for families with young children, and adults can spend hours exploring the multitude of easy and scenic trails. This is a great place for running and horseback riding, and the opportunities for mountain-bikers are fantastic. Open an hour before sunrise to an hour after sunset every day, the park has toilets and many picnic tables and picnic areas near the parking area. Dogs must stay leashed. There is a pump with drinkable water for horses, people, and canines. No camping is allowed, and motor vehicles are prohibited on the trails.

At the trailhead are park maps and information about John Walker and his Stanley Steamer races of the 1910s. At Walker's "castle" and his never-completed Summer White House are panels offering further history. Nearly all of the trails in the park are easy, and—true to the park's name—this is a beautiful area to catch sight of raptors and other wildlife, in addition to spectacular meadows full of wildflowers. A wildfire burned through here in 1989; you can see part of the scorched burn area near the trailhead.

THE WALK

You can explore any number of well marked, crisscrossing paths and loop hikes throughout the park. The route described here makes a nice out-and-back hike to the walls of Walker's once-lavish home and, beyond that, the cornerstone of his Summer White House. A bit hilly, the hike might be a slight challenge for the littlest hikers. But if they make it even as far as the "castle," then its dramatic, crumbling walls, complete with upper-story fireplaces, offer them a memorable reward for their accomplishment.

From the trailhead, simply follow the signs for Castle Trail and start walking southeast. At about 0.4 mile you'll turn left, still on Castle Trail, and go up a slight incline along a meadow to the remains of Walker's home. Continue on Castle Trail about another 0.75 mile to Walker's Dream Trail, which cuts north and uphill about 0.3 mile to the site of the Summer White House foundation. This spot offers a nice canyon view, where you'll have a good chance to catch sight of falcons or other raptors in flight. It also looks out onto Red Rocks Park (see Hikes 27 and 28).

Return the way you came. If you would rather take a longer loop back, the Meadow Trail traverses a large central section of the park and accesses side trails such as the Tower Trail, which leads to the Eagle Eye Shelter and a lookout tower on Mount Falcon.

Above and below: *The burned-out remains of the "castle," John Walker's home on Mount Falcon*

Hildebrand Ranch

THE PASSING OF THE PIONEER

Historians, novelists, and screenwriters have used the term "pioneer" so much that it has become almost meaningless. For many of us, the word conjures a generic vision of a westward-bound covered wagon driven by a leather-skinned farmer. Seated next to him is his beautiful bonneted wife, who dabs sweat from her brow with one hand while holding a loaded Springfield rifle in the other. The kids sit in the back, page

through well-worn *McGuffey Readers*, and never ask, "Are we there yet?"

In the early 1900s, people had a more exact definition of a pioneer. To the Sons of Colorado, an exclusive historical society consisting of "all white males of good moral character who were residents of the Territory of Colorado," plus any other Colorado-born white males over the age of 21, a pioneer was anyone who settled here before 1876.

The Sons of Colorado pub-lished a monthly newsletter called *The Trail* that included an obituary

Deer Creek School

section titled "The Passing of the Pioneer." The March 1916 issue contains an obituary for Mrs. Elizabeth Hildebrand, a 70-year-old who died at her Deer Creek home from "a combination of ailments attending old age." The single paragraph mentions her German heritage, her long-term residency in Jefferson County, and her surviving family members.

Of course, being a pioneer involved more than long-term residency. According to Maria Davies McGrath, author of *The Real Pioneers of Colorado*, a pioneer was "one who goes before to prepare the way for another." In her reference book, she limited her pool to 1,400 notables who arrived in what is now Colorado prior to its establishment as a U.S. territory in 1861.

Elizabeth Hildebrand and her husband Frank made the cut. McGrath documented that Frank and Elizabeth left their native Germany and came to America "in their youth." In 1859, Frank, like thousands of others, caught gold fever. He hitched up an ox team to the proverbial covered wagon and joined the throngs of sojourners who hoped to cash in on Rocky Mountain gold.

After arriving in Denver City, Frank settled north of Denver at the mouth of Clear Creek near present-day Commerce City. Here he stayed, probably as a farmer, until the great flood of 1864 ruined his home and prompted him to find employment elsewhere. Frank freighted cargo between Denver and Cheyenne for two years before

Region 4: Denver

locating a suitable homestead with a small log cabin and good land south of Littleton on Deer Creek. Elizabeth joined him soon after he settled in.

The existing cabin became the nucleus of the current Hildebrand house. Instead of demolishing or abandoning the original log structure, Frank and Elizabeth added to it as their family grew. In the 1880s, they built a kitchen, two bedrooms, and a nursery. They used the cabin as a formal parlor. Clapboard siding and smooth plaster interior walls masked the home's rustic heart.

The Hildebrands and their sons, Francis and Albert, raised corn, wheat, hay, hogs, chickens, milk cows, and more than 600 Herefords. They watered the fields with two irrigation ditches, which they dug by hand or with help from horses and primitive machinery. Up to four ranch hands worked the fields and tended cattle in the summer. Each of them earned the right to be called "pioneer" one day at a time.

Today, many of the cars racing past Hildebrand Ranch on C-470 have special "pioneer" license plates bearing an image of the familiar wagon. Obtaining the plates is easy: Colorado drivers need only prove that an ancestor lived in the state a century ago. So, with every passing year, more and more families are eligible—all of them proving that history is not made by any single group, but by everyone.

LOCATION:	Chatfield Nature Preserve
DESCRIPTION:	Starting or ending at the Hildebrand Ranch structures, located directly west of the preserve's pay station, this short loop travels through riparian and wetland ecosystems.
DISTANCE:	1.5-mile loop
HIKING TIME:	1 hour
RATING:	Easy
TRAILHEAD ELEVATION:	5,500 feet
MAXIMUM ELEVATION:	5,500 feet
MAP:	*Colorado Atlas & Gazetteer,* p. 40, D2
CONTACT:	Denver Botanic Gardens, (303) 973-3705, www.botanicgardens.org/
GETTING THERE:	From Denver, take Wadsworth Blvd. south just past C-470 and turn right (west) on Deer Creek Canyon Rd. The entrance road is 0.4 mile ahead on the left.
GOOD TO KNOW:	The preserve is open daily, 9 a.m. to 5 p.m., and is closed on major holidays. Annual events include a pumpkin festival and corn maze in the fall and Earth Day cleanup festivities. The visitor center, housed in a one-room schoolhouse next to the parking lot, is not always open. Water and restrooms are available on the north side of the parking area. Pets are prohibited. Admission is charged (Denver Botanic Gardens members and walk-in guests get in free), but the pass is valid for all other Colorado state parks on the same day. Consider combining this short history walk with a trip to nearby Roxborough State Park (see Hike 31). Bird-watchers, don't forget your binoculars!

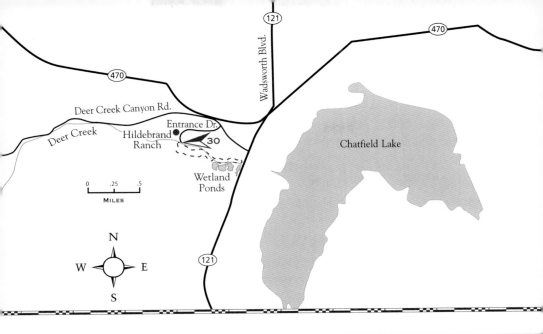

THE WALK

Begin at the one-room schoolhouse and take the paved path east past the picnic area. Follow the trail along the edge of the cottonwood trees that line Deer Creek and take your second right into the trees. This is the Dora and Pauline Roberts Riparian Trail. Continue east along the creek for about 0.5 mile and do not cross either of the two bridges leading to the other side. Watch for a rectangular stone foundation on your left; this was the schoolhouse's original location.

The riparian trail curves south over Deer Creek near Wadsworth Blvd. and connects to the Moras L. Shubert Wetlands Trail. This path encircles four ponds surrounded by cattails on the southern side of the creek. Choose any of the several paths and watch

A variety of branding irons

for blue herons and other birds as you make your way west to a wildlife observation blind on the northwest side of the westernmost pond.

From the blind, head west past an intersection with a dirt road toward some farm structures now used as maintenance buildings and administrative offices. A little farther on, turn right just past a circular building resembling a yurt and head north into the trees. Take your first left, walk a few dozen yards, take the next left, then cross a meadow and follow the trail south to a small wooden bridge. The Hildebrand Ranch is on the other side of the creek. Don't worry if the numerous side trails in this area confuse you. They all lead to the ranch or to another bridge that connects you to the picnic area and visitor center. After exploring the ranch buildings, head east toward the preserve's parking lot.

Fountain Valley Trail to Persse Place

"A PLACE FOR POETS"

Would-be real estate developer Henry Persse had big dreams. Fortunately for today's hikers, naturalists, and history buffs, he failed to realize them.

In 1889, Persse settled on a scenic homestead about 20 miles southwest of Denver. Overwhelmed by the area's natural beauty—and economic potential—he bought additional parcels until he had acquired enough land to develop a full-fledged resort. His plans, publicized by the *Denver Republican* in 1907, called for a "first-class 200-room hotel, golf links, a club house, a well-stocked lake, charming driveways, and comfortable cottages, all placed in surroundings said to be the most beautiful." If all went well, an electric tramway would connect the resort with Denver.

Roxborough Park's sandstone formations, photographed by William Henry Jackson around 1870

Hoping to earn support for his scheme, Persse entertained well-to-do businesspeople and political leaders in his two-story stone house. Built in 1903, the home backs up to a rock formation that resembles George Washington in repose. The area was originally named for this presidential profile, but because Denver already had a park with that name, Persse renamed the place after his family's Roxborough estate in Ireland.

Mayor Robert W. Speer, a politician known for expanding Denver's park system, was among Persse's visitors. Before leaving, he added a prophetic note to Persse's guestbook. Roxborough Park, he wrote, "should be owned by the city for the free use of the people." Though Persse's reaction to the note is unknown, it is safe to assume that "free use" did not figure into his business plan.

Persse continued to dream big, but his resort idea never materialized. He died in 1918 after being struck by a Denver City Tramway car. He was trying to cross the same tracks that he had once hoped would be extended from Englewood to Roxborough.

Even without convenient rail access, people continued to recognize the park's potential value. Taking up Speer's cause, the Colorado Mountain Club tried to convince the City of Denver to buy the property and preserve it as a public park. The

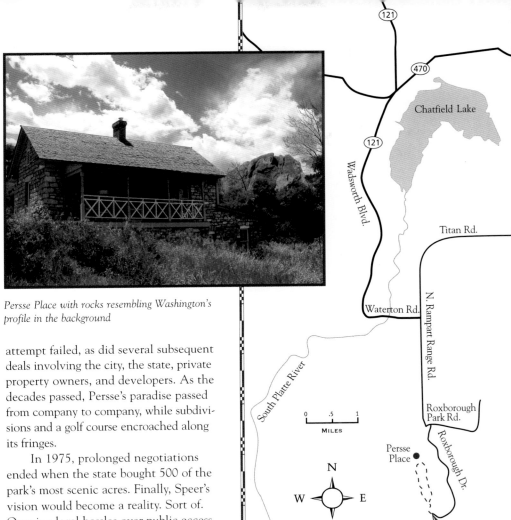

Persse Place with rocks resembling Washington's profile in the background

attempt failed, as did several subsequent deals involving the city, the state, private property owners, and developers. As the decades passed, Persse's paradise passed from company to company, while subdivisions and a golf course encroached along its fringes.

In 1975, prolonged negotiations ended when the state bought 500 of the park's most scenic acres. Finally, Speer's vision would become a reality. Sort of. Ongoing legal hassles over public access kept the gates closed through 1986. The battles prompted a *Rocky Mountain News* reporter to write that Roxborough Park is "a place for poets to find words that conjure feelings simple sentences cannot. It's a place to feel your soul stir, yet a place that mocks the failings and feuds of man. And the lawyers are *still* involved."

Additional purchases boosted the park's area to 3,319 acres. The park's new stewards, charged with educating the public about the area's natural and cultural resources, undertook comprehensive archaeological and historical research projects. Results confirmed that Persse was not among the first people to call Roxborough home. In fact, he was among the last.

Researchers found dozens of archaeological sites within the park's boundaries, most of which reflected prehistoric occupation. Rock shelters, buried campsites, and ancient quarries dating from about 5000 B.C. to A.D. 1000 proved that a variety of cultural groups from many different time periods found the area's sheltered environment and abundant wildlife attractive.

These attributes caught the attention of Major Stephen Long in 1820 and writer Francis Parkman in 1846. Both travelers noted the presence of Ute Indians, a mountain tribe who stopped here on their way to and from hunting grounds on the plains.

Today, the archaeological sites (accessible on guided tours only) and Persse's home remind visitors that Roxborough Park is more than a geological wonderland.

LOCATION:	Roxborough State Park
DESCRIPTION:	This mostly level loop leads through dramatic uplifted sandstone rock formations to Henry Persse's 1903 home and ranch.
DISTANCE:	2.2-mile loop
HIKING TIME:	2 hours
RATING:	Easy
TRAILHEAD ELEVATION:	6,200 feet
MAXIMUM ELEVATION:	6,320 feet
MAP:	*Colorado Atlas & Gazetteer,* p. 50, A2
CONTACT:	Roxborough State Park Visitor Center, (303) 973-3959, www.parks.state.co.us/
GETTING THERE:	From Denver, take Wadsworth Blvd. south past C-470 and Chatfield State Park. Turn left on Waterton Rd. and continue 1.6 miles until it ends at N. Rampart Range Rd. Turn right (south) on N. Rampart Range Rd., continuing south for 2.2 miles. Turn left onto Roxborough Park Rd. and take the next right just past the fire station (50 yards) to enter the park. Look for a crumbling brick structure on the right. This was the Silicated Brick Company's kiln and is all that remains of the Western Feldspar Mining Company, which manufactured distinctive white bricks using the area's feldspar deposits.
GOOD TO KNOW:	Visitors must purchase a daily or annual Colorado State Parks pass. The park is open for day use only, usually from 8 a.m. to dusk. In order to protect wildlife, no pets, bicycles, or horses are allowed in the park. Rock climbing is prohibited, but cross-country skiing and snowshoeing are permitted. The visitor center has restrooms, archaeology and wildlife exhibits, and a gift shop. Contact the park for details on Persse Place open-house events. To avoid potential crowds, plan your visit for a weekday. Because this is a short hike, you might want to consider combining it with a visit to the Chatfield Nature Preserve, which maintains the historic Hildebrand Ranch and riparian nature trails (see Hike 30). Your State Parks pass will get you into the preserve at no additional charge.

THE WALK

The sheltered valley occupies a transition zone between the plains and mountains that features several distinct ecosystems. The natural diversity attracts many kinds of wildlife, including mule deer, black bears, bobcats, golden eagles, and an occasional mountain lion.

Begin at the visitor center and hike 0.2 mile north along the Fountain Valley Trail. At the fork, go left and continue north 1 mile through the valley to Persse Place. The red sandstone rocks belong to the Fountain formation, while the yellowish orange rocks make up the Lyons formation. Gambel oaks, which grow unusually tall here, line the trail.

Benches near the Persse house offer a good place to rest and have a snack. On most days, the two-story stone structure is locked. If you want to see the interior, call ahead and ask about special guided history hikes (usually held in May during Archaeology and Historic Preservation Month). The rock formation with George Washington's profile is visible from the east side of the house, as you look west.

Return to the visitor center by following the trail as it turns south. Depending on the season and time of day, you might see a herd of mule deer on the way. Halfway to the visitor center, a side trail leads to the Lyons Overlook. The view more than justifies the 0.4-mile detour.

Formations along the Fountain Valley Trail

Castlewood Dam

WALL OF STONE, WALL OF WATER

In 1903 the Denver Sugar, Land and Irrigation Company published a pamphlet promoting real estate in the newly established South Denver Fruit District. Employing a pitch that would make a used car salesman blush, its author mapped "a sure road to prosperity" for folks willing to buy and farm 5- and 10-acre plots between Denver and Franktown near Cherry Creek. Sellers offered easy credit terms on inexpensive land with good soil. Even city dwellers with no experience behind the plow could pay off the principal and turn a profit in a few short years. As proof, the booklet listed high per-acre prices on the district's most recent strawberry, raspberry, onion, squash, and bean crops.

To sway any remaining doubters, the pamphlet's author assured potential buyers that they would never lack for a Colorado farmer's most precious resource: water. The district's irrigation ditches drew from Castlewood Reservoir, a 5,300-acre-foot lake that eliminated the possibility of drought (an acre-foot will supply a family of four for one year). Furthermore, the reservoir dam, "a wall of stone" thrown across the mouth of a small canyon "no less firm or permanent" than the canyon walls themselves, would protect downstream inhabitants from seasonal floods. "In the course of every summer, without fail," the pamphlet asserted, "there have been two

Lucas Homestead

or three or more heavy rains in the upper basin of the Cherry Creek Valley. Before Castlewood Dam was completed, these rains used to make dangerous floods." Would-be farmers did not know that the most destructive flood was still to come. And the dam itself would be the cause.

Cherry Creek drains part of an area known as the Black Forest. The ponderosa pines that give the forest its name blanket the Palmer Divide, an elevated region extending eastward from the foothills to the plains, separating the South Platte and Arkansas River basins. On its way toward Denver, Cherry Creek flows through Castlewood Canyon, a dramatic chasm in an otherwise flat or rolling landscape. The creek has flooded many times in recorded history, usually when heavy summer rains hit

Castlewood Dam, 1890

the Palmer Divide. During the Pikes Peak gold rush, when prospectors first settled in Denver City and Auraria where Cherry Creek flows into the South Platte River, Cheyenne and Arapaho Indians warned people not to build near the water. The settlers ignored the advice and suffered the consequences: In May 1864, a great flood of Cherry Creek swept 19 people to their deaths.

In the 1870s, the Black Forest region attracted lumber companies that supplied ties to the Kansas Pacific and other railroads. Later, farmers took advantage of the Cherry Creek basin's good soil, adequate rainfall (some would say too adequate), and proximity to Denver markets. In 1890, a group of investors doing business as the Denver Land and Water Storage Company developed the area's agricultural potential further by financing Castlewood Dam. They hoped to earn a profit by selling 16,000 acres of irrigated land in 40-acre units.

Chief engineer A.M. Welles designed a 70-foot-high, 600-foot-wide rubble-filled dam that closed a narrow gap in Castlewood Canyon's northern end. Its riprap core was faced with masonry blocks sealed by concrete mortar. Eighty-five men completed the project in just over one year. The first crack appeared six months later.

City of Denver inspectors found a small longitudinal fracture along the top of the dam "resulting from settling of the structure." They also discovered a leak under the foundation. A contractor insisted the leak was a spring. The inspectors replied to this assertion with humor, stating that "if it is a spring, it is a fine one, [producing] about one million gallons per twenty-four hours."

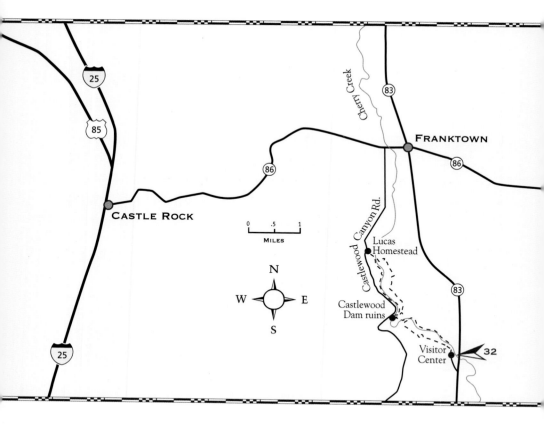

More cracks appeared after a heavy rainfall in 1897 but resulted in no further visible damage. Nervous people living downstream eyed the skies over the Black Forest every time it rained. After an exceptionally wet April in 1900, engineer Welles addressed these fears by writing a letter to the editor of the *Denver Times:* "The Castlewood dam will never, in the life of any person now living, or in generations to come, break to an extent that will do any great damage either to itself or others from the volume of water impounded, and never in all time to the city of Denver." His words would be reprinted 33 years later.

On the evening of August 2, 1933, Hugh Paine watched Castlewood Reservoir's water level rise. It had been raining hard for a week. Still, the dam's caretaker thought the wall of rock would hold. Then, at about 1:30 a.m., he heard a "rumbling" and rushed outside. Water was pouring over the dam's top. He tried to call the authorities, but the lines were dead. Paine woke up his neighbor, Ed Hall, and the two drove 12 miles through thunder, lightning, and pouring rain to get to the nearest telephone exchange in Castle Rock.

August Deepe, the owner of the Parker telephone exchange, got Paine's call. He went out to check the water level while Nettie Driskill, his sole employee, began to call local subscribers who lived in the path of the oncoming flood. A journalist from *Time* magazine credited her with saving dozens of lives. "I don't remember feeling in danger or like a hero," she reported later.

Other telephone operators stayed at their switchboards throughout the night, telling farmers to get their families and livestock to higher ground. In Denver, fire-fighters and policemen spread the warning. Their combined efforts outpaced the 15-foot-high wall of water and kept the damage and death toll to a minimum. Two people, a rancher in Franktown and a Denver man, died that night. The torrent destroyed bridges in downtown Denver 35 miles downstream from the dam.

One witness remembered seeing a horse, cows, sheep, ducks, dogs, and other flood-borne animals swept up against an old bridge that crossed Cherry Creek on Colorado Boulevard. Debris caught underneath the bridge trapped the animals until they formed a single living mass struggling for safety. But the force of the water was too great. None could escape. The sound of the frightened animals—the neighing, mooing, bleating, quacking, and barking—was too much for the witness, a 17-year-old student, to bear. Finally, some ranchers and policemen arrived and asked everyone to leave the area. The boy heard rifle shots and the noises stopped.

In the following days, Denver newspapers reported that the worst flood since 1864 had killed two people and caused $1 million worth of damage. Men employed by the Civilian Conservation Corps, a Depression-era work relief program, helped clean up after the disaster. In the following years, a few leaders suggested that Castlewood Dam should be rebuilt. But nothing happened until 1950, when the U.S. Army Corps of Engineers completed a new dam and reservoir farther downstream near Denver. Though Denver city officials state that it is perfectly safe, they admit that its unlikely failure would cause "flooding of historic proportions."

Castlewood Dam ruins

LOCATION:	Castlewood Canyon State Park
DESCRIPTION:	The suggested route offers dramatic views of Castlewood Canyon from its rim, stunning vistas that include Pikes Peak and other Front Range fourteeners, a pleasant creekside stroll within the canyon, and access to Castlewood Dam and the Lucas Homestead ruins. The route combines several trails totaling 8.4 miles, but it may be shortened to as little as 2.7 miles by excluding the Canyon View Nature Trail and the Lucas Homestead from the hike.
DISTANCE:	2.7 to 8.4 miles*
HIKING TIME:	2 to 4 hours* *Varies according to the trail or combination of trails hiked. See walk description for details.
RATING:	Moderate
TRAILHEAD ELEVATION:	6,600 feet
MAXIMUM ELEVATION:	6,600 feet (but hikers must descend into and climb out of the canyon)
MAP:	*Colorado Atlas & Gazetteer*, p. 51, B4
CONTACT:	Castlewood Canyon State Park, (303) 688-5242, www.parks.state.co.us/

GETTING THERE: From Denver take I-25 south to Castle Rock and exit east on CO 86. Follow the road through downtown Castle Rock to Franktown and turn south on CO 83 (S. Parker Rd.). Drive 5 miles to the main park entrance, turn right, and continue 0.5 mile to the visitor center. After paying the entrance fee, park at the visitor center, or continue northwest a short distance to the Juniper Rock or Canyon Point parking lots. Castlewood Dam can be reached from any of these three starting points.

Alternatively, to reach the park's west entrance and a different trail to the dam beginning at the Lucas Homestead ruins, follow CO 86 east from Castle Rock and turn south on Castlewood Canyon Rd. just before reaching Franktown. Drive 2 miles south to the west entrance parking lot and the Homestead Trailhead. Although the suggested route starts at the park's east end (near the main entrance), hikers starting from the west entrance can access Castlewood Dam by completing the Creek Bottom–Rimrock Trail loop portion of the hike.

GOOD TO KNOW: The park is open from 8 a.m. to sunset. The daily pass is valid from the day purchased until noon the following day. Restrooms, water, information, and a gift shop are located inside the visitor center. Restrooms, picnic areas, and water fountains are also available at the Juniper Rock and Canyon Point parking lots. Pets must be leashed and camping is prohibited.

THE WALK

Trails leading to Castlewood Dam and the Lucas Homestead ruins may be reached via the Canyon View Nature Trail that runs along Castlewood Canyon's south rim. This trail may be accessed from the visitor center and the adjacent Bridge Canyon Overlook parking lot or the Juniper Rock parking lot. Start at the visitor center to enjoy the entire 1.2-mile nature trail or cut its distance significantly by starting at the Juniper Rock lot. For direct access to the Inner Canyon Trail and to shorten the hike, begin at the Canyon Point parking lot. Keep to the canyon's south rim and proceed northwest to the Inner Canyon Trailhead. Hikers starting at Canyon Point should head north and follow the signs for the Inner Canyon Trail.

The Inner Canyon Trail dips into the canyon just north of its intersection with the nature trail. Descend to Cherry Creek, cross the bridge, and then follow the stream northwest through stands of Gambel oak, juniper, and ponderosa pine and past rock formations made of a natural concrete called Castle Rock conglomerate. The canyon opens up near a fourth wooden bridge at 1.2 miles. Stay to the right and proceed across the bed of the old reservoir 0.3 mile to the Castlewood Dam ruins. Hikers opting to shorten the route by excluding the Lucas Homestead ruins may follow the dam access trail back to the wooden bridge, cross the creek, and follow the 0.8-mile Lake Gulch Trail uphill back to the Canyon Point parking lot.

As you face the ruins from the south, the trail forks left and right. Take the right fork past the eastern remnants of the dam to the Rimrock Trail. Follow moderately steep switchbacks up to the canyon's north rim, and then proceed northwest. This is a perfect place to view the dam's ruins and Pikes Peak to the south. Cairns mark the trail's path over the flat, rocky surface, though hikers cannot get lost if they stay close to the canyon's edges. Hikers with children or dogs should be wary of the steep cliffs.

About 2 miles past the dam, the Rimrock Trail descends to Cherry Creek through a forest of Gambel oak. Cross the creek over another wood bridge and continue northwest past the Creek Bottom Trailhead 0.3 mile to the Lucas Homestead historic site. Ruins include the picturesque remnants of a concrete house and several other structures. This was the first ranch to be affected by the 1933 flood, though it is not known whether the damage to the house was caused by the raging torrent.

After visiting the ruins, follow the Homestead Trail back to its intersection with the Creek Bottom Trail. Follow this shady path along Cherry Creek's south side past the falls 1.7 miles to Castlewood Dam. Take the Dam Trail 0.3 mile to the wooden bridge where the Inner Canyon Trail ended. Cross the bridge and proceed southeast up the Lake Gulch Trail 0.8 mile to the Canyon Point parking lot.

Hikers beginning at the park's west entrance near the Lucas Homestead may access Castlewood Dam via the Creek Bottom–Rimrock Trail loop.

Devil's Head Fire Lookout

THE LONE FOREST RANGER

On an August morning in 1898, 18-year-old Bill Kreutzer walked into Colonel William T.S. May's Denver office carrying nothing more than a letter from his father. In the letter, the elder Kreutzer informed his son that the U.S. Congress had finally appropriated money to manage the nation's forest reserves. Colonel May, the new forestry superintendent for Colorado, needed men to put out fires and to enforce timber and grazing regulations. Though young, Bill Kreutzer knew he could handle the job; he had grown up in the mountains southwest of Denver and had doused his share of fires.

Devil's Head Fire Lookout

After a short meeting and a long lunch, Kreutzer left Denver with two additional items: a shiny new badge and another letter. The letter confirmed his appointment as the first official forest ranger in the United States.

Kreutzer wore his badge with pride as he rode back to the Plum Creek Timber Reserve near Sedalia. When he reached the summit of a ridge near Indian Creek in the Rampart Range, he noticed smoke rising from several small fires in a region that encompassed tens of thousands of acres. The immensity of his job sharpened his appetite for action and he spurred his horse home. The next day Kreutzer borrowed an axe and a shovel from his father and then single-handedly suppressed his first fire by clearing a pathway around its edges and letting it burn itself out. During the following days he put out several more conflagrations—spotted from peaks such as Devil's Head —by enlisting help from local residents. Exhausted and excited by his new profession, Kreutzer had no idea extinguishing fires might be less hazardous than his other duties.

One day while Kreutzer patrolled a trail on the reserve, a bullet ripped through the air near his head. Four more shots followed as he jumped from the saddle and drew his .45-caliber pistol. Ascertaining the direction of the assault, he returned fire until his unseen assailant stopped shooting. Although he never caught the gunman, he suspected members of an outfit that had been cutting timber on public lands without a permit. He had even been tipped off that the outfit had set fires to cover up their activities. Kreutzer knew that he had created enemies by enforcing government regulations that required permits and fees for using timber, grass, or other forest reserve resources. Lumber companies, ranchers, and others viewed government forests and grazing land as part of the public domain to be used without restriction.

Kreutzer learned later that his badge, the very symbol of his authority, had almost cost him his life during the shootout. Reportedly, the badge's shiny silver surface reflected the sun and made a nice target from a distance. From then on, Kreutzer hid the badge from view and tried to resolve public land battles diplomatically. In time, lumber companies and cattlemen accepted the concept that forest resources should be managed for sustained use. And Kreutzer calmed their fears by dispelling rumors about excessive government restrictions and penalties.

Today, forest rangers patrol Kreutzer's stomping grounds, now part of Pike National Forest, from Devil's Head Fire Lookout. From their perch 9,748 feet above sea level atop a granite formation resembling a devil's face (although some say it looks more like Elvis), these rangers spot 30 to 40 fires per season. Built in 1912 and reconstructed in 1951, the lookout post offers visitors 360-degree views of mountains and plains up to 100 miles away.

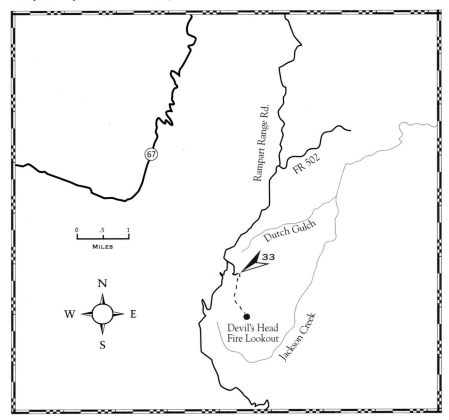

LOCATION:	Pike National Forest
DESCRIPTION:	The Devil's Head National Recreation Trail leads to the last of the seven original Front Range fire lookout towers, which offers panoramic views.
DISTANCE:	2.8 miles, out and back
HIKING TIME:	2 hours
RATING:	Moderate
TRAILHEAD ELEVATION:	8,800 feet
MAXIMUM ELEVATION:	9,748 feet
MAP:	*Colorado Atlas & Gazetteer*, p. 50, C2
CONTACT:	South Platte Ranger District, (303) 275-5610, www.fs.fed.us/r2/psicc/spl/

🗼 👫 🐕

GETTING THERE:	From Denver, take US 85 south to Sedalia. Turn right (west) on CO 67 and proceed approximately 10 miles. Turn left (south) on Rampart Range Rd.—which is gravel, but is well maintained and suitable for two-wheel-drive vehicles—and proceed 8.5 miles south to the trailhead. On the way you'll pass several campgrounds, turnouts, and trailheads set aside for off-road motorcycle and four-wheeler enthusiasts.
GOOD TO KNOW:	Restrooms and a water spigot are available at the trailhead. An outhouse is also available at the end of the trail near the stairway leading to the lookout. The lookout is open during the fire season (usually late spring to early fall, but call ahead if you are unsure) and is supervised by a forest ranger. Remember that the ranger is on duty as a fire lookout, not a tour guide. They are friendly and will be happy to answer your questions, but their job takes precedence. Note the fire finder in the center of the structure, a circular instrument that helps rangers determine the exact location and distance of fires. This is a heavily used trail, so please leash your dog.

Note the weather when you begin; the lookout closes during lightning storms. In the summer, start early to avoid the usual afternoon thunderstorms.

THE WALK

The trail begins on the south side of the parking lot. A sign invites visitors to read interpretive markers along the way that explain the local ecology and history. However, at this writing most of the signs were missing or damaged. Although the trail is only 1.4 miles long, it gains 948 feet in elevation. Several benches provide pleasant places to catch your breath and enjoy the scenery. The first 0.25 mile goes through an aspen grove that fairly glows with yellow light in the fall. Beyond the grove, the trail leads hikers on a series of switchbacks up the mountainside with occasional views of the mountains to the north and west and the plains to the east.

The Devil's Head National Recreation Trail cuts through sunlit aspen groves.

The trail ends in a small meadow just below the Devil's Head rock formation. You will find a ranger's house, restrooms, benches, and a narrow steel stairway leading to the lookout structure. The stairway's 143 steps might not seem like much as you start out, but they can elevate even the fittest hiker's heart rate. Supervise children, as the stairway is narrow with dramatic drop-offs.

Return by the same route.

Colorado Springs

Above: *Early-day tourists freely scrambled to the tops of petrified tree stumps at Florissant Fossil Beds, pictured here around 1900.*

Left: *Ore sorting house, Vindicator Valley*

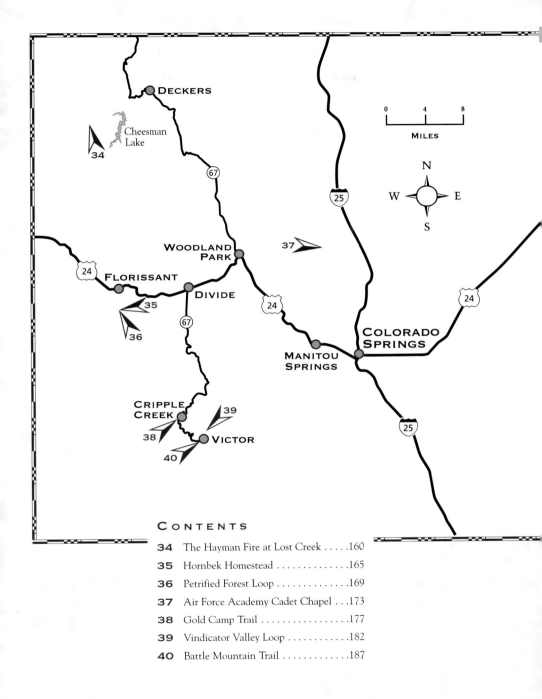

DECKERS

Cheesman
Lake

34

67

25

0   4   8
MILES

N
W ◇ E
S

37

WOODLAND
PARK

24
FLORISSANT

DIVIDE

35

67

36

24

COLORADO
SPRINGS

24

MANITOU
SPRINGS

CRIPPLE
CREEK

39

38

VICTOR

40

25

CONTENTS

The Hayman Fire at Lost Creek

AN EPIC WILDFIRE

Randy and Brenda Myers were cooking a chuckwagon dinner for the latest group of patrons at their M Lazy C Ranch, a guest ranch they operated at a hundred-year-old homestead near Lake George in the Pike National Forest. It was the evening of June 8, 2002—a warm night during a drought season of hot days and high wildfire danger. With wildfires burning here and there in Colorado and elsewhere in the West, Forest Service staffers were patrolling trails and campsites to keep on top of the situation and ensure that the ban on campfires was being observed. Forest Service employee Terry Lynn Barton, an acquaintance of the Myerses', was scouting campsites and picnic grounds near the ranch to ticket anyone not observing the fire ban.

Busily cooking dinner on the back porch while entertaining the guests, Randy Myers looked up to see a plume of smoke rising through the forest just three-quarters of a mile away. "Randy jumped on an all-terrain vehicle and rode closer," Brenda Myers recounts. "He called the Lake George fire department, and when he got over to the smoke, Terry was there and asking if we had seen anyone coming from our direction."

Shafthouse remnants in the Lost Creek Wilderness escaped the ravages of the Hayman Fire.

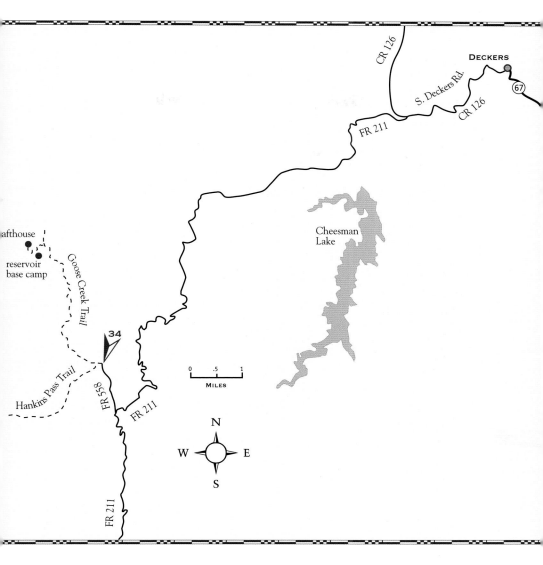

The fire quickly took hold, and Randy and Brenda Myers spent a sleepless night watching it. "We got up every hour the first day and checked the wind direction," Brenda says. What they saw was an incredible sight. The fire consumed 30,000 acres in its first 24 hours. Already, the newly dubbed Hayman Fire was the biggest in Colorado's recorded history. It raged out of control, moving northeast and showing no signs of stopping. The sky glowed red at the fire zone, and the heat it created reached 1,100 F—hot enough to melt lead. Animals fled and waterways filled with ash.

The fire grew so massive and hot that it continued to spread even at night—something wildfires rarely do. "At 87,000 acres, it was big enough to create its own weather," wrote Becca Blond of the *Denver Post*. "Thunderstorms erupted, collapsing part of the smoke plume." For weeks firefighters battled the blaze without rest, sometimes without hope. When it reached 90,000 acres, officials declared it uncontrollable. They would do what they could, but only nature's cooperation could stop the blaze. They brought in reinforcements from around the country to fight the fire, setting prescribed burns to intercept its momentum when possible.

Newscasters nervously reported the fire's progress as it crept northward, closer and closer to the Denver metropolitan area, some 50 miles from where it had begun. In Denver, ash fell visibly and the sky turned an ominous gray. Asthma sufferers suffered and the air smelled strongly of smoke. The fire's plume could be seen in Wyoming. With the Hayman Fire and others raging, Colorado tourism took a nose-dive, especially after Governor Bill Owens anxiously stated on national television that "all of Colorado is burning."

Aided by shifting winds, exhausted firefighters had the blaze contained by July 2, 2002, nearly a month after it had begun. The Hayman Fire had consumed an unfathomable 138,000 acres. The fire was more than five times the size of the biggest previous fire in Colorado history: the Lime Creek Burn of June 1879, a fire of mysterious origin that burned 26,000 acres near Silverton. The Hayman Fire had destroyed 133 homes in four counties and dozens, maybe hundreds, of other structures. Remarkably, the Myerses' M Lazy C Ranch less than a mile from the fire's flashpoint was unscathed.

After days of questioning, Forest Service worker Terry Lynn Barton confessed to having accidentally set the fire herself. She started it, she said, when she stopped at a fire pit and burned the papers detailing her separation agreement with her estranged husband. Barton pleaded guilty to federal fourth-degree arson charges. She received a 12-year sentence and was ordered to pay millions in restitution.

Heavy rains the following spring aided the regrowth, which continues. After the fire, planes spread grass seed over thousands of acres, and helicopters sprayed mulch slurry and dry mulch to aid regeneration and slow erosion. Biologists and other scientists are monitoring and documenting the landscape's recovery.

In 2004, the Colorado Court of Appeals threw out half of Barton's sentence because the Teller County judge who had ordered it had failed to report that he and his acquaintances and an employee had been affected by the fire. He had added time to Barton's sentence because she was a Forest Service worker and because of the fire's disastrous effects, both of which the appeals court ruled he should not have done. The court reduced Barton's time to the six-year federal portion of the original ruling; her sentence ends in June 2008.

From her Fort Worth–area prison, Barton told a reporter, "I can never replace it. If I could be out there, I would be out there planting every tree I could." In December 2004 she was teaching health and fitness classes to the other inmates for 12 cents an hour. Any hint of fire or smoke—even cigarette smoke—still made her nervous.

LOCATION:	Lost Creek Wilderness
DESCRIPTION:	A trail leads through the burn zone of the infamous Hayman Fire before a gorgeous canyon unfolds, where workers once tried to dam an unstoppable stream.
DISTANCE:	About 7 miles, out and back
HIKING TIME:	4 hours
RATING:	Moderate
TRAILHEAD ELEVATION:	8,200 feet
MAXIMUM ELEVATION:	8,750 feet
MAP:	*Colorado Atlas & Gazetteer*, p. 49, C7
CONTACT:	South Park Ranger District, (719) 836-2031, www.fs.fed.us/r2/psicc/sopa

GETTING THERE:	From Colorado Springs, take US 24 west to Woodland Park, then turn right (north) on CO 67 and go to Deckers. From Deckers, turn west on CR 126 (South Deckers Rd.) and drive for about 2 miles until you see a little sign for Cheesman Lake and some ranches. This is FR 211, a wide dirt road; turn left.
	Bear right and stay on FR 211. At 3 miles you'll come to a Y in the road; follow the sign left to Goose Creek Campground. After a total of about 11 miles on FR 211 you reach a sign for the Goose Creek Trailhead. Turn right at the sign, go 0.5 mile farther to the trailhead, and park.
	If you're coming from Denver, take US 285 to Pine Junction. Turn south on paved CR 126 (South Deckers Rd.) through the towns of Pine and Buffalo Creek for a total of about 22.5 miles. This is a beautiful drive, and Pine is a historic district. Toward the end of the drive, you can see where the road occasionally acted as a firebreak during the Hayman Fire. At the 22.5-mile point, turn right at the little sign that points the way to Cheesman Lake and some ranches. (The sign is easy to miss; if you get to Deckers, you've gone about 2 miles too far.) Once you are on FR 211, follow the directions in the previous paragraph to reach the trailhead.
GOOD TO KNOW:	The Goose Creek Trailhead has a large parking area but no facilities or picnic tables. *Watch for rain* on this road; flash floods are a common hazard after a fire the magnitude of Hayman.
	This hike is within the Lost Creek Wilderness. The trail follows a diminutive creek up its narrow canyon to the spot where it emerges from the rocks as Goose Creek, having disappeared into them as Lost Creek. Bicycles are prohibited in the wilderness area. Molly Gulch Campground is closed (as of early 2006) due to Hayman. When you get on FR 211, you enter the Hayman Fire Restoration Area. You will drive through 11 miles of the fire's devastation, and it is an eerie sight. Notice how the extreme amounts of smoke and ash turned some of the region's dramatic red granite formations a dull gray.
	The fire damage has closed a number of area trails. This hike offers an opportunity to witness firsthand the devastation of the Hayman Fire, the gradual regeneration of the burn area as it comes back to life, and the jaw-dropping natural beauty of this wilderness.

The Goose Creek Trail leads hikers through the devastation of wildfire, and the forest's gradual and beautiful regrowth.

THE WALK

The hike begins within the far northern section of the Hayman burn area. The devastation is obvious, and it's all around you. Most of the trees are charred, and burnt logs lie scattered. The ground cover has grown back in profusion, however, so you'll see a wealth of wildflowers and, late in the season, skunk cabbage growing where the fire wiped out the previous growth. You'll leave the burn area within the first mile of the hike and begin to see the majestically sculpted granite domes, half domes, cones, and spires that lend a mysterious allure to the secluded canyons of this wilderness.

After about 2.5 miles of up-and-down hiking, you'll see a sign that says "historic buildings." Follow the sign to the buildings left behind at the base camp for an ill-fated attempt to dam the creek a century ago. Beginning in 1891, the local Antero and Lost Park Reservoir Company pumped cement into the crevices between the rocks through which the creek disappears just upstream. The workers gave up the attempt in 1913, having (thankfully) come no closer to creating the would-be Lost Park Reservoir. Their sturdy cabins of hand-hewn timbers were spared by the Hayman Fire, which stopped short of this narrow canyon. Several campsites are in the area of the buildings, as well as along the trail. A grave beside the biggest of the two standing cabins and in the shadow of a solitary pine marks the resting place of a prospector. The cabin boasts an impressive fireplace, as well. At the cabins, another sign leads you about 0.5 mile to the remains of the shafthouse at the attempted dam site. No house remains, but the machinery still perches there, looking out over the valley that would have formed the reservoir had the project panned out.

The shafthouse site marks the endpoint of the hike. With the rest of your day, however, you might want to continue north for another few miles on the stunningly beautiful Goose Creek Trail. Or, you might opt to explore the Hankins Pass Trail, which branches off from the Goose Creek Trail near the beginning of the hike and leads straight west into even more of the Hayman burn zone.

Hornbek Homestead

A Woman of Enterprise

"I am the head of a family. My husband Elliott A. Hornbek abandoned me over ten (10) years ago, since which time I have supported myself and family. My said husband did not pay for these improvements nor any portion thereof."

So wrote Adeline Hornbek in 1885 when she filed the final homestead papers for the impressive ranch she had established in a lush meadow near Florissant, Colorado. Some 35 miles west of Colorado Springs and in the shadow of nearby Pikes Peak, the site for Hornbek's homestead was as shrewdly chosen as it was picturesque. The town of Florissant, 2 miles to the north, had begun life as a ranch but had recently grown to offer a trading post, mercantile, and overnight accommodations to travelers passing through the Florissant valley along the Ute Trail. The trail steered those travelers—miners, explorers, freighters, early tourists, and the Ute Indians with whom area settlers

Adeline Hornbek's homestead, where she managed a prosperous ranch for 27 years

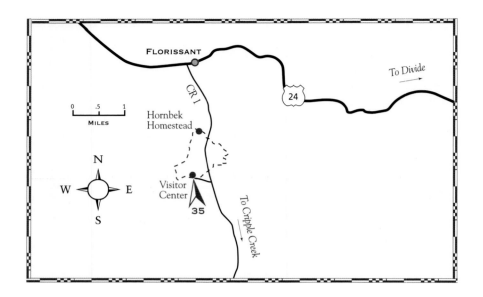

enjoyed largely affable relations—around the massive obstacle of Pikes Peak and straight through the valley where Hornbek raised her cattle and grew her crops. The traffic provided her with a constant and ready market, and for a time she supplemented her ranch income with extra cash earned working at the Castello trading post in town.

Hornbek's own road to Florissant had been a rocky one. The tall, red-haired settler arrived at the valley with four children, long widowed from her first husband and newly (and mysteriously) separated from her second.

She was born Adeline Warfield in Massachusetts in 1833. Twenty-five years later in present-day Oklahoma, she married Simon A. Harker, an Englishman who worked with Adeline's brother at his trading posts among the Creek Indians. Within three years the couple, with their two young children Frank and Annie (born just 10 months apart), had left Indian territory and the growing tensions of the Civil War behind. They headed west by wagon to the two-year-old town of Denver. "I exposed myself too much when buying cattle," Simon wrote, "and am afraid I may have injured my constitution." Like so many others, they sought relief for Simon's illness in the much-touted dry and high-altitude climate of Colorado.

Just north of Denver they began farming and raised cattle, making a comfortable living in an area that was thriving as a supply center for prospectors mining in the nearby mountains. Adeline gave birth to a third child, George, in 1863. But the following year brought one of the most devastating floods in Denver's history. The couple's farm along the banks of the South Platte River was hard-hit. Compounding the tragedy, Simon died shortly after. Still, Adeline was able to buy their 80-acre homestead claim in 1866, and that same year she married Elliott Hornbek.

The records of Elliott Hornbek's life are largely a blank, and 10 years later the couple was no longer together. Adeline, young Elliott, Jr., and Adeline's three children by Simon Harker were making their way south to a new life in the

Florissant valley—a valley recently grown famous for its remarkable petrified forest (see Hike 36).

There, a master craftsman built for Adeline the handsome and sturdy house that still stands today. She had chosen the spot for her new homestead while living in the Colorado Springs area, and the advantages of that spot were many: the meadow—stretching across the bed of what was once the primitive Lake Florissant—offered rich soil, lush native grasses, good ponderosa pines all around, and an ideal location near a populated supply station for travelers and the region's gold and silver miners. Wagon, stagecoach, and soon railroad traffic all passed through Florissant. Hornbek's home was the first two-story house in the valley, and it became a center of gatherings, dances, and celebrations—many of which played out to the music of the pump organ in her ornately furnished parlor. Adeline's daughter, Annie, was married in the parlor on Christmas Day of 1883.

In her first year alone, Hornbek cut 20 tons of hay. Her ranch eventually grew to include more than 20 horses and 100 head of cattle. In addition to a few year-round ranch hands, she employed seasonal help for harvests, roundups, and branding. The civic-minded Hornbek also served as secretary of the local school board.

One by one Hornbek's children moved on. Her sons Frank and George Harker founded their own homesteads (after the oldest, Frank, tried his hand at prospecting), and Elliott worked as a stagecoach driver on the line between Florissant and Cripple Creek; he later served as a deputy sheriff in Rio Blanco County. Adeline's daughter, Annie, lived near the town of Woodland Park but died after giving birth to her second child in 1889.

When she was 66 years old, Adeline Hornbek married 45-year-old German immigrant Frederick Sticksel. The two were together for five years, the remainder of Adeline's life, during which time they stayed at the Florissant valley ranch she had worked so hard to establish. In all, Adeline spent 27 years at the homestead. Adeline Hornbek Sticksel died in June 1905 at age 71 after suffering what was most likely a stroke.

In addition to the main house, Hornbek had also built outbuildings, a barn, a carriage shed, a bunkhouse, and a large corral to support her 160-acre cattle ranching operations. Of these structures, only the home remains today; it is listed in the National Register of Historic Places. The other buildings were torn down and a few of them were replaced as the years passed and subsequent owners made use of the homestead Hornbek had pioneered. The outbuildings that sit at the site today were moved there from throughout the valley, and the root cellar was reconstructed in the same spot based on the design and some surviving timbers of the original. The Hornbek Homestead lives on as a testament to the first ranch founded in the region that would one day become Florissant Fossil Beds National Monument.

LOCATION:	Florissant Fossil Beds National Monument
DESCRIPTION:	A nature loop encircles the home of an intrepid homesteader and her sprawling mountain ranch.
DISTANCE:	4-mile loop
HIKING TIME:	2.5 hours
RATING:	Moderate
TRAILHEAD ELEVATION:	8,300 feet
MAXIMUM ELEVATION:	8,600 feet
MAP:	*Colorado Atlas & Gazetteer,* p. 62, A1
CONTACT:	Florissant Fossil Beds National Monument, (719) 748-3253, www.nps.gov/flfo/
GETTING THERE:	From Colorado Springs, drive west on US 24 for 35 miles to the town of Florissant. Turn left (south) on CR 1 at the sign for Florissant Fossil Beds National Monument. Go 2.4 miles to the monument entrance on the right. As you follow the signs to the visitor center, you'll first pass the homestead (which has a parking area), but you do need to continue to the visitor center and pay a usage fee before hiking the trail.
GOOD TO KNOW:	The visitor center has toilets, several picnic tables, and a bookstore, which offers information about the Hornbek Homestead and the adjacent fossil beds (see Hike 36). The visitor center and hiking trails are open year-round. The center's hours are from 8 a.m. to 7 p.m. from June 7 through Labor Day weekend, and 8 a.m. to 4:30 p.m. the rest of the year. The Hornbek Homestead structures are open during summer between 2 and 4 p.m., staff permitting. The national monument also offers summer Junior Ranger programs on Saturdays and Sundays at 1 p.m., summer Wildflower Walks on Fridays from 10:30 a.m. to noon, and other seminars. In July, Hornbek Homestead Days recreates the valley's 1880s pioneer life. Call the visitor center first or check in at http://florissantfossilbeds.areaparks.com/parkinfo.html, as schedules for these activities can change. No dogs are allowed on any of the trails.

THE WALK

At the visitor center is the well-marked trailhead for the Hornbek Wildlife Loop. Overall, it is an easy trail with two steeper stretches toward either end of the hike. The trail starts with a moderate climb up a hillside into woods of ponderosa pine and aspen across the road from the homestead, then gradually drops back down into the valley that was once the prehistoric Lake Florissant. True to its name, the scenic Hornbek Wildlife Loop provides habitat for elk, deer, coyote, rabbits, birds, and an abundance of wildflowers. This is an excellent trail for cross-country skiing and snowshoeing. Toward the end of the hike, you might choose to take a side trail that leads about 0.6 mile to a quirky natural feature dubbed "the Caves."

Petrified Forest Loop

PLUNDERING THE PAST

Thirty-four million years ago, Lake Florissant stretched for 15 miles through a damp valley dense with pine, redwood, and cedar towering over hickory, maple, and oak. Along the lake's banks was a lush carpet of ferns and shrubs. In and around its waters and the valley's many streams were thousands of fish, insects, and tinier organisms. Mammals and birds populated the valley and the lake's shores. Those 34 million years ago, humans were, well, about 34 million years away. Dinosaurs had been extinct for some 30 million years. The valley (and all of today's Colorado) was warmer than it is now. It was a land of mild winters and humid summers.

And volcanoes. A huge cluster of volcanoes began erupting around Lake Florissant —first in tremendous rumblings, then in a massive spray of lava, ash, and dust. The debris buried the entire valley as mudflows and ash covered everything in their path. Giant redwoods and pines burned off at the tops as the remaining stumps were covered in 15 feet of mud. Fish, insects, and other valley life were trapped in the dust, ash, and mudslides. The eruptions came and went for several hundred thousand years.

As the minerals from volcanic debris seeped into the buried tree stumps and the remains of insects, leaves, and twigs, they preserved their inner cell structures, turning all to stone and creating fossils that lay in compressed layers of shale.

Fast-forward 34 million years to A.D. 1871. Nineteen-year-old Theodore Mead, a student at Cornell, was visiting the area, collecting butterflies. When locals told him about the fossils near Florissant—which the Ute Indians had known about for hundreds of years—he decided to make a side trip to check them out. "Visited some petrified stumps thirty miles from our stopping place," Mead wrote in a letter, "and beside the wood secured about 20 fossil insects from the shale

A Colorado Midland wildflower excursion train stops to let tourists gather fossils at the Florissant Fossil Beds in 1902.

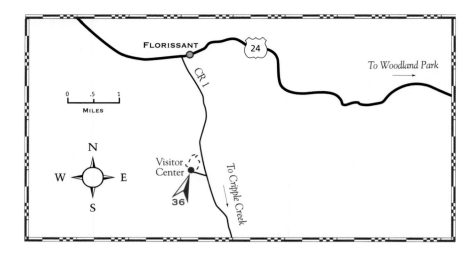

nearby." Mead's collection represented the first scientific holdings of Florissant samples. Two years later, a member of the federal Hayden Survey made a side trip to the valley, as well. "About one mile south of Florissant, at the base of a small hill of sandstone," he wrote in his report, "are 20 or 30 stumps of silicified wood. This locality has been called 'Petrified Stumps' by the people in the vicinity." Widely anticipated and keenly read, the survey report made the curious fossil formations known to the world at large.

A group of Princeton students spent two days in the summer of 1877 gathering fossils of vertebrates; their finds are still some of the most important ever collected. Samuel H. Scudder, a paleoentomologist who had written about Florissant after studying other collectors' findings, decided to make his own visit, arriving just days after the Princeton group's departure. One of his partners for the study was Arthur Lakes of Golden, Colorado (see Hike 28). Lakes and Scudder spent evenings in the cabin at their base camp, feasting on elk meat while gently prying samples of shale apart with butter knives to expose the fossils within. The team's findings and Scudder's later reports included rare samples of prehistoric butterflies and beetles. The ensuing decades brought study after study of the fossilized stumps and preserved relics of ancient animal and plant life at Florissant.

In the meantime, the fossils were fast becoming one of the most talked-about attractions in the region. In the late 1880s, the Colorado Midland Railway began running wildflower excursion trains through the valley and into the surrounding peaks. The trains made stops at Florissant, allowing the tourists to scramble up the hillsides to gather fossils. By the 1920s, the managers of new stump excavations allowed tourists to gather fossils exposed in the diggings. Landowners and quarry operations around Florissant permitted fossil collecting to go on for decades. Even Walt Disney came. In 1956, he bought one of the biggest petrified stumps and hauled it away; the stump sits today at Disneyland, in the park's Frontierland attraction. The 1960s brought plans for a subdivision of A-frame cabins to go up within the fossil beds of Florissant.

Enough was enough. So said a group of citizens who in the late 1960s mobilized against the ongoing plundering of the fossil beds. Calling themselves the Defenders of Florissant, they mounted an organized opposition to the area's development. In 1969, Congress established the Florissant Fossil Beds National Monument, halting development and setting aside the fossil beds as a protected area.

LOCATION:	Florissant Fossil Beds National Monument
DESCRIPTION:	A brief jaunt takes you back millions of years into Colorado's fossilized past.
DISTANCE:	1-mile loop
HIKING TIME:	1 hour
RATING:	Easy
TRAILHEAD ELEVATION:	8,300 feet
MAXIMUM ELEVATION:	8,300 feet
MAP:	*Colorado Atlas & Gazetteer,* p. 62, A1
CONTACT:	Florissant Fossil Beds National Monument, (719) 748-3253, www.nps.gov/flfo/
GETTING THERE:	From Colorado Springs, drive west on US 24 for 35 miles to the town of Florissant. Turn left (south) on CR 1 at the sign for Florissant Fossil Beds National Monument. Go 2.4 miles to the monument entrance on the right. Follow the signs to the visitor center, where you'll need to stop and pay a usage fee before hiking the trail.
GOOD TO KNOW:	The visitor center has toilets, several picnic tables, and a bookstore, which offers information about the fossil beds and the adjacent Hornbek Homestead (see Hike 35). The center has on display many of the finest specimens of fossil flora and fauna that have been found in the region, as well as abundant information about the area's prehistory. The visitor center and hiking trails are open year-round. The center's hours are from 8 a.m. to 7 p.m. from June 7 through Labor Day weekend, and 8 a.m. to 4:30 p.m. the rest of the year. The Hornbek Homestead structures are open during summer between 2 and 4 p.m., staff permitting. The national monument also offers summer Junior Ranger programs on Saturdays and Sundays at 1 p.m., summer Wildflower Walks on Fridays from 10:30 a.m. to noon, and other seminars. In July, Hornbek Homestead Days recreates the valley's 1880s pioneer life. Call the visitor center first for information or check in at http://florissantfossilbeds.areaparks.com/parkinfo.html, as schedules for these activities can change. No dogs are allowed on any of the trails.

Massive petrified stumps remain from the giant redwoods and other trees swallowed in volcanic lava and ash some 34 million years ago.

THE WALK

This is a short loop in a beautiful valley that was once prehistoric Lake Florissant. The path is a smooth, wide, well-marked trail that offers a number of side hikes in addition to the main Petrified Forest Loop. The sites of the many well-preserved petrified tree stumps and other natural features are surrounded by wooden fences and often marked by numbers corresponding to a self-guided tour booklet available for free at the visitor center. At varying heights and circumferences, these petrified stumps, which sometimes cluster in groups of two or three, are amazing relics of the valley's prehistoric flora. Wildlife, including deer, elk, red fox, and rabbits, is abundant in the valley, which is radiant with wildflowers that bloom throughout the spring and summer. Across the valley to the east, the broad profile of Pikes Peak rises to an elevation of 14,110 feet.

Air Force Academy Cadet Chapel

DIVINE INSPIRATION

To architect Walter Netsch, winning the commission to design the campus of the Air Force Academy was "the greatest opportunity for an architectural firm at its time." His company, Skidmore, Owings and Merrill Associates (SOM), outclassed dozens of other firms in a national competition, including Frank Lloyd Wright's Kittyhawk Associates. Netsch and the rest of the team at SOM relished the opportunity to realize the Air Force's vision for the academy's built environment. "We want the Academy to be a living embodiment to the modernity of flying," Air Force Secretary Harold Talbott told Congress.

Netsch felt less enthusiastic about the project after he and the rest of the design team unveiled conceptual plans for the academy at an exhibition hosted by the Colorado Springs Fine Arts Center in 1955. Air Force brass invited 88 members of Congress, plus the press and the public at large. Response to the sleek, rectilinear glass, steel, and aluminum structures was lukewarm. Senator John Stennis expressed disappointment "in the modernistic and futuristic type of architecture" and maintained that "the traditional and conventional type of structure would create more of an atmosphere of learning." Then he focused his opinion on Netsch's chapel, calling its tipi-like design "a cruel twist to the whole subject of religion and spiritual instruction."

Crushed by criticism, Netsch sat at the back of the room and wept. His colleagues tried to cheer him up by putting the whole design process into perspective. SOM had been hired to create nothing less than a national monument that combined space-age function with military tradition. Controversy was inevitable.

Hikers returning from the AFA Cadet Chapel

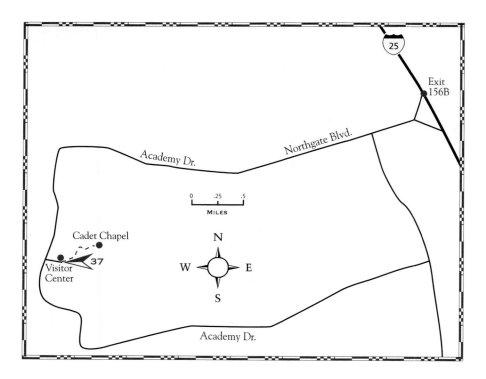

For Congress and the general public, the Cadet Chapel symbolized the academy itself. President Eisenhower signed the Air Force Academy Act in 1954, ending a 30-year struggle to establish a formal college training institution for the nation's professional Air Force officers. Its founding in the nation's highest state reflected America's need to maintain air superiority over the Soviet Union in a post–World War II era colored by fears of massive thermonuclear retaliation and mutually assured destruction. The academy would not only teach the next generation of leaders how to fly, it would inculcate character, discipline, and honor. Congress wanted the Cadet Chapel to facilitate those goals by instilling spiritual strength in those future leaders.

After his design was shot down, Netsch took some time off from work to regain perspective. He went on a Lake Michigan fishing trip with his father and then traveled around Europe on a meager $250 per week salary, looking at sacred places for inspiration. He started in England at Stonehenge, then went to France to see the great Gothic cathedrals. "Sainte-Chapelle made a tremendous impression on me, being flooded with colored light," he reported later. Then he drove to Chartres, glimpsing it for the first time over a wheat field. Its connection to the natural environment reminded him of the academy's mountain surroundings. "It had all the guts and strength I didn't see in Notre Dame," he remembered. In Italy, the church of St. Francis of Assisi gave him the idea for placing multiple chapels in the same building on separate floors.

Netsch returned to the United States without photographs or notes of any kind. "I came home with this tremendous feeling of how can I in this modern age of technology create something that will be as inspiring and aspiring as Chartres, and with the light of Sainte-Chapelle." Working with his engineer, he came up with an idea of stacking aluminum tetrahedrons into 17 triangular spires 150 feet high. By adding vertical bands of inch-thick, chipped stained-glass windows to each spire, he invested the structure with an unmistakable Gothic atmosphere. The final design, approved by Congress in 1958, achieved a perfect blend of past and present that quelled the controversy.

In 2004, the Air Force Academy Cadet Area, including the chapel, was designated a National Historic Landmark, the federal government's highest official recognition of nationally significant properties.

Right: *The colorful interior of the AFA Cadet Chapel*

Below: *Cadets stand at attention in the Honor Court of the Air Force Academy*

LOCATION:	U.S. Air Force Academy
DESCRIPTION:	This short walk offers public access to the Air Force Academy Cadet Chapel, recognized as one of the most important modernist structures in the world.
DISTANCE:	0.6 mile, out and back
HIKING TIME:	1 hour
RATING:	Easy
TRAILHEAD ELEVATION:	7,200 feet
MAXIMUM ELEVATION:	7,250 feet
MAP:	*Colorado Atlas & Gazetteer,* p. 50–51, D4
CONTACT:	U.S. Air Force Academy, (719) 333-2025, www.usafa.af.mil/
GETTING THERE:	From Colorado Springs, take I-25 north to the N. Academy Entrance (Exit 156B). Drive west on Northgate Blvd. past the guard station. Continue west as Northgate turns into Academy Dr. Follow the road around the athletic fields to the visitor center parking lot.
GOOD TO KNOW:	Because of increased security at the Air Force Academy, visitors without a military or Department of Defense identification may only visit the visitor center, Cadet Chapel, Field House, Arnold Hall, and the Honor Court. The chapel is only accessible via the nature trail and is open Monday through Saturday, 9 a.m. to 5 p.m., except during special services. Before visiting, call (719) 333-2025 to make sure the chapel will be open. Protestant and Catholic worship services are open to visitors on Sundays. Call (719) 333-3817 to confirm service times. The visitor center has restrooms, a gift shop, and exhibits on the academy's history.

THE WALK

Begin at the trailhead southeast of the visitor center entrance. Walk 0.3 mile along the paved path through a natural foothills landscape of scrub oak, ponderosa pine, and dry grass to the chapel. Interpretive panels describe the area's flora and fauna and a short spur leads to a scenic overlook with views of the academy, the Rampart Range, and Colorado Springs. Near the end of the trail, the chapel's tetrahedron spires emerge above the horizon. Approaching the landmark from the forest preserves the architect's personal conviction that natural settings intensify the spiritual power of religious places. Return by the same path.

Gold Camp Trail

WOMACK'S FOLLY

Bob Womack came to Cripple Creek from Kentucky via his father's common sense. Fearing woeful consequences due to his home state's recent secession from the Union, the elder Womack gathered his kin and abandoned the South for the golden promise of the West. Father and son learned lode mining in Idaho Springs, made about $10,000, and settled the family on a cattle ranch near Colorado Springs.

Bob, by then in his 20s, never took to cowboy life. He herded his charges with one eye on the ground, looking for telltale signs of the next great bonanza. To his often whiskey-addled mind, the knowledge he gained about the Pikes Peak region's geography and mineralogy more than compensated for the loss of a few cows.

Womack's fortune-seeking prospects improved when his brother bought Levi Welty's Cripple Creek ranch west of Pikes Peak in 1876. He didn't know it then, but the property fit within an area that F.V. Hayden and a band of government surveyors had described as an ancient volcanic formation that might hold gold-bearing ore. Bob filed on an adjacent quarter section, named it Poverty Gulch, and resumed his duties as a derelict ranch hand.

Miners working the Nightingale mine in the "world's richest gold field."

Hikers shaded by aspens on the Gold Camp Trail

Two years later, Womack discovered a small gray piece of rock called "float." Miners define float as a type of rock that breaks off of an outcropping and washes downstream. Exposed to air, it becomes lighter than its source material. He sent the sample to a Denver assay office and learned that it came from gold-bearing ore worth $200 per ton. Womack spent the next dozen years searching for the float's source.

He found it on October 20, 1890, but nobody believed him. All of his potential investors—Colorado Springs folks with the cash to develop his mine—had been burned by the Mt. Pisgah Hoax. Six years earlier, con men had salted a bogus mine near Mt. McIntyre, about 13 miles west of Poverty Gulch. They dug a hole and salted the tailings with a small amount of bona fide ore from somewhere else. This ore assayed at an incredible $2,000 per ton. They yelled "Eureka!" to the press and the rush was on. Fortune seekers poured in from everywhere. Cañon City merchants, being closer to the discovery than Colorado Springs, got most of the business. They passed some of that cash under the table to the con men.

Unhappily for Womack, newspapers mistakenly reported that the rush was happening "on the eastern slope of Mt. Pisgah" instead of its true location, which was on Mt. McIntyre. When miners exposed the ruse, papers got it wrong again, calling it the "Mt. Pisgah Hoax." So when Womack announced that he had discovered gold in Poverty Gulch, which happened to be just east of Mt. Pisgah, nobody took him seriously. People joked about his vision for Cripple Creek's development into a great gold camp while his precious ore sat in the display window of the J.F. Seldomridge and Sons grain store in Colorado Springs. He was just another drunken prospector crying wolf.

But Womack's penchant for binge drinking eventually paid off. One January evening in 1891, the Colorado Springs police arrested him for public drunkenness and threw him in the city hall's jail to sober up. When he came to the next morning, he clamored for someone to let him out. Jimmie Doyle, who was upstairs manning the fire hoses for the local hook and ladder company, released him. The liberated prospector immediately pitched his mine, and, to his surprise, Doyle seemed interested. What's more, Doyle's friends were also interested. Pretty soon, Womack had company in Poverty Gulch.

Four months later, a group of pioneer prospectors gathered at the Broken Box ranch to form a mining district. They considered many names, but settled on the obvious choice. Somebody stood on a chair and toasted Bob Womack, the discoverer of the Cripple Creek Mining District. Bob drank his whiskey and listened to the meeting's attendees sing his praises. He was happy. His dream was about to come true. And then, according to historian Marshall Sprague, "he passed out cold."

Womack watched as Cripple Creek became a town, and then a city of some 12,000 souls by 1894. Gold production increased to $200,000 per month, and Winfield Scott Stratton became the district's first millionaire that same year (see Hike 40).

El Paso Gold King mine, Poverty Gulch

But Womack's fortunes did not match the district's rise to distinction as the world's greatest gold camp. Some say he sold the El Paso Lode for $500 in dollar bills and a bottle of booze. Then he stood on a street corner and handed out the singles to children. In any case, he never reaped financial rewards for his life's labor. The El Paso became part of the Gold King mine and eventually produced $5 million for its owners. Womack didn't see a dime.

Womack left Cripple Creek and settled in Colorado Springs. When his health declined, he lived on handouts from millionaires he helped create. Some old-timers, the sons and grandsons of miners who lived and worked in Cripple Creek during its golden age, claim that Womack was not a drunk; he just liked searching for something more than he liked finding it.

LOCATION:	Cripple Creek
DESCRIPTION:	The Gold Camp Trail begins in Cripple Creek and heads up Poverty Gulch, where gold was first discovered in what became the world's greatest gold camp. The trail ends at the Hoosier mine on CR 83.
DISTANCE:	6 miles, out and back
HIKING TIME:	2 to 3 hours
RATING:	Moderate
TRAILHEAD ELEVATION:	9,500 feet
MAXIMUM ELEVATION:	10,313 feet
MAP:	*Colorado Atlas & Gazetteer,* p. 62, C1
CONTACT:	City of Cripple Creek Parks and Recreation, (719) 689-3514, www.cripple-creek.co.us/prec.html
GETTING THERE:	From Colorado Springs, take US 24 west through Woodland Park to Divide. Turn left (south) on CO 67 and drive 18 miles to Cripple Creek. CO 67 becomes 5th St. in town. Take 5th St. to Bennett Ave. and park at the Cripple Creek Welcome Center, which is adjacent to the Cripple Creek & Victor Narrow Gauge Railroad and the Cripple Creek District Museum (both highly recommended stops).
GOOD TO KNOW:	This sometimes steep trail winds through inactive mines and deteriorating structures. For your safety, stay on the trail at all times. Hikers, horses, leashed dogs, mountain bikers, and cross-country skiers are welcome. Restrooms and water are available at the welcome center. The trail begins at 9,500 feet; use sunscreen and stay hydrated.
	This hike is part of the American Discovery Trail, a 6,800-mile coast-to-coast nonmotorized recreational trail. To get more information, visit www.discoverytrail.org.

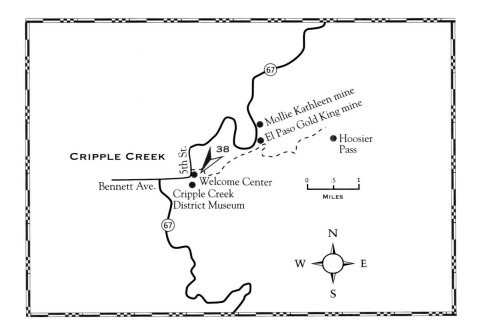

THE WALK

Begin at the Gold Camp Trail sign in the welcome center's parking lot. Walk north to Carr Ave. and head a short distance east to a trailhead bordered by a split-rail fence. The path leads south up a steep hill that offers a good view of Cripple Creek and Mt. Pisgah before it bends eastward and leaves town. Another split-rail fence marks the place where the trail heads over a hill toward Poverty Gulch. Interpretive signs identify an abandoned railroad trestle and headframes on the mountains that rise to the south.

The trail descends into the gulch through a small aspen grove just past the Deadwood headframe sign at an intersection with a mining road. Follow the path to the Gold King mine sorting house. Behind the structure is the El Paso Gold King mine, discovered in 1890 by rancher and prospector Bob Womack. This claim started the last great gold rush in the Lower 48. The Mollie Kathleen mine, located in 1891 by Mollie Kathleen Gortner—the first woman in the Cripple Creek Mining District to register a mining claim in her own name—is farther up the hill to the north. (The mine offers daily tours April through October; call 719-689-2466.) Hike past the sorting house to the C.O.D. mine, which put Spencer Penrose and Charles Tutt on the road to wealth and fame. Penrose later established the posh Broadmoor Hotel in Colorado Springs.

The trail continues uphill through aspen and pine groves past other abandoned mining structures and reclaimed hillsides. This section borders an active mining area operated by the Cripple Creek and Victor Gold Mining Company. The trail ends at an outdoor display of mining equipment on CR 83 across from the Hoosier mine. Return by the same route.

Vindicator Valley Loop

NOT A POOR MAN'S CAMP

At 2:15 a.m. on June 6, 1904, a train pulled into Independence Depot just north of the Vindicator mine. The Cripple Creek Mining District was busy, even at this hour. About 25 workers stood on the platform, waiting to go home after a long shift in the mines. When the engine's whistle blew, someone hiding nearby pushed a button that set off 300 pounds of dynamite that had been placed under the platform. The explosion killed 13 men instantly, wounded six others, and destroyed the depot. Rescuers found severed heads, arms, and legs 500 feet away. This event escalated an ongoing labor strike into a bloody battle for control of the district's working conditions.

Life in the mountainous region west of Pikes Peak had been much different 14 years before the explosion. When Bob Womack discovered gold in Poverty Gulch (see Hike 38) and posted a sign above a hole in the ground reading "El Paso Lode," cows outnumbered people 10 to 1. Cripple Creek itself, legend tells us, was named after a lame cow. But demographic conditions reversed quickly as prospectors poured in from Colorado Springs and beyond.

A local newspaper watched the camp develop and prophesied that "it will take time and money [and] a good deal of them" to explore the district. "Cripple Creek is not a poor man's camp." The paper was referring to the fact that the district contained no "free gold" that could be panned from gravel streambeds or crushed and sifted from rock by methods requiring little capital investment. Millennia ago, volcanoes erupted here, leaving fissures that filled with gold-bearing ores brought upward

Independence Depot, just after an explosion that killed 13 miners

by salt solutions. To release the gold, these calaverite and sylvanite ores must be pulverized, then heated to hellish temperatures and treated with chemicals. The capital required to build and operate headframes, hoists, mills, and smelters was beyond the means of any single prospector. Only wealthy individual owners or corporations could create the economies of scale that would transform Cripple Creek ore into pay dirt.

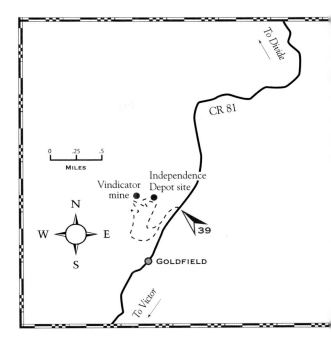

By degrees, Bob Womack's cow pasture became an industrial center. Workers, many of them refugees from Colorado's failing silver camps, poured into new towns like Victor, Goldfield, Altman, Gillett, Independence, and Anaconda. The district's total population swelled from 15 in 1890 to 50,000 in 1900. Many were first- or second-generation immigrants from Ireland, Canada, Wales, Scotland, Sweden, Germany, and France.

Inevitably, the miners and other laborers clashed with owners over pay, hours, and working conditions. Hard-rock miners had legitimate concerns: They worked underground with dynamite and heavy drills, tram cars, and hoists. Tunnels often collapsed. When Isabella mine superintendent H.E. Locke told his employees that he was extending the workday from 8 to 10 hours in 1893, unionized laborers called a strike. The newly formed Western Federation of Miners (WFM) won an 8-hour day for their members, but only after the arrival of the Florence & Cripple Creek Railroad to the district decreased the owners' transportation costs and increased profits. The capitalists could afford to cede the battle but prepared for a longer future war.

The WFM, trumpeting its motto "Labor creates all wealth; wealth belongs to the creator thereof," fired the first shot in 1903 by calling a strike to support Colorado City's mill and smelter employees. There, management had returned to 12-hour workdays despite the recent institution of the 8-hour workday through a state constitutional amendment. In response, the district's businessmen and politicians formed the Cripple Creek Mine Owners Association and the Cripple Creek Citizens Alliance to foster the idea that owners, not unions, should determine working conditions. Governor James H. Peabody, a Cañon City businessman, sympathized with the owners.

Both sides used intimidation, propaganda, and violence. When mine operators imported nonunion workers, armed strikers barricaded rail lines and roads leading to the district. The WFM published "scab lists" with pictures of the nonunion laborers. Owners blacklisted union members by requiring all employees to sign a card stating that they would not join a union. Governor Peabody sent in the militia to "protect lives and property," but the WFM suspected that the soldiers were there at the owners' request to safeguard mines, mills, and strikebreakers.

Popular opinion turned against the miners on June 6, 1904, when newspapers reported the Independence Depot explosion. Because the dead miners had been strikebreakers, most people blamed union terrorists. The next day, Mine Owner's Association leader Clarence Hamlin incited a riot by delivering an antiunion speech in front of the Union Hall in Victor. Two more men died in the resulting melee, while the owners' henchmen wrecked offices and presses at the pro-union *Victor Record* and deported 73 strikers to the Kansas border.

Organized labor in the Cripple Creek Mining District never recovered from the defeat, though industrial warfare continued for the next decade. Violence also spread to Colorado's coalfields and culminated in 1914 with the Ludlow Massacre (see Hike 48).

Theresa mine headframe with ore house, Vindicator Valley

LOCATION:	Off CR 81 near Goldfield
DESCRIPTION:	The Vindicator Valley Trail loops through part of what was once the richest and most active gold mining district on earth. It passes dozens of standing, and barely standing, structures that still have the power to suggest the massive scale of late 19th-century mining activity. The entire trail features signs interpreting each major structure's history.
DISTANCE:	2-mile loop
HIKING TIME:	2 to 3 hours
RATING:	Easy
TRAILHEAD ELEVATION:	10,000 feet
MAXIMUM ELEVATION:	10,200 feet
MAP:	*Colorado Atlas & Gazetteer*, p. 62, C2
CONTACT:	Victor Chamber of Commerce, (719) 689-2284; Southern Teller County Focus Group, www.web-xpres.com/stcfgtrail.htm

🛷 🐻 👫 🚲 🐕

GETTING THERE:	From Colorado Springs, take US 24 west through Woodland Park to Divide. Turn left (south) on CO 67 and drive 13 miles to a sign for CR 81 leading to Victor. Turn left and proceed 6 miles to a turnout with a large wooden sign that reads, "Welcome to Historic Colorado Mining Country." The small town of Goldfield is just ahead on the left side of the road. Park in the gravel lot at the trailhead.
GOOD TO KNOW:	This trail winds past more inactive mines and deteriorating structures than any other hike in this book. For your safety, stay on the trail at all times. Hikers, horses, leashed dogs, mountain bikers, and cross-country skiers are welcome. Bring plenty of water. The trail begins near 10,000 feet in elevation, so use sunscreen and stay hydrated.
	This hike is part of the American Discovery Trail, a 6,800-mile coast-to-coast nonmotorized recreational trail. To get more information, visit www.discoverytrail.org.

THE WALK

From the trailhead, hike south along the fence-lined gravel path toward the Theresa mine's hoist house, office, change room, and towering headframe with an attached ore house. The trail branches off to the left. Keep to the right. The trail loops back to this spot.

Walk along the trail to the right of the headframe and then go around the bend to the right. The trail overlooks the valley before turning right and heading up a steep hill past the Anna J. mine to a kiln-shaped powder magazine. Here a short spur veers off to the right and leads to the Golden Cycle mine.

Backtrack to the main trail and then follow it as it meanders uphill past the half-buried Christmas mine, a Pikes Peak viewpoint, and another powder magazine.

The number of existing powder magazines indicates the amount of blasting that took place in the past. In fact, you may see, hear, and smell blasting in the active mining operation on the mountain northwest of the trail.

Continue along the trail past the Lillie (C.C.) Gold Mining Company, Ltd., mine to the Bebee House, where the district superintendent once lived. An alternate trailhead starts here. Next to the Bebee House is the Vindicator mine, which produced an incredible 1,244,000 troy ounces of gold during its operation.

Past the Vindicator's headframe and surface plant is an overlook with views of the American Eagles Mine group, the Hull Placer, and the former Independence townsite. A sign indicates their locations. Winfield Scott Stratton owned the Eagles, which at 10,570 feet was the highest mine in the district. It also boasted the deepest shaft—it went down 1,540 feet below the surface.

Continuing downhill, the trail leads past the largest standing structure in the area, the Vindicator ore house. From here, the trail winds down past a hillside that demonstrates how this intensively mined area is being reclaimed. Heading back toward the trailhead, the path passes the Dunham, Longfellow, Clyde, and Keystone mines and numerous other abandoned homes and structures.

The loop returns to its starting point at the Theresa mine.

Abandoned mine structures on the Vindicator Valley Loop

Battle Mountain Trail

THE BARON OF BATTLE MOUNTAIN

In 1879, mining mogul Horace Tabor hired a handyman to place a silver dollar–shaped metal disc on top of a bank in Leadville. The handyman—a slender, sinewy, and conspicuously melancholy fortune hunter from Colorado Springs—had been prospecting near the booming silver camp without success and fell back on his carpentry skills in

Independence mine headframe, Battle Mountain

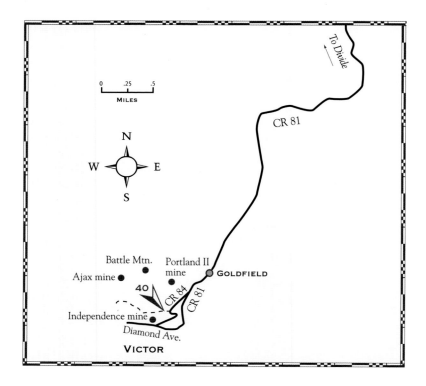

order to make ends meet. Tabor, who could afford to put up extravagant references to the source of his wealth, paid the man well. The transaction meant little at the time; a few paper bills and coins passed from one hand to another. Looking back now, it is easy to imagine the men exchanging entire fortunes.

The handyman was Winfield Scott Stratton, known to posterity as the "Midas of the Rockies." He came to Colorado in 1872 and set up shop as a carpenter in Colorado Springs. On weekends he read books on mineralogy and prospected in the mountains west of his home. As his hobby became his passion, he spent more time in the hills and in classrooms. Stratton invested in a mine in the San Juans, worked in a Breckenridge reduction mill, and studied metallurgy at the Colorado School of Mines. Despite his ambition and know-how, luck eluded him for 17 years. With every failure, he proved the adage that "gold is where you find it, not where it is supposed to be."

Then, on the night of July 3, 1891, while sleeping near Pikes Peak under the stars, Stratton had a vision. A dream revealed a fabulously rich mine on Battle Mountain's south slope, a short ride from a booming gold camp called Cripple Creek. "I tried to reason with myself," Stratton said later, "but the mysterious something told me it was no time for reasoning, but for action." The following morning, he mounted his burro, rode to Battle Mountain, and staked two 1,500-by-300-foot claims. Remembering the holiday, he named them Independence and Washington.

Stratton developed the Washington mine first, made some money—but not a fortune—and then focused his resources on the Independence. Two years passed without success. Frustrated, he decided to sell his "vision mine" to a San Francisco syndicate for $5,000 down and $150,000 payable in 30 days. Afterward, he went belowground to clear out his gear.

Subsequent events became legend, with various versions appearing in different publications. Historian Marshall Sprague told it like this: While recovering tools and lamps from an abandoned crosscut, Stratton discovered a vein with at least $3 million worth of gold in plain sight. He remembered the 30-day option: Although the mine no longer belonged to him, the buyer could cancel the deal within 30 days if the mine looked unpromising. So Stratton cleared out his things, piled some debris up in front of the crosscut to obscure his discovery, and left.

Stratton sweated for a month while the new owners worked the mine. The day before the contract expired, he took L.M. Pearlman, the syndicate's representative, to dinner. Pearlman admitted that his workers had not found enough gold to make the mine pay, though they had yet to explore an abandoned crosscut. Not wanting to waste another day's wages on what looked like a barren mine, he offered to return the Independence immediately. Stratton trembled and told the man to throw the contract in the fire.

By most accounts, the one-time carpenter extracted $4 million worth of gold from 18 miles of tunnels and drifts before selling the Independence for $11 million. He controlled the Portland, too, another fabulously rich mine just up the slope on Battle Mountain. Stratton, who grew up with eight sisters and couldn't stand women, took Lady Luck's hand and danced with her all the way to the bank.

As Stratton developed his claims, the rest of the mining district boomed, too. The last great gold rush in the Lower 48 transformed Cripple Creek from a cow pasture with a few wooden shacks to a metropolis with 50,000 people, electric lights, and an interurban train. New communities formed, including the town of Victor at the base of Battle Mountain below the Independence. It became known as the "City of Mines" for its proximity to the area's richest producers. After platting its streets and lots, brothers Warren, Frank, and Harry Woods commenced work on a hotel. While excavating for the foundation, they hit pay dirt and decided to dig a mine instead. Remnants of their Gold Coin mine can still be seen from the Battle Mountain Trail today, just behind the town hall.

While Cripple Creek and Victor boomed, Colorado's silver industry went bust. Trying to fix a weak economy, Congress sent the state into instant recession by repealing the Sherman Silver Purchase Act in 1893. Intended to repair an ailing monetary system, the act's repeal devalued silver and put thousands of miners out of work. Horace Tabor, Stratton's erstwhile Leadville employer, lost his entire fortune.

Stratton never became comfortable with his money. Unlike Tabor, he disdained ostentatious displays of wealth. He "dressed well but unobtrusively" and always wore boots made by a Swiss cobbler who was also his best friend. When miners and mill workers clashed with owners over wages and long working hours in 1894, he broke with his peers and sought compromise. And though he treated his enduring melan-choly with regular doses of whiskey, he was also addicted to kindness. Citizens of Colorado Springs benefited the most from his generosity. He donated the land for a post office and city hall, gave money to the School for the Deaf and Blind, and left $6 million to establish the Myron Stratton Home for the Sick and Aged, named for his father. "This fortune was not given to me for myself," Stratton once told a friend, "but to do good with."

LOCATION:	Victor vicinity
DESCRIPTION:	The trail begins near one of the Cripple Creek Mining District's largest and richest mines, offers close-up views of Victor from above, and continues along the base of Battle Mountain, "the richest hill on earth."
DISTANCE:	1 mile, out and back
HIKING TIME:	1 hour
RATING:	Easy
TRAILHEAD ELEVATION:	9,800 feet
MAXIMUM ELEVATION:	10,000 feet
MAP:	*Colorado Atlas & Gazetteer,* p. 62, C2
CONTACT:	Victor Chamber of Commerce, (719) 689-2284; Southern Teller County Focus Group, www.web-xpres.com/stcfgtrail.htm or www.victorcolorado.com/
GETTING THERE:	From Colorado Springs, take US 24 west through Woodland Park to Divide. Turn left (south) on CO 67 and drive 13 miles to a sign for CR 81 leading to Victor. Turn left and proceed 6.2 miles to Victor. Stay on CR 81, which becomes Diamond Ave. in Victor. Turn right on gravel CR 84 and follow it up the hill 0.25 mile. The trail's parking lot is on the left.
GOOD TO KNOW:	This trail passes by inactive mines and deteriorating struc-tures. For your safety, stay on the trail at all times; dogs must be leashed. Bring plenty of water. As the trail begins near 10,000 feet in elevation, use sunscreen and stay hydrated. Make sure to stop by the Victor Town Hall on Victor Ave. for more information on historic attractions and local businesses.

THE WALK

Start at the parking lot and head west toward the tall Independence mine headframe. On the way, look left and notice the maze of concrete foundations. These once supported the Independence Processing Mill, which sorted, crushed, and ground the ore from Stratton's fabulously productive mine (later owned by the Ventures Corporation and the Portland Gold Mining Company). Take some time to look at the ore-sorting exhibit next to the headframe and then continue west over a metal bridge and up the hill to the base of Battle Mountain.

Mining structures and tailings piles mark the landscape around Victor and Cripple Creek.

This mountain, which looks more like a gargantuan pile of rubble, supported many of the district's most productive mines. As the trail levels out on the old Midland Terminal Railroad grade, stop at the bench and interpretive sign for a bird's-eye view of Victor. The Gold Coin mine, discovered by town fathers Warren, Harry, and Frank Woods while excavating the foundation for a hotel in 1894, is visible behind the golden-spired town hall. Look for a large hoist amid earth-filled brick foundations. The Portland I, Portland II, Cresson, and Ajax mines were located above the trail on the mountain.

The official trail ends on the far western side of Battle Mountain where the yellow-orange mine dumps end. However, the Southern Teller County Focus Group might extend it along an existing path that continues westward around Squaw Mountain to Arequa Gulch, where the Cripple Creek and Victor Gold Mining Company is still extracting gold from the Cresson mine's ore. In the meantime, you can view current surface mining operations by driving farther north along CR 84 to the American Eagles Scenic Overlook.

Pueblo

Top: *A refrigerator car drifts into a commercial building in front of Union Station during Pueblo's great flood of 1921.*

Bottom: *The Arkansas River snakes downstream from the Royal Gorge, beside a historic rail line and the Tunnel Drive hiking trail.*

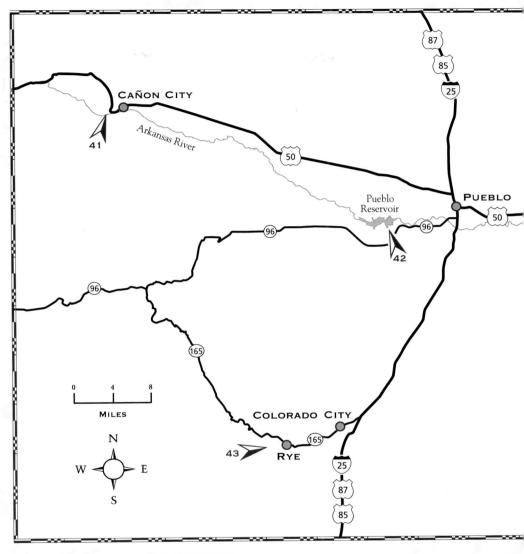

CONTENTS

Tunnel Drive

BATTLING FOR CUSTODY OF THE "BABY ROAD"

Turf battles were nothing new. Railroads had been fighting each other since well before 1877. But this fight raged for two years, and the prize was none other than the Royal Gorge.

Controlling traffic along rail lines could mean life or death, economically speaking. And this narrow stretch of Arkansas River canyon—more than 1,000 feet deep at its deepest—was the only logical passage from point A to point B. Point A was Cañon City, where the Denver & Rio Grande Railway was. But the Atchison, Topeka & Santa Fe was already at Pueblo, a mere 35 miles away. Point B was the new mining district that would soon give rise to Leadville, about 100 miles northwest and the site of a raging bonanza in silver and lead ore. Both railroads wanted control of the traffic to and from Leadville and the mining regions beyond. And both were willing to fight for it. That meant gaining control of the stretch known as the "Baby Road" for its narrow passageway and skinny set of tracks; with just 3 feet between these narrow-gauge rails, trains could better navigate the winding, rocky paths the companies blasted through Colorado's mountains. As if the railroads needed more incentive, access to Leadville meant getting one step closer to Salt Lake City and an eventual transcontinental rail line.

Both railroads were struggling financially. General William Jackson Palmer's north-south Rio Grande line had overreached itself, stretching south into New Mexico to hold on to the route along the Santa Fe Trail, whose foot and oxen traffic was fast

Three tunnels remain from the trail's origins as the route of a wooden water pipeline.

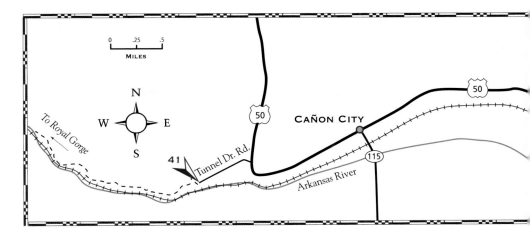

growing obsolete. A tendril into Leadville made sense, but the company was easing back on expenses to survive. Palmer stubbornly—many said arrogantly—held on.

No stranger to money crunches, William B. Strong wanted control of the Leadville traffic for his Santa Fe line. And although railroads often shared the same routes, parts of the Royal Gorge were only wide enough for one line. The clash came to a head in the great "Railroad War" over the narrow-gauge line.

By 1878, both railroads had laid tracks to the Arkansas River valley, and both claimed to have gotten there first. Suddenly, Cañon City was the focus of tension and excitement as railroad crews cut telegraph wires and intercepted mail to sever each other's lines of communication. "Both sides rushed in re-enforcements, each trying to buy off the other's men with offers of higher wages," wrote historian Robert Athearn. On April 20, Santa Fe engineer DeRemer "took a small party of men up the canyon to occupy the Royal Gorge, circled around the Atchison company's camp at the mouth of that defile, swam the river to the north bank, and laid claim to the vital entrance." That slick strategy proved unnecessary, however, when the Santa Fe management obtained an injunction prohibiting the Rio Grande from going any farther.

Now the real fight was in the courts. But in the meantime, the crews battled on. "The Rio Grande men attacked the Atchison workers, drove them from the grade and threw their tools into the river," wrote Athearn. When a U.S. circuit court judge ruled that neither railroad could build in the canyon but that the Rio Grande line could build *above* it, a cold war ensued. Both railroads had to discharge hundreds of workers while the construction largely stopped. An engineer for the Rio Grande line painted "Dead-Line" on a tie and planted it across the rail bed 20 miles beyond Cañon City. Just past it, he and other crewmen built a stone fortress. Thirteen miles beyond that, they built another. "Arsenals were maintained by both sides and the siege kept up for months," Athearn wrote. "It was a noisy but bloodless war, most of the warriors using blanks."

Both companies were allowed to proceed as long as they didn't interfere with one another—an impossible condition. Palmer's Rio Grande laid tracks through the narrow north end of the canyon, where it was only wide enough for one line. More stone forts went up, and armed crewmen patrolled the riverside. Meanwhile, the

Santa Fe sued Palmer for interfering with its own line to Leadville. Out of resources, Palmer reluctantly agreed to lease out his line.

Locals were delighted, glad to see an end to the tactics that had halted a lucrative rail line through their towns. Soon, the Santa Fe was using arrogant tactics of its own: manipulating freight rates in favor of Kansas City shippers who used the Santa Fe's eastern lines, cutting out the Denver shippers who used Palmer's leased lines. Meanwhile, the Santa Fe finished laying tracks through the Arkansas River canyon and Royal Gorge.

Palmer's final attempt to break the lease sparked a last round of violence, this one resulting in the fatal shootings of a few workers. Federal courts intervened, and after a bitter struggle that went all the way to the U.S. Supreme Court, the two railroads signed a treaty in March 1880. The truce gave Palmer access to the line at a cost of nearly $2 million. With the fight finally settled, the tracks crept into Leadville by July 1880.

By 1882, the Royal Gorge route was the most scenic stretch of a transcontinental railroad. And soon, the "Baby Road" was no more: The narrow-gauge rails were replaced with standard gauge to conform with the rest of the line.

Below the hiking trail, railroad tracks traverse the sites of "Royal Gorge Railroad War" skirmishes.

LOCATION:	Just west of Cañon City
DESCRIPTION:	A popular Cañon City–area jaunt follows 2 miles of the historic Royal Gorge Route scenic railroad line.
DISTANCE:	4 miles, out and back
HIKING TIME:	2 hours
RATING:	Easy
TRAILHEAD ELEVATION:	5,400 feet
MAXIMUM ELEVATION:	5,500 feet
MAP:	*Colorado Atlas & Gazetteer,* p. 72, A1
CONTACT:	Cañon City Chamber of Commerce, (800) 876-7922 or (719) 275-2331, www.canoncitychamber.com/

≈ ✕ 👤 🚲 🐕

GETTING THERE:	In Cañon City, drive west on US 50. From the junction of US 50 and CO 115 in town, it's just 1.25 miles to Tunnel Drive Rd. (watch for the little sign on the left). Turn left onto the road. Keep going straight (don't take the right turn), and drive 0.5 mile to the trailhead and parking area.
GOOD TO KNOW:	For an easy walk along a scenic stretch of river, this hike is a gem. The trail takes you into the mouth of the Royal Gorge, traversing the first 2 miles of this beautiful stretch of the Arkansas River canyon. You're likely to see a few trains pass through the canyon along the Royal Gorge Route scenic railroad line, and you might see some river rafters, as well. This is a popular running trail, owing in part to the convenience of the mileage markers posted every 0.25 mile. This is a great trail for families and dogs, too. Pets must stay on a leash. Mountain biking and horseback riding are permitted. There is no overnight camping, and campfires are prohibited. The trail is open from dawn to dusk, and restrooms are posted near the trailhead.
	Benches are set all along the route and overlook the river, as do picnic tables. With reservations, handicap-accessible vehicles are allowed up the first 0.25 mile of the trail; reservations are available for two vehicles. Parking for the vehicles is available beside a bench at a spot overlooking the river. Beyond this point, the trail is not open to motorized vehicles.

THE WALK

The beautifully maintained Tunnel Drive Trail begins at the east entrance of the Arkansas River gorge. From the trailhead, the trail passes through three tunnels in the granite walls of the canyon. It climbs gently for a very short stretch, then parallels the river and the railroad tracks for the rest of the walk. The trail is level after the first slight climb as it winds along the cactus-dotted foothills and overlooks the river. Posts indicate every 0.25 mile of distance. At the 2-mile post, the trail ends; beyond this point is railroad property.

The tunnels were dug for the Redwood Stave irrigation pipeline, a wooden waterway built in the late 1800s and later used for Cañon City's water line. The aqueduct was abandoned in 1974, and along the trail you can see its remnants.

Conduit–Arkansas Point Trails

PUEBLO OF THE ARKANSAS

At about 8 p.m. on June 3, 1921, Pueblo residents heard a loud, familiar whistle. During World War I the public address system had been used to announce American victories in Europe. But this time, its tone was more ominous. For those who lived near the Arkansas River and had watched its water level rise after three days of rain, the whistle's extended shriek meant something else: A flood was coming.

The Arkansas River has been Pueblo's lifeblood since the town's establishment as a frontier trading post in 1842. Traders and mountain men—such as George Simpson, Jim Beckwourth, and Robert Fisher—knew that their adobe fort would attract Ute Indians from the mountains where the Arkansas originated, as well as American,

Widespread devastation from the flood of June 3, 1921

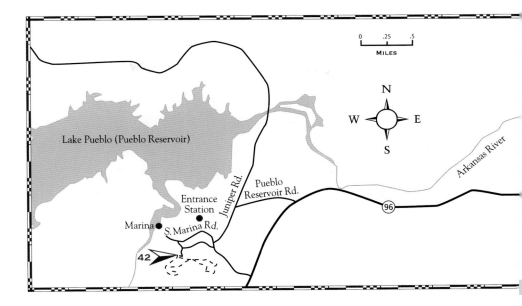

Map showing Lake Pueblo (Pueblo Reservoir), Arkansas River, Entrance Station, Marina, Juniper Rd., Pueblo Reservoir Rd., S. Marina Rd., Highway 96, and trail 42.

French, and Hispanic traders operating from opposite ends of the Santa Fe Trail (see Hike 44). Native hunters would supply the hides and pelts, while the traders —some working from St. Louis, Missouri, and others from Taos, New Mexico— supplied manufactured items such as blankets, guns, utensils, and liquor. The plan worked until the Utes attacked the fort on Christmas Day, 1854, killing nine people.

Years later, Colorado's gold rush brought a fresh stream of settlers to the Pueblo area. As miners prospected in the Arkansas Valley, farmers and ranchers took up land near the site of the abandoned fort and built ditches to irrigate fields of alfalfa, corn, wheat, and vegetables. Formalizing their reliance on the water, residents called their town "Pueblo of the Arkansas River." By 1882, three communities had formed: Pueblo, South Pueblo, and Central Pueblo. The towns consolidated in 1886, creating the nucleus of today's city.

By the 1890s, Pueblo boasted five railroads and a mature economy based on manufacturing. Colorado Fuel & Iron (CF&I), the only integrated iron and steel plant in the West before World War II, employed 6,000 people—many of them first- or second-generation immigrants—and controlled 75 percent of the state's coal production. The company relied on nearby coalfields (see Hikes 47 and 48) and Pueblo's web of rail connections to the outside world, but it couldn't operate at all without water. To prevent factory shutdowns during Colorado's frequent periods of drought, CF&I built the Arkansas Valley Conduit, a canal that delivered water from the river near Florence to reservoirs south of the company's Minnequa Works in Pueblo.

Hikers stroll along the Conduit Trail.

CF&I got more than it needed on June 3, 1921. Shouting followed the prolonged whistle as policemen rushed ahead of the oncoming wall of water, trying to warn residents. At about 8:30 that evening, the rising river broke through levees and flooded much of the city, including the downtown business district, the steel and iron plants, and a railyard. Two passenger trains tried to outrun the deluge but were derailed before they could escape. Most people climbed through windows, jumped into the water, and swam to safety. Seven of them drowned.

Lights dimmed across the city after the water shorted out a power plant, but the darkness did not last. Within minutes, the sky glowed orange from fires. "It seemed impossible that fire could live between flood and rain," said former Congressman John Martin, "and yet these fires burned fiercely for hours and threatened at one time to destroy all that had escaped the destructive maw of flood."

In the end, authorities estimated that the disaster caused more than $19 million in property damage (in 1921 dollars). But the loss of life made the monetary figure seem insignificant. Official lists counted 78 dead, but that number did not include missing persons. Newspapers reported the recovery of bodies for months after the flood. Many victims were buried downstream in the flood's debris and were never found.

Hoping to prevent another catastrophe of this kind, the Colorado General Assembly passed a bill authorizing the creation of the Pueblo Conservancy District. Financed by bonds, the district rerouted the Arkansas River's course through town in a massive concrete aquifer.

The conservancy district's work foreshadowed the more ambitious Fryingpan-Arkansas Water Diversion Project. In 1936, the U.S. Bureau of Reclamation looked into the possibility of diverting water from Colorado's Western Slope to the Eastern Slope for irrigation purposes. Intensive planning resulted in congressional approval for a transmountain diversion system that would siphon water from the Fryingpan River near Aspen, shunt it through the Continental Divide, and pour it into the Arkansas River. Construction on the project's main components, including five dams and 27 miles of tunnels, began in 1964 and finished in 1975.

While the project's main goal was to provide supplemental water for agricultural, industrial, and municipal use, it also provides flood-control benefits to Pueblo and other Arkansas River communities. The main line of defense against another calamity is the Pueblo Dam. The reservoir created by this massive concrete structure has a maximum capacity of 357,678 acre-feet of water (an acre-foot will supply a family of four for one year), but it stores much less. In the event of another three-day deluge, the reservoir would fill up and release a controlled flow through the city.

Today, Pueblo views its relationship with the Arkansas River in a different way than it did in 1921. Lake Pueblo State Park has become one of the region's most popular recreational attractions. It offers 4,646 acres of surface water for boating, 18 miles of hiking and biking trails, and 401 campsites. And warning whistles are rarely heard anymore, except when one of the lake's Mississippi River–style paddlewheel boats pulls away from the marina for a tour.

LOCATION:	Lake Pueblo State Park
DESCRIPTION:	The Conduit–Arkansas Point double loop leads to several mesa-top overlooks with views of the CF&I Arkansas Valley Conduit remnants, Lake Pueblo (Pueblo Reservoir), and the reservoir's 10,500-foot-long dam.
DISTANCE:	1.7-mile double loop
HIKING TIME:	1 hour
RATING:	Easy
TRAILHEAD ELEVATION:	4,900 feet
MAXIMUM ELEVATION:	5,150 feet
MAP:	*Colorado Atlas & Gazetteer,* p. 73, C5
CONTACT:	Lake Pueblo State Park Ranger Station, (719) 547-2343, www.parks.state.co.us/

GETTING THERE:	From I-25 in Pueblo, go west on US 50 for 4 miles, go south on Pueblo Blvd. (CO 45) for 4 miles, and then go west 6 miles on CO 96 (Thatcher Ave.) to the park. From the entrance station, follow S. Marina Rd. and take the first left to the Arkansas Point Campground parking lot and ranger station.
GOOD TO KNOW:	Lake Pueblo State Park, with 60 miles of shoreline and an 11-mile-long body of water, is one of Colorado's most popular water-sport venues. The park has 401 campsites that accommodate tents, towed campers, trailers, and RVs. The Arkansas Point Campground features restrooms, showers, laundry facilities, and electrical hookups. The visitor center, located just off the main road into the park, has wildlife and history displays, a gift shop, and restrooms. Visitors must purchase a daily park pass. Keep pets on a leash.

Lake Pueblo from the Arkansas Point Trail

THE WALK

The Conduit Trail loop begins at the brown Arkansas Point Trail System sign on the southwestern side of the Arkansas Point Campground parking lot. Head south between two low hills and follow the trail as it bends to the left around the western end of the bluff and turns east. Turn left at the sign for the Conduit Trail and go up the hill and back around the western end of the bluff. A large brown sign points out remnants of the CF&I Arkansas Valley Conduit directly to the west across Bogg's Cove (which might be dry). Follow the trail as it curves right around to the bluff's north side and heads east. Look for a rock on the right side of the trail with small, orange, tubular markings. The marks are fossilized worm tunnels. Keep going straight east past a green bench to the Arkansas Point Trail junction.

Turn right at the trail intersection and head south up the hill. Stay to the right until you reach the top of the bluff. On top, you may follow a side trail that heads west and affords views of the Spanish Peaks to the south and the Wet Mountains and Sangre de Cristo Range to the southwest, or stop at the bench and take in the view to the north, which encompasses the lake, dam, and Pikes Peak on the horizon. Before going back down, go a little farther east to a post that marks the location of a survey marker indicating an elevation of 5,148 feet. Go back to the main trail and descend via several switchbacks with steps built out of railroad ties to the foot of the bluff. Continue west until you reach the bench and head back to the parking lot.

Greenhorn Trail

FIERCE FIGHTERS MEET

In the 18th century, with Spain's empire reaching north into New Mexico, Santa Fe was the center of a vast region of trade. As New Mexicans broadened their trade networks, and as relations with the Plains Indians grew ever better, little stood in the way of Spain's northward momentum. Even the Apaches—long resistant to encroachment—had made increasing concessions to peace and were generally willing to adopt Spanish and Pueblo Indian customs in order to take advantage of the growing trade opportunities.

But the Comanches had other ideas. A nomadic mountain people who raided Spanish colonists and Indian pueblos alike, the Comanches developed a reputation as fierce fighters. A leader of their raiding parties was Chief Cuerno Verde—"Green Horn"—so named for his striking leather headdress with a prominent green-colored buffalo horn. Cuerno Verde's father had died battling the Spaniards, and Cuerno Verde had taken up where his father left off. In 1779, New Mexico's governor Juan Bautista de Anza mounted an expedition north from Santa Fe with 600 soldiers, vowing to do away with the threat that Cuerno Verde posed.

A photogenic ranch marks the Greenhorn Trailhead.

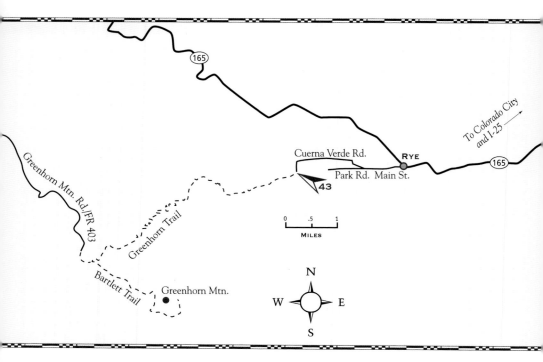

Anza's father, too, had died in battle, fighting against Apache raiders. Juan Bautista de Anza continued his father's tradition of battling Apaches, and his victories landed him the post of military commander at the southern Arizona settlement of Tubac. After a successful colonizing expedition into California, Anza was made governor of New Mexico and took up residence at Santa Fe. In August 1779, enjoying much improved relations with the Apaches, he and his 600 men struck north on horseback into Colorado—the courageous Cuerno Verde's domain. Anza considered Cuerno Verde "the cruel scourge of this kingdom," accusing him of exterminating entire pueblos, "killing hundreds and making as many prisoners whom he afterwards sacrificed in cold blood." En route to Cuerno Verde's land, he even managed to take on some Apache and Ute volunteers, who were equally determined to wipe out Cuerno Verde's raiders.

Governor Anza chose an unusual route, traveling north through the Ute-dominated San Luis Valley, then east over the mountains near today's Colorado Springs—then south again into the heart of Cuerno Verde's territory. "Thus," Anza wrote in his journal, "I shall not suffer what has always happened so often, that is to be discovered long before reaching the country in which the enemy lives." That country was today's Greenhorn Mountain Wilderness.

The strategy worked. On August 31, Anza's forces encountered a band of Comanches, attacked the warriors, and took the women and children hostage; from his prisoners he learned of Cuerno Verde's whereabouts. On September 3 his forces surprised Cuerno Verde and his own horse-mounted followers, armed with captured muskets and camped at the base of the mountain that today bears the name of Greenhorn. Anza managed to separate Cuerno Verde from the bulk of his followers. Still, Cuerno Verde defiantly paraded his horse in front of Anza's soldiers, infuriating the New Mexican commander. At that moment, Anza wrote, "I determined to have his life."

Vastly outnumbered and cut off from most of his warriors, Cuerno Verde was trapped. "Cuerno Verde perished," said Anza, "with his first born son, the heir to his command." Also killed were "four of his most famous captains, a medicine man who preached that he was immortal, and ten more." Anza claimed that the casualties could have been much greater, but he was too determined to see Cuerno Verde dead. Among the New Mexican forces, he added, "We had no greater disaster than a slight bullet wound received by a light-horse soldier." Anza had eliminated the foremost threat to Spanish settlement in southern Colorado.

After the victorious battle against the Comanche fighter, the New Mexican soldiers climbed high up the slopes of Greenhorn Mountain. Looking out toward the plains, they could see the cloud of dust that signaled the retreat of the surviving Comanche warriors.

The defeat of Cuerno Verde set the stage for a peace treaty that, seven years later, Anza and another Comanche leader made official. True trade relations among New Mexicans and Comanches began, and the treaty was never broken. The arrival of Americans decades later even saw the Comanches and New Mexicans join together loosely in retaliation against this new occupation.

A stormy autumn afternoon in the Greenhorn Wilderness

In honor of the legendary Comanche chief Greenhorn, myriad features near the site where he fell have taken his name, including the sprawling Greenhorn Mountain, the creek along whose banks the battle likely unfolded, a 22,000-acre wilderness area—and a hiking trail.

LOCATION:	Greenhorn Mountain Wilderness, outside Rye
DESCRIPTION:	A strenuous trail traverses the creek, mountain, and wilderness area named for one of the bravest—and fiercest—Comanche warriors in history.
DISTANCE:	4 to 15.6 miles*
HIKING TIME:	2 to 7 hours*
RATING:	Easy to difficult*
TRAILHEAD ELEVATION:	7,460 feet
MAXIMUM ELEVATION:	11,340 feet* *Varies according to the portion of trail hiked. See the walk description for details.
MAP:	*Colorado Atlas & Gazetteer,* p. 82, A3
CONTACT:	San Carlos Ranger District, (719) 269-8500, www.fs.fed.us/r2/psicc/

GETTING THERE:	Take I-25 about 20 miles south from Pueblo or 60 miles north from Trinidad to Colorado City. Turn west on CO 165 and drive 8 miles to the town of Rye. The highway becomes Main St. in Rye. Stay on Main St. through town; just past town the street becomes Park Rd. Soon you'll see a soft right for Cuerna [*sic*] Verde Rd.; take it. Stay on the road 1.5 miles to where it makes a hard left. Continue about 0.2 mile farther to the sign for the Greenhorn Trailhead. Park in the little parking area.
GOOD TO KNOW:	This is Trail 1316 of the San Isabel National Forest. There are no services at the trailhead, but there is a lovely place for picnicking at a shady, level spot by the creek just down the hill a few dozen yards from the trailhead. A set of steps makes the walk easy for kids and older folks. It's a long, steep hike to the summit of this trail, but there are great camping spots at the summit.
	The region you are in was the site of the pivotal 1779 battle between New Mexico governor Juan Bautista de Anza and Comanche chief Cuerno Verde (Green Horn). The trail follows Greenhorn Creek for the first few miles of its length; it is believed to be somewhere along this creek, at the foot of Greenhorn Mountain, that Anza and Cuerno Verde had their fateful encounter. Historians will probably never pinpoint the battle's precise location, but a bronze marker at Greenhorn Meadows Park, on CO 165 a few miles east of Rye (and 4 miles west of Colorado City), commemorates the event.

THE WALK

If you are looking for an easy, family-friendly hike, just follow the trail for its first mile or two as it gently parallels Greenhorn Creek. The trail passes through beautiful flat stretches of deep woods, with the rippling waters of the creek always nearby. A Greenhorn Mountain Wilderness sign near the trailhead includes a map of area hiking trails.

For a much more challenging climb, follow the trail for its entire 7.8-mile length to its end, for a total gain of about 4,000 feet in elevation. After the first, easy stretch, the trail gets considerably steeper and a few switchbacks take you up to a fairly level section of trail that runs west along a ridge that looks across a narrow valley toward Greenhorn Mountain. The views from this part

of the trail are very impressive, and this is a particularly gorgeous hike in the fall when the leaves are changing. At about 2.5 miles you reach a formidable rockslide—a popular destination among the locals.

After you pass the rockslide, the trail will get steeper and begin trending a bit more to the south. If you follow it all the way, the trail climbs up several more steep and sometimes rocky switchbacks beyond timberline to the saddle between North Peak and Greenhorn Mountain. (From the saddle, the Bartlett Trail goes southeast 1.8 miles across the tundra

A cool Colorado forest awaits hikers on the Greenhorn Trail.

to the summit of Greenhorn Mountain at 12,347 feet.) At the end of the trail are spectacular views looking out on the plains and south toward the Spanish Peaks. There are also plenty of places for camping.

La Junta

Top: *A stop along the Barlow and Sanderson stage line in 1878. The company built one of its stations in the spring-fed oasis of Vogel Canyon.*

Bottom: *Inside Picketwire Canyon, adobe ruins and crumbling homesteads intermingle with ancient rock art and dinosaur tracks.*

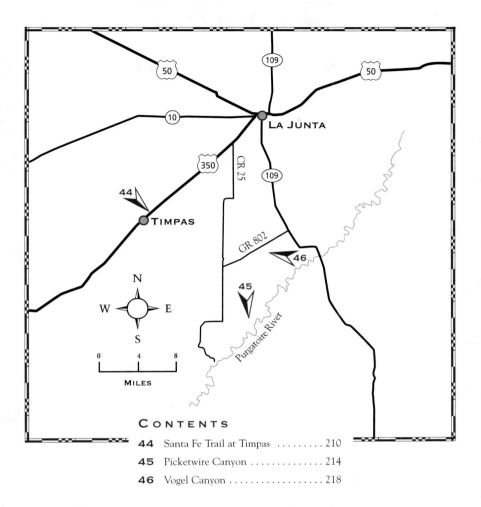

CONTENTS

Santa Fe Trail at Timpas

A FRAGILE OASIS

From 1821 onward, the Santa Fe Trail provided a vital trade corridor from Missouri through Kansas, into Colorado, and south into New Mexico—ultimately to the market metropolises of Taos and Santa Fe. For most of the route's 800-mile length, little save natural landmarks, waterways, and an occasional set of wagon ruts guided the travelers' way.

Through Colorado's southeastern corner passed the trail's "mountain branch" —so called because it crossed into New Mexico by traversing the rugged Raton Pass south of Trinidad. Trail travelers invariably stopped near today's La Junta at Bent's Fort —a bustling supply outpost where mountain men, fur traders, American Indians, and the military gathered and bartered. From there, they forged on, anxious to traverse this near-final stretch of the trail and arrive at the all-important mercantile centers

of Taos and Santa Fe. Travelers called this section the Taos Trail—a reflection of a key destination that lay in their sights. The Taos Trail also served as a critical military route between Bent's Fort and Taos. Having stocked up at the fort, General Stephen W. Kearney's Army of the West took this route in the summer of 1846, headed toward their invasion of New Mexico in the United States's war with Mexico.

The trail functioned into the 1870s, when the arrival of stagecoaches (a slight improvement over ox-drawn wagons) and finally railroads made it obsolete. Then came the homesteaders, several of whom settled around Timpas at the turn of the century. They resolutely worked rocky, slowly yielding ground to the point at which they could grow crops, graze livestock, and make a go of living off this high prairie land. And they did— but at a price they couldn't pay. Plowing and overgrazing led to the destruction of

No hiking path marks the Santa Fe Trail. Instead, follow the stone markers set at intervals along this historic trade route.

The local headquarters of FDR's Soil Conservation Service now serves as the trailhead for this hikeable high-plains stretch of the Santa Fe Trail.

habitat for the native grasses that had thrived here for thousands of years. Attempts at irrigation never panned out. When in the early 1930s several seasons went by with barely a drop of rain, the result was Dust Bowl devastation. With heavy winds came massive clouds of dirt, as nothing held it down and little blocked the wind's path. Many farmers and ranchers simply had to abandon the land and move on.

In 1938, President Franklin D. Roosevelt's Soil Conservation Service established a local headquarters at Timpas. Workers built a camp and set about the long process of repairing eroded farmland and reseeding native grasses. When the Writers' Program of the Works Progress Administration assembled its guide to Colorado in 1941, the writers described lonely Timpas as "a few weather-beaten houses, a station, and general store," all supporting a population of 80. "South of Timpas a 20-mile belt has been ravaged by floods; deep gorges slash the prairies, and once-rich grazing land has been ruined," the guide continued. "Only a few stunted cedars, sagebrush, and cane cacti relieve the desolate scene."

But the success of the soil conservers' efforts is visible today: Though this is still a high, windy, often unforgiving prairie land, it is once again a stable environment of native grasses and other wildlife. The region forms a part of the federally designated Comanche National Grassland; the Forest Service, local communities, and area ranchers work together to retain the area's use for grazing while supporting the conservation of wildlife species and their habitats.

As for the Santa Fe Trail, in 1987 Congress designated it a National Historic Trail in recognition of its many cultural legacies.

LOCATION:	Comanche National Grassland
DESCRIPTION:	A deceptively strenuous walk follows an arid stretch of the Santa Fe Trail.
DISTANCE:	7 miles, out and back
HIKING TIME:	4 hours
RATING:	Moderate
TRAILHEAD ELEVATION:	4,400 feet
MAXIMUM ELEVATION:	4,400 feet
MAP:	*Colorado Atlas & Gazetteer*, p. 100, A2
CONTACT:	Comanche National Grassland, (719) 384-2181, www.fs.fed.us/r2/psicc/coma/

🏕 ⚔ 🚐 🚶 🚴 🐕

GETTING THERE:	Drive about 16.5 miles southwest of La Junta on US 350 to the well-marked Timpas Rest Area.
GOOD TO KNOW:	Foot travel, bikes, and horseback riding are all permitted on this 3.5-mile section of the Santa Fe National Historic Trail. The picnic area offers covered tables, grills, a nice restroom, and a trail register. A low stone wall surrounds the rest area and a few wood-frame buildings sit nearby— all remnants of the New Deal–era local headquarters of the Soil Conservation Service. Several interpretive panels explore the region's Santa Fe Trail past and its settlement following the Homestead Act, as well as the Soil Conservation Service's efforts to repair the land and the Forest Service's current work to protect soil, native plants, and wildlife habitats.

THE WALK

From the rest area, follow the signs to the left (west) beyond the stone wall and onto the nature trail. The short nature trail leads through grasses, cacti, and other native plants and out toward the site of the Santa Fe Trail.

Once you get beyond the nature trail, there is no longer a trail per se. Markers of "post rock" limestone with trail insignia embedded in them, set in the ground every 0.25 mile, guide your way. Keep following the markers to the northeast all the way to the Sierra Vista Overlook, 3.5 miles from the trailhead. The trail generally parallels the tiny stream of Timpas Creek. The highway is always nearby, but it is not heavily traveled enough to intrude on your experience. You will occasionally need to go past a fence or through a gate, as the trail traverses private ranch property. Please be sure that you close all gates behind you and cross fences *only* at designated spots.

This is a level and arrow-straight route, but its "moderate" rating reflects the fact that this trailless turf can make for laborious going. The hike might take longer than you expect; the footing is soft and sandy, and you'll need to pick your way through clumps of low brush and around the other native vegetation. You might

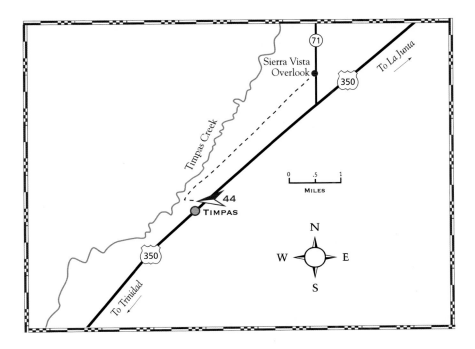

gain an appreciation of the persistence that was involved in traveling mile after mile of the Santa Fe Trail. But as a hiker, you'll be rewarded by the occasional glimpse of a wagon rut and by the experience of immersing yourself in this quiet stretch of high prairie. What you see today has changed little from what the Santa Fe Trail travelers gazed upon as they slowly rolled their way from Bent's Fort, aimed toward Trinidad and the trade centers of New Mexico beyond. (From Timpas, you're walking in the opposite direction, then heading toward Trinidad on your way back.)

The other reward is seeing that wildlife abounds when at first it might not seem so. Many species of birds inhabit the area, some of which build tiny nests and guard their eggs in the brush and short grasses underfoot. Meanwhile, hawks and eagles soar overhead. You might see the tracks of animals in places where mud has dried. Skinks and other lizards—and snakes—make their homes among the rocks. Small wildflowers and a profusion of cacti bloom in the spring. Short grasses, sagebrush, yucca, and mesquite abound.

After about 1.5 miles of walking, you'll begin to notice scattered debris, such as an iron woodstove, a washtub, fencing, bedsprings, and shattered crockery, all remnants of settlers past. Your destination, the Sierra Vista Overlook, is the easily recognizable rise straight ahead of you. There's a good reason the Santa Fe Trail passed beside the overlook: it gave travelers a vantage point from which to get a look at the route ahead (and the ever-reliable guideposts of the Spanish Peaks) and reassure themselves that they were on the right path.

Nearly desertlike terrain, high-prairie vistas, steady winds, and reminders of a historic past create a mysteriously beautiful atmosphere along this hike with no trail.

Picketwire Canyon

WALK OF AGES

There was no Picketwire Canyon 150 million years ago. There also were no Rocky Mountains. All through southeastern Colorado was a smoothly undulating landscape filled with streams whose waters gently rolled down shallow limestone valleys. The climate was warm and wet, and at the site of today's Picketwire Canyon was a vast, shallow freshwater lake.

Though humans would not appear for tens of millions of years, there was abundant wildlife. But none was as formidable as the dinosaurs. As they walked along the lakeshore, the massive meat-eating allosaurs and the even grander vegetarian brontosaurs left deep footprints behind for future discovery, trampling plants and clams and leaving them in their muddy wake.

The Purgatoire River flows through Picketwire Canyon.

Some 14 feet high at the shoulder, the gentle brontosaurus weighed 30 tons and walked on all fours. With its long neck and even longer tail, it stretched to a length of 70 feet—though its brain was about the size of an apple. The brutal allosaurus was smaller, weighing about 4 tons and walking on its three-toed hind feet; it could run on those back feet with a 6-foot stride. The talons on its front feet grew to 6 inches long, making this ferocious hunter and scavenger an efficient ripper of flesh.

Hundreds of these dinosaurs lived here, and they all came to the shores of the lake. Hunting alone or in packs, the meat eaters roamed those shores, back and forth, looking for an unsuspecting meal—a meal that sometimes included a brontosaurus. Social creatures, the brontosaurs traveled in herds, walking along the lakeshore in a westerly pattern that they established and followed together.

As the years passed, layer upon layer of mud buried the footprints of these giants, and eventually the mud turned to stone. Millions of years afterward, as the Purgatoire River formed, its waters carved away at those layers of stone, again revealing the footprints along these solidified limestone flats.

Thus was exposed the largest known dinosaur tracksite in North America—a site containing 1,300 tracks from about 100 dinosaurs, all extending for 0.25 mile. The site comprises part of the same Morrison Formation that makes up the Dakota

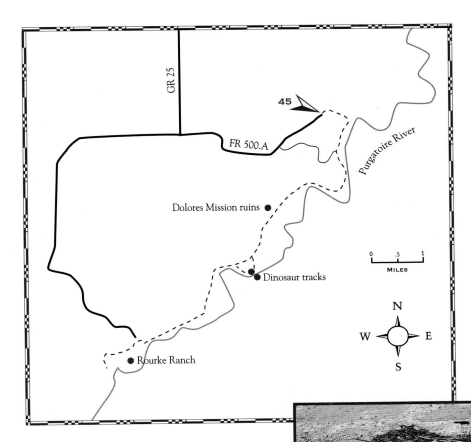

Ridge hogback southwest of Denver (see Hike 28). Here at the Picketwire Canyon site are the tracks of young brontosaurs who once walked side by side, foraging for plants to munch on. In fact, those parallel tracks were the first discovered evidence of these dinosaurs' social behavior. Even more plainly visible are the three-toed prints of the allosaurus. Ripples and cracks in the mud offer proof that the Picketwire site formed at the edge of an enormous lake, as do the fossil remains of the fish, clams, and microscopic animals that lived in the lake's waters.

The powers of nature are not easily held at bay. As the living, coursing Purgatoire River continues its downhill flow, its waters will keep eroding the mud flats that remain from

Picketwire Canyon is home to the largest known site of dinosaur tracks in North America.

the primitive "Dinosaur Lake." Only erosion-control measures can help protect this Jurassic gold mine. By repositioning blocks of the limestone foundation in which dinosaur tracks are embedded, the Forest Service is hoping to ensure that the forces that gradually exposed the tracks will not just as gradually wash them downstream.

LOCATION:	Comanche National Grassland
DESCRIPTION:	A vigorous hike plunges you into one of the most historically diverse canyons in Colorado.
DISTANCE:	10.6 miles, out and back
HIKING TIME:	6 hours
RATING:	Moderate
TRAILHEAD ELEVATION:	4,500 feet
MAXIMUM ELEVATION:	4,500 feet (with a low elevation of 4,000 feet)
MAP:	*Colorado Atlas & Gazetteer,* p. 100, B3
CONTACT:	Comanche National Grassland, (719) 384-2181, www.fs.fed.us/r2/psicc/coma/

GETTING THERE:	From La Junta, drive south on CO 109 for about 13.5 miles. Turn right (west) on GR 802 and go about 8 miles. Turn left (south) on GR 25 and go another 6.2 miles. At FR 500.A (also marked as GR B), turn left (east) and go 0.75 mile to a small gate beside a bulletin board. The road is rougher after this point, but four-wheel-drive vehicles or passenger cars with relatively high clearance shouldn't have any trouble. Drive through the gate and go 1.2 miles to a fork in the road; bear left and go 1.4 miles to the parking area.
GOOD TO KNOW:	If your car isn't up to the stretch of road beyond the gate and bulletin board, you can park at the large parking area there and hike the 2.6 miles to the trailhead. The trailhead parking area has plenty of space for cars, and toilets are available. There is another toilet at the site of the dinosaur tracks.

At the trailhead, a pipe gate marks the trail descending into the canyon. The trail is open to hiking, bikes, and horseback travel only. The area is open from dawn to dusk, and no overnight camping is permitted. This can be a very hot and dry hike; be sure to bring (and drink) plenty of water. This is a fantastic trail for mountain biking or horseback riding. Horses and bikes must stay on the trail, but hikers are free to roam and find canyonside boulders with American Indian rock art created hundreds and even thousands of years ago. The oils from your hands can damage the art, so please don't touch.

Because this area is so rich in historical artifacts, the warning posted by the Forest Service is worth repeating: "Any person who, without an official permit, injures, destroys, excavates, or removes any historic or prehistoric ruin, artifact, or object of antiquity on the public lands of the United States is subject to arrest and penalty of law."

THE WALK

After you cross through the pipe gate at the trailhead, hike down the canyon toward the river. The first short stretch is a steady and steep hike downhill to the cottonwoods and the river; the trail drops about 500 feet in elevation from the trailhead. When you get to the bottom of the canyon, bear right at the old four-wheel-drive road. From here, it is an easy and level hike for the rest of the way as you follow the course of the slow-moving Purgatoire River, whose name

Centuries of human habitation span Picketwire's past.

became Picketwire among the area's settlers. Juniper, sage, cactus, and wildflowers populate the riverside landscape. Wildlife here includes pronghorn antelope, coyotes, rabbits, snakes, songbirds, and raptors.

Not long after you get down to the river is a set of ruins from a brick, adobe, and wood structure. Rock art is hidden away on boulders throughout the canyon, but the first narrow boulder-strewn stretch, along fairly steep canyon walls, is a particularly good place to find examples of the art. After about 3 miles you'll find the remains of a homestead across the canyon to the left.

About 3.7 miles from the trailhead are the remains of the Dolores Mission. Beginning around the 1870s, Mexican settlers came to this valley. They built this particular settlement—complete with adobe chapel and cemetery—sometime between 1871 and 1889; about 11 families lived here. Graves and tombstones remain at the cemetery, as do the crumbling remains of the mission structure. Again, look but please don't touch.

About a mile past the mission is a kiosk with panels describing the canyon's history and prehistory. Along a well-marked side trail, about 0.2 mile beyond the sign, are the dinosaur tracks. After you look at the impressive sets of allosaurus tracks on this side of the river, shed your shoes and wade to the other side to view many more sets of allosaurus and brontosaurus tracks. More than 1,300 dinosaur tracks are visible over a distance of 0.25 mile.

Return the way you came, or if you want to go even farther (and this is a good reason to bring your bike), the Rourke Ranch site, also known as the Wineglass Ranch, is about 3.4 miles beyond the dinosaur tracks. Established by Eugene Rourke in 1869 as a 40-acre operation and managed by three generations of his family, this cattle and horse ranch grew into one of the region's largest at more than 52,000 acres. The family sold the ranch in 1971 after a century of operation.

Vogel Canyon

A HIGH PLAINS HAVEN

Throughout history, not only has the oasis of Vogel Canyon offered shelter; it has been the stuff of artistic inspiration.

At the same time that it is starkly beautiful, the landscape south of today's La Junta can be barren, windswept, and truly harsh. For thousands of years, tiny Vogel Canyon has meant one thing: shelter. Two natural springs feed the canyon, providing the water and attracting the wildlife that have drawn people here and sustained them. Over the years, the people who found a haven in Vogel Canyon etched patterns and figures inspired by its denizens—snakes, deer, humans—into the sandstone faces of its cliffs.

A network of trails crisscrosses Vogel Canyon for easy access to rock art and other remnants of the past.

Nomadic hunters and gatherers came to Vogel Canyon some 7,500 years ago in search of the deer, elk, pronghorn, bison, and rabbits that frequented the canyon. Beginning around A.D. 100, hunting societies started taking permanent shelter in rocky overhangs. Thus protected from the elements and enjoying the bounty of wildlife and springwater, they stayed for hundreds of years and even did some farming. More recently, Plains Indian tribes made the canyon their home. Arriving around 1500, tribes such as the Comanche frequented the canyon for nearly 400 years. Increasingly fierce conflicts with explorers, traders, and settlers drove them away.

The sandstone walls of the canyon's cliffs bear the reminders that these people called the canyon their home. They left their mark in the form of petroglyphs carved into stone, some telling stories and some just fanciful drawings. The surviving glyphs date from around 300 to 800 years ago. Today it is these cultural resources that largely draw visitors into Vogel Canyon, just as the canyon's natural resources long ago drew the artists who etched them.

No doubt equally impressed by the petroglyphs were travelers who stopped at the Barlow and Sanderson stagecoach station that sat within the protection of the canyon for a few years. Established in 1872 to carry mail and passengers between Trinidad and Las Animas, the stage line was a spur of the Santa Fe Trail, the trade route that extended from Missouri to New Mexico (see Hike 44). Trail travelers had long known Vogel Canyon as a place to water their horses and rest, so the canyon was a logical

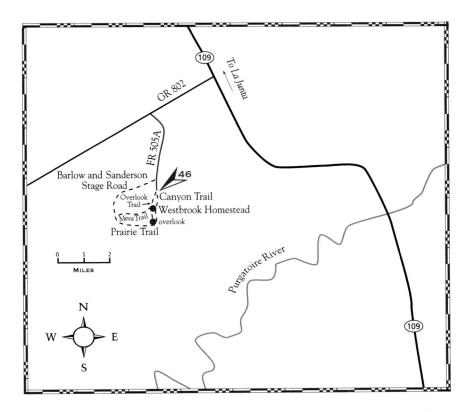

site for a stage stop. The station remained in use until 1876, by which time the railroads' arrival had quickly made stagecoaches a thing of the past. Disappearing one by one as the rails advanced to the west and south, the last stagecoaches rolled into Santa Fe in 1880.

The Homestead Act of 1862 had offered free land to anyone who could sustain a living on it—even here on the high plains, where low rainfall made it next to impossible. The act gave homesteaders 160 acres of land as long as they could show they had worked and improved it for five years. The first homesteaders to make a go of it along the Purgatoire River arrived a few years after the act went into effect. Ranchers came, too, raising cattle and sheep. Again, Vogel Canyon—with its steady supply of water and its shelter from the driving wind—offered promise.

"The boom, however, was short lived," writes historian Paul D. Friedman. "Dry years in 1888 and 1889 soon had the new homesteaders convinced that southeastern Colorado was not the agricultural paradise they had been promised....The drought of the 1880s was followed by a national depression in the early 1890s, and many of these homesteaders were forced off the land." But gradually, homesteaders came back, thanks in part to the Enlarged Homestead Act of 1909 and the Stock Raising Homestead Act of 1916, which made concessions to homesteaders and ranchers who eked out livings on arid lands. Another homesteading boom was in the making.

One such family of homesteaders, the Westbrooks, came to Vogel Canyon and built a sandstone house, barn, and outbuildings on a high rise that still enjoyed some of the shelter of the canyon walls. They weathered the economic depression of the 1920s only to be hit by the drought and Dust Bowl of the 1930s. As a trailside marker relates, "On April 14, 1935, the biggest dust storm ever to rage across southeastern Colorado billowed several miles high. The sun was completely blotted out and skies were dark for 24 hours....Many families had no choice but to abandon their homesteads." The Westbrooks were among them. By 1937, they were gone, too. Today, only the crumbling ruins of their once-promising homestead remain— another reminder of the past occupations of Vogel Canyon.

LOCATION:	Comanche National Grassland
DESCRIPTION:	Trails lead to the sheltering walls of a narrow river canyon and reminders of ancient and historic peoples.
DISTANCE:	5-mile loop
HIKING TIME:	4 hours
RATING:	Easy
TRAILHEAD ELEVATION:	4,400 feet
MAXIMUM ELEVATION:	4,400 feet (but hikers must descend into and climb out of the canyon)
MAP:	*Colorado Atlas & Gazetteer,* p. 100, A3
CONTACT:	Comanche National Grassland, (719) 384-2181, www.fs.fed.us/r2/psicc/coma/

GETTING THERE:	From La Junta, drive south on CO 109 for about 13.5 miles. Turn right (west) on GR 802 and go about 1.3 miles. Turn left (south) on FR 505A and drive 2 miles to the picnic area.
GOOD TO KNOW:	The picnic area includes many parking spaces, a toilet, shaded picnic tables with charcoal grills, hitching rails for horses, and parking for trailers. There is no camping along the trail, but overnight camping is allowed at the parking area (no drinking water is available). Horseback riding is permitted. This is a very accessible canyon for viewing American Indian rock art, but be sure not to touch any of it. The oils from your hands can deteriorate both the art and the rocks.
	Before you start, take the easy stroll along the Overlook Trail to see the overview of the canyon. From the picnic area, this short, graveled, wheelchair-accessible path takes you gently uphill and across two wooden bridges to the overlook. From here you can see down into the canyon; across the canyon to the left are huge stone faces incised with rock art (sadly, some of it vandalized), and to the right are the scant ruins of the Barlow and Sanderson stagecoach station. There is a bench at the overlook, and interpretive markers explore the canyon's history.

THE WALK

From the picnic area, walk south on the Canyon Trail down toward the canyon. The trail takes you into an arid landscape of juniper and cactus. On a warm May afternoon, when the cacti were blooming everywhere, we saw hawks, an owl, several skinks, and a gopher snake that was sunning itself on the rocks. Make sure to keep your eye out for rattlesnakes.

After about 0.5 mile you'll see the stone ruins of the Westbrook Homestead to your right. The ruins include the remains of a house, barn, outbuilding, and a lone chimney. After visiting the homestead site, resume your hike down the Canyon Trail. You'll start to see petroglyphs incised into the sandstone cliffs. Many are identified and explained in panels posted beside them, and separate paths lead up to the stone faces along the steep canyon walls. One rock face alone boasts no fewer than 49 identifiable petroglyphs. The panels also discuss the ravages of vandalism—a major problem in this canyon.

While exploring the rock art, continue south along the Canyon Trail. Just over a mile from the trailhead is one of the two springs that feed the tributary stream of the Purgatoire River that flows through this canyon; cottonwoods and cattails surround the spring. Continue on the trail, toward the right, until you reach the Prairie Trail (a total of 1.75 miles from the trailhead). Walk west along the Prairie Trail. Across to your right are the stone walls of the 1870s Barlow and Sanderson stage station.

From here, keep walking west on the Prairie Trail, through the canyon. Pass the ruins of two stone structures just before the junction with the Mesa Trail. Continue on the Prairie Trail. About 1.5 miles from where it began, the Prairie Trail starts its curve north, gradually rising up out of the canyon and onto the short-grass prairie. At this point you're following wagon ruts, apparently made deeper from more recent ranch use. At about 2 miles past the starting point of the Prairie Trail, you'll come up out of the canyon and arrive at a prominent sign that marks the main Barlow and Sanderson Stage Road. Turn right and keep following the ruts, continuing east for the last mile toward the road you drove in on. Here the ruts are much more faint; the occasional cairn helps to mark the path until you reach the road. Turn to the right (south), and walk the short distance back to the parking area.

Stone walls and foundations remain from the canyon's days as a stage stop.

Trinidad

Top: A scene from the Berwind Canyon coal camp of Tollerburg.
Austrian saloonkeeper Giacomo Toller is at the wheel.

Bottom: West Spanish Peak as seen from one of
ranger Asa Arnold's trails near Bear Lake

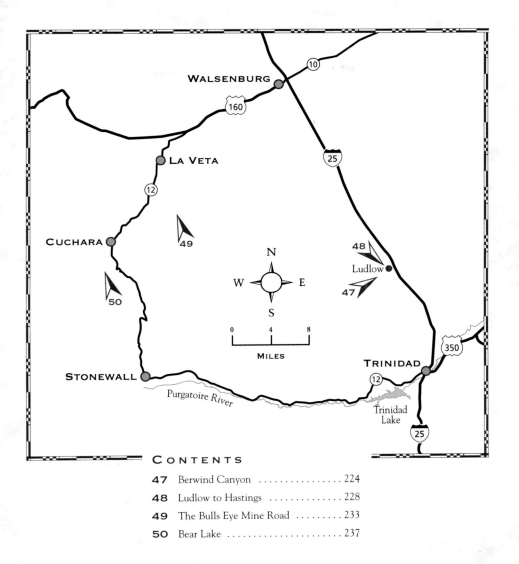

CONTENTS

Berwind Canyon

A HIGH-GRADE HERITAGE

In the rapid-fire industrialization of the 1880s, Pueblo's steel mills needed ton after ton of coke to fire the furnaces that burned day and night to keep up with the nation's demand for steel. Fueling those furnaces by the trainload were the enormous coal-fields of southern Colorado. Those fields stretched for miles—straight north, south, and west of Trinidad. One of the earliest known and richest veins of that coal was in Berwind Canyon, a high-grade hub of coal-mining activity.

El Moro No. 2 began producing coal in 1888 and incorporated in 1890 as the town of Berwind, taking its name from Edward J. Berwind, board chair of Colorado Fuel & Iron—the company that would dominate Colorado's coal industry for decades to come. The town slowly grew and by 1900 had a population of 450 residents. Throughout the region, the rosters of coal miners reflected the ethnic mix that poured in to meet the demand for labor: Hispanos, Japanese, Russians, Slavs, Irish, English, and others. As many as 10 African American families lived and worked at Berwind, too.

CF&I established the camp of Tabasco in 1900, further extending its Berwind Canyon coal operations. In addition to a butcher shop, a barbershop, and two saloons, Berwind was home to the first Catholic church in a CF&I camp. Tabasco eventually boasted another saloon, a YMCA, and more than 300 coke ovens, with a mine employing up to 350 men a year. "The people made their purchases from a general store at Ludlow, from the company store, or from a visiting huckster wagon," write authors George McGovern and Leonard Guttridge in their classic study of the

Coal cars and company housing in the coal camp of Berwind

1913–1914 strike, *The Great Coalfield War.* "And whether at home, at school, or in one of Berwind's four saloons, no one could escape the soot mists and unburned gases from the long rows of coke ovens at Tabasco." Because of Tabasco's precarious location in this narrow canyon, the town suffered the wrath of a torrential thunderstorm in 1905 when flooding destroyed several houses and killed 11 of the town's residents. Berwind would eventually grow to support a population of more than 1,000, three pool halls, a Presbyterian church, and a hotel.

A few miles up the canyon, CF&I founded a camp called Tollerburg in 1907. Named for (and by) Austrian saloonkeeper and store owner Giacomo Toller and his brother, Angelino, the camp had a mine with two shafts and a daily output of more than 800 tons of coal. In another reflection of the camp's diversity, Hispano miners served as union delegates. And as with so many of the region's coal camps, danger was a tragic fact of life. On a July morning in 1909, nine men making the day's first descent into the mine died instantly when their lamps apparently ignited a pocket of gas. March 1913 brought further tragedy when two more miners met a similar fate.

Above: *The miners' boardinghouse and hotel at Vallorso still stands and, like many structures in Berwind Canyon, is private property.*

Below: *The old jail at Berwind*

Up the canyon from Tollerburg was Vallorso, founded in 1918 as the farthest camp up Berwind Canyon and the farthest extension of the Colorado & Southern, the rail line that linked all of the camps. The C&S hauled coal down from the Berwind Canyon mines and connected the camps to the rail hub of Ludlow (see Hike 48). Three mines operated at Vallorso—two were functioning for about 10 years, but a third, the Bear Canyon Mine, ran for nearly 50 years before shutting down in 1953.

Once the canyon's largest coal producer, Berwind shut down in 1928 with the drop in demand for coal. Its smaller neighbor, Tabasco, had quit operation some 10 years earlier. (Bulldozers claimed Tabasco's many coke ovens in 1982, but the piled brick remains are still plainly visible.) The Great Depression claimed Tollerburg in 1932.

LOCATION:	About 20 miles north of Trinidad
DESCRIPTION:	A hike along a little-used county road takes you up into a historic coal-mining canyon.
DISTANCE:	About 6 miles, out and back
HIKING TIME:	3 hours
RATING:	Moderate
TRAILHEAD ELEVATION:	6,400 feet
MAXIMUM ELEVATION:	6,800 feet
MAP:	*Colorado Atlas & Gazetteer*, p. 93, B6
CONTACT:	Trinidad/Las Animas Chamber of Commerce, (866) 480-4750 or (719) 846-9285, www.tlac.net/chamber/

GETTING THERE: On I-25, drive north from Trinidad or south from Walsenburg to Exit 27. You'll see a sign for the Ludlow Monument. Take the exit and drive west 0.8 mile to the monument. (Make note of your odometer reading at this point, or set it back to zero.) Just past the monument, turn left on CR 61.5 to the remains of the town of Ludlow, 0.5 mile down the road. At 1.25 miles from the monument, turn right (west) onto CR 40.2 and drive under the railroad overpass. Continue driving through the site of what was once the town of Tabasco (roughly between the 2- and 2.5-mile marks), which today appears mostly as a set of ruins up on the bluffs to your right.

When you've gone about 3.2 miles from the Ludlow Monument and see sections of a long stone wall along the road and a profusion of other wall fragments, foundations, and structures, you are at the site of Berwind. Park along the side of the road and start walking west from here.

GOOD TO KNOW: On your way to this walk, you will pass the Ludlow Monument (see Hike 48) and the remains of the tiny town and rail stop of Ludlow. Please remember that all structures are on private property and absolutely no trespassing is allowed.

Like Hike 48, this stroll follows a well-maintained county road. This is a perfect route for mountain biking through a slice of Colorado history. Because these roads serve local ranchers and other area residents, you'll probably be sharing the route with some auto traffic, but not much. Many remnants of the coal camps are on private property, so it is best to simply stay on the road.

THE WALK

This walk follows the route of an abandoned stretch of the Colorado & Southern rail line (as you go up, the tracks were to the left of the roadway, so keep your eyes peeled for a few remaining stretches of railroad bed). This is a winding, somewhat hilly road through a semiarid landscape of juniper, sage, and cactus. As you start walking through the abandoned town of Berwind, an unmistakable sight is the two-cell jailhouse on the right, about 0.5 mile into town. The jail is on private

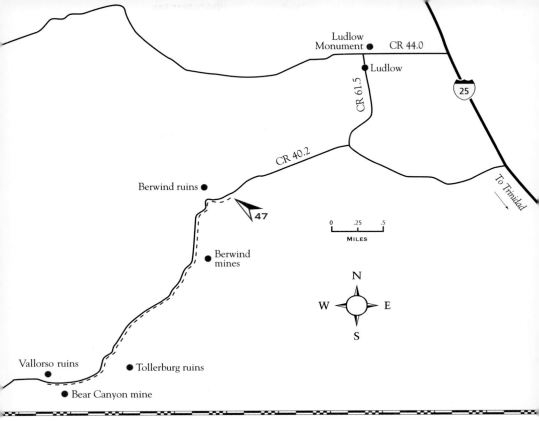

property and sits behind a gate. To the left of the roadway you can see three mine portals alongside one another, as well as others throughout the hillsides.

About 1.5 miles past Berwind is the site of Tollerburg, another of the coal camps. On the right side of the road is a large section of stone wall alongside a set of steps that once led to a house. The home belonged to the family of Giacomo Toller, the Austrian-born landowner and former miner who developed the town under its original name of Tollerville. Later the home served as the offices of the camp's doctor. Other than a few more walls and foundations, little else remains of Tollerburg.

As you walk beyond the site of Tollerburg, you'll see some modern houses above the roadway, sprinkled within some lovely scenery. Walls, foundations, an old red-brick house, and other mining camp remnants also dot the way. When you've gone about 3 miles from the starting point at Berwind, you'll be at the camp of Vallorso, at the junction of Berwind (or Road) Canyon and Bear Canyon. Off to the left you will see a huge brick structure, the old Vallorso Mercantile. Now a hay barn, the mercantile once housed a general store, pool hall, and barbershop. You'll also see a section of railroad trestle near the junction. The left fork is Bear Canyon Rd., which leads into the private Tamburelli Ranch. The town of Vallorso was the final coal camp established up Berwind Canyon and along the Colorado & Southern line, so this road junction marks the end of the history hike. However, continuing straight—up what is now marked as Road Canyon—takes you farther into some beautiful country, so you might want to keep hiking or biking to your heart's content.

Ludlow to Hastings

TRAGEDY TIMES TWO

In the annals of Colorado labor history, no single word strikes as resounding a chord as "Ludlow." By the 1890s, the massive Colorado Fuel & Iron was foremost among the companies that ran mining operations throughout the sprawling coalfields of southern Colorado. At brand-new company towns in the high sagebrush hills around Trinidad and Walsenburg, CF&I set up housing, facilities, schools, and the company stores that brought the miners' families the basics they needed, at great cost. Most miners were immigrants, having traveled with their wives and children to these isolated coalfields from Mexico, Eastern Europe, Italy, Greece, and elsewhere. Periods between labor strife were marked by relative calm—as calm as could be expected given the dangers of mining—but at times the close-knit group of families helped each other to survive.

In the summer of 1913, the United Mine Workers of America launched a major effort to mobilize the miners, with union recruiter John Lawson overseeing its activities in the southern coalfields. Aiding him was the outspoken 80-year-old socialist organizer, Mother Jones, whose fiery rhetoric helped expand union rosters and inflamed passions on both sides of the unionization issue. As mine operators and the union reached an impasse, the union officially struck in September.

Mine operators recruited spies and strikebreakers, and miners took up arms. The miners saw in the strike an opportunity to effect real change and obtain an 8-hour workday; a 10-percent wage increase; impartial oversight to ensure that the coal they brought out of the ground was weighed accurately and their wages tallied fairly; the right to choose their own living quarters and doctors; and official recognition of the United Mine Workers of America, the union that they believed could keep the mine owners accountable in the years ahead.

Ludlow

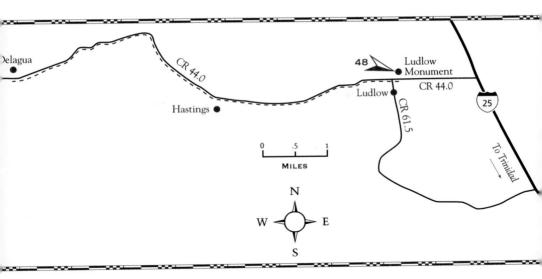

As violence flared, CF&I took extreme measures: Striking miners, company officials reasoned, had no right to live in company-owned quarters, so CF&I evicted the workers and their families. The union and aid organizations quickly set up tent colonies, temporary communities that would offer basic shelter until strikers and the company reached a resolution. As the families moved in, snows fell, and they kept falling. A blizzard set in, covering the entire Front Range with the deepest snows the state had experienced in all of its recorded history. The residents of the makeshift tent colonies hung on—largely because the snowstorm had brought relatively mild temperatures. Still, the simple act of survival was once again not so simple.

As the months passed, miners and mine operators returned each other's attacks. Several strikers died in the hostilities. Las Animas and Huerfano County officials called Governor Elias M. Ammons, and he called the Colorado National Guard. Militia troops came from Denver and martial law was declared.

On the cold spring day of April 20, 1914, the troops descended on Ludlow, determined to quell the back-and-forth violence centered there. Bullets flew and the tent colony's 900 occupants fled. Suddenly tents were burning, and within moments the entire colony was ablaze. Families ran from the burning colony, gathering at safe distances to regroup and count their numbers. The flames leveled the colony, with charred bed frames, stoves, and other smoldering remnants of the temporary homes littering a grim scene. Militia troops captured Louis Tikas, the colony's Greek-born leader, then shot him three times in the back. In the aftermath of the blaze, searchers made a tragic find. In one of the cellars lay the bodies of 2 women and 11 children who had sought refuge from the flames and gunfire, only to suffocate.

For 10 days, enraged miners torched and dynamited area mines. "Remember Ludlow!" became a rallying cry for labor organizers everywhere.

Following the tragedy at Ludlow, the United Mine Workers of America bought 40 acres at the massacre site. On the third anniversary of the tragedy, the union dedicated the site in a ceremony that drew thousands of miners and their families, who paraded together from Tollerburg (see Hike 47).

But exactly a week later, tragedy struck again—this time at Hastings, just a few miles up the road. Managed by the Victor-American Fuel Company, Hastings had grown from a tiny clump of houses to a coal operation that produced 2,000 tons a day. Established in 1889, Hastings by 1917 supported a school, a church, a boarding house, two barbers, saloons, and an opera house of sorts, but a 1912 explosion that took the lives of a dozen miners had left it with a reputation as a dangerous mine.

On the morning of April 27, 1917, miner Frank Milatto "was guiding a string of empty coal cars into 'Hastings No. 2,'" writes local author F. Dean Sneed. "About one-half mile from the main portal, Milatto encountered a cloud of thick, black smoke rising up the shaft towards him. He immediately abandoned the cars and ran back to the surface shouting 'FIRE!' as he went." As rescue parties searched the scene, they found that an explosion had ripped through a seam 8,000 feet underground. No one aboveground had even felt it. Most likely, the blast occurred when safety inspector David Reese had tried to relight his lamp, instead igniting the huge pocket of gas that had probably doused its flame in the first place. In the deadliest mining accident in Colorado history, the Hastings explosion killed 121 miners, nearly all of whom died of carbon monoxide asphyxiation. It took seven months to remove the bodies, a few of which were never found. Of the miners in Hastings No. 2, Milatto had been the only survivor.

The mines at Hastings operated for only another six years. In 1923, they shut down for good and the portals were sealed. The town was abandoned about 15 years later. In 1960, a simple granite marker was erected in memory of the miners killed.

In 1918, the United Mine Workers of America erected the grander monument that commemorates the Ludlow Massacre and honors the children, women, and miners who died on that day. The union still maintains the site.

One of the scattered hillside remnants of the coal-mining heyday at Hastings

LOCATION:	About 17 miles north of Trinidad
DESCRIPTION:	A dusty road leads from the site of a tragic event in U.S. labor history to the location of Colorado's deadliest mining accident.
DISTANCE:	5 miles, out and back
HIKING TIME:	3 hours
RATING:	Easy
TRAILHEAD ELEVATION:	6,260 feet
MAXIMUM ELEVATION:	6,400 feet
MAP:	*Colorado Atlas & Gazetteer*, p. 93, B6
CONTACT:	Trinidad/Las Animas Chamber of Commerce, (866) 480-4750 or (719) 846-9285, www.tlac.net/chamber/

GETTING THERE: On I-25, drive north from Trinidad or south from Walsenburg to Exit 27. Look for a sign for the Ludlow Monument. Take the exit and drive west 0.8 mile to the monument's large parking area.

GOOD TO KNOW: The Ludlow Monument includes a covered patio with picnic tables, historical information, and an outhouse. The monument, inside a gated plot with a sign-in sheet, rises beside the field where the tent colony once stood. At the plot is also the underground pit where the victims of the Ludlow Massacre died. The walls have been cemented, and a set of concrete steps leads down into it. The United Mine Workers of America restored the monument after a recent incident of major vandalism.

Like Hike 47, this walk follows a well-maintained county road. Ranchers and others drive the road, so you'll likely get some dust blown your way. But the ground you'll cover is so rich in history that walking or (best of all) mountain biking the route is highly rewarding. This is a hot walk in the summer, with little opportunity for shade; you'll be exposed to the windy elements during winter.

On your way to Hastings or after you return, be sure to take a side trip, by car or on foot, to see what remains of the town of Ludlow. From the Ludlow Monument, you can see the cluster of buildings about 0.5 mile up CR 61.5, which leads left (south) from the road toward Hastings. The structures are protected by a fence and are on private property; no trespassing is allowed.

THE WALK

Set out walking due west on the road from the Ludlow Monument toward the Spanish Peaks. The walk is easy and slopes gently uphill along an abandoned stretch of railroad (the tracks were to the right of the roadway). You'll stroll alongside arroyos and bluffs to your right with a nice view of the Spanish Peaks ahead of you. The road passes through private ranchland; occasional cottonwoods mark streams, and wild turkeys are among the elusive wildlife you might spot.

The sealed entrance to the Hastings No. 2 mine, the site of a 1917 explosion

At 0.6 mile are the remains of a store that operated for several years during the mining heyday. At 2.1 miles you pass a small abandoned bridge, and at 2.2 miles look for some coal tailings on your right and a few structures and foundations on the left. At this point, you're walking along rangeland of short grasses, cedar, sage, juniper, and cactus.

At about 2.5 miles is the site of Hastings. A modest granite marker just left of the road honors the 121 miners killed in the 1917 explosion. Remaining from the camp are the sealed entrance to Hastings No. 2 several yards behind the marker, many foundations, a few partial structures, and some brick and stone walls. Across the road is a long row of coke ovens. Be sure to respect all fences and stay off private property.

For a more ambitious walk or bike ride and a look at more of the region's history, you can keep going up the road to the site of Delagua, a former coal camp 6 miles west of the Ludlow Monument that time has reduced to foundations and coal dumps.

The coke ovens at Hastings

The Bulls Eye Mine Road

AN ARROW IN THE HEART OF A WILDERNESS?

Like twin pyramids, the easternmost promontories of the Rocky Mountains jut from the High Plains to elevations surpassing 13,600 and 12,600 feet. Both West and East Spanish Peaks have been the stuff of legends for centuries. Strikingly visible from across the plains and radiating more than 250 wall-like volcanic dikes that sometimes stretch for miles, the peaks have long been held sacred by American Indians and served as guideposts to explorers, settlers, and travelers along the Taos branch of the Santa Fe Trail (see Hike 44). Juan Bautista de Anza refers to them in journals of his 18th-century expedition into the region (see Hike 43).

In the 1870s, silver prospectors began their scramble up the sides of the peaks. On the taller West Spanish Peak was the Lincoln lode, so named because it was one of several properties held by Robert Lincoln—the nation's secretary of war and the son of Abraham Lincoln.

High in the tundra along a rocky gulch on the peak's northern flank, other prospectors struck silver and dubbed their lofty mining claim the Mountain Monarch. The Monarch—owned by a group of Iowa investors—was one of many strikes in a flurry of activity at West Spanish Peak. Soon, Monarch miners were working consecutive 8-hour shifts, day and night, boring new tunnels and extracting not only silver but gold, lead, zinc, and copper.

By May 1882, the mine was so lucrative that a local paper reported on "talk of starting a town at the Mountain Monarch to be known as Monarch City." A crew had begun the final section of a toll road up to the mine. By the end of June, with yet another silver strike proving the mine's richness, workers were finishing the last stretch of today's Bulls Eye Mine Road. By August the

The old Bulls Eye Mine "Road" quickly reaches timberline and beyond.

miners were sacking the ore as quickly as they pulled it out of the mountain, shipping it to smelters in Pueblo. The Monarch's owners kept their mine running into the 1890s, when the Silver Crash took its toll on mines throughout Colorado.

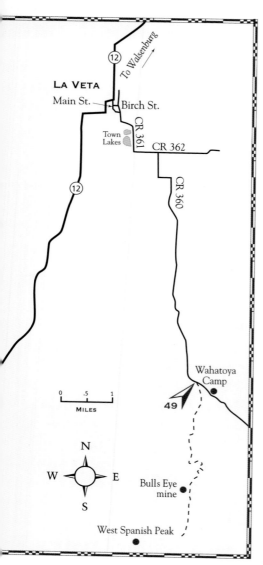

But the legacy of the Monarch—renamed the Bulls Eye—didn't end there. Today the scant remains of the Bulls Eye mine lie perched at the edge of the 18,000-acre Spanish Peaks Wilderness, signed into existence by President Bill Clinton in 1999. Locals know the Bulls Eye mine well—and they know the road even better because it sparked a heated debate over land use in the newly designated wilderness.

Wilderness designation reserves a region for such uses as hiking, camping, and horseback riding; it also means the end of motorized traffic. In the decades after the mine's closure, the steep road had become a popular jeep route, but by the time of the wilderness designation, it had fallen out of such use and had become a hiking and horseback-riding trail. Opposition to the wilderness measure came from locals who feared losing vehicular use of the Bulls Eye Mine Road. Republican Senator Wayne Allard backed the proposed wilderness but offered a bill that excluded the road from the measure. As the *High Country News* described the proposed legislation, "A vein of unprotected land, called a 'cherry stem' by the Forest Service, would line the road." Allard's press secretary said that the local community had requested that the road be cherry-stemmed so they could one day jeep up the mountain again. But as Jeff Widen of the Colorado Environmental Coalition argued, "There is no practical use, demand, or really logic to cherry-stemming that road all the way up to the mine. That would really be an arrow in the heart of the Spanish Peaks Wilderness."

The Forest Service agreed, insisting that vehicles would diminish the area's value as wilderness while creating erosion, lessening water quality, and incurring high maintenance costs. In the end, though, the road was indeed cherry-stemmed and is not subject to wilderness restrictions. But in a compromise, the Spanish Peaks Wilderness Act specifies that the secretary of agriculture (who oversees the Forest Service) must approve any opening of the road to vehicular traffic, in consultation with the local community. As the AP wrote, "The new law gives the Forest Service authority to manage the road, and the compromise satisfied some environmentalists." Because opening the road would mean some $100,000 in maintenance over a five-year period, the AP reported, forestry officials had no intention of opening it.

The historic Bulls Eye Mine Road is now open only to hikers and horseback riders, who can enjoy a trek to the trail's end free from the noise of rumbling engines.

LOCATION:	Spanish Peaks Wilderness
DESCRIPTION:	A steep and rocky walk leads up the side of West Spanish Peak to the Bulls Eye mine.
DISTANCE:	7 miles, out and back
HIKING TIME:	5 hours
RATING:	Difficult
TRAILHEAD ELEVATION:	8,200 feet
MAXIMUM ELEVATION:	11,900 feet
MAP:	*Colorado Atlas & Gazetteer,* p. 92, A3
CONTACT:	San Isabel National Forest, (719) 553-1400, www.fs.fed.us/r2/psicc/

GETTING THERE: From Walsenburg, drive west and then south (left) on CO 12 (the Scenic Highway of Legends, also marked as US 160 at Walsenburg) for 17 miles to the town of La Veta, where the highway becomes Main St. From Main, turn left and go one block to Birch St. Turn right (south) on Birch and go straight out of town. You'll pass the two Town Lakes on your right, then take a left at the "Huajatolla Valley" sign, and then take the first right (onto CR 360). After you have driven about 6.5 miles past La Veta, you'll see the trailhead (with a sign and a Forest Service road marker) to the right. The trailhead marker says "Wahatoya Trail 1304," which the marker identifies as FR 442. There are a few wide spots in the road for parking.

GOOD TO KNOW: A high-clearance road goes straight up the north side of West Spanish Peak; locals call it the "Bulls Eye Mine Road." Today, it's only open to hikers and horseback riders—although we do not recommend this hike for horses because of the talus fields on the approach to the mine. To get to the road, first you hike 2 miles' worth of the equally strenuous Wahatoya Trail. Climbing to an elevation of about 12,000 feet, the hike takes you past timberline to the remnants of the old Bulls Eye mine and a few smaller prospects. You cannot get to the summit of West Spanish Peak from this side of the mountain; rather, the hike will take you into the heart of a supremely lonesome alpine cirque, where an old stone shelter awaits among the rocks.

The hike begins near Wahatoya Camp, a collection of homes and cabins both old and new along Wahatoya Creek, a stream that once held gold. (Wahatoya Camp has drawn a wealth of Kansans into its ranks for more than a century.) It is best to get your walk started early in the day, as the weather at trail's end can be capricious and afternoon rain, snow, sleet, and whipping winds can blow through at any time of year.

View from the top of the Bulls Eye Mine Road

THE WALK

Your strenuous hike up the Wahatoya Trail kicks off with a fairly straight uphill stretch. After about 1.5 miles you hit the first big switchback, at about 9,900 feet in elevation, as well as a trail junction. To the left is the continuation of Wahatoya Trail, which crawls its way southeast between the two Spanish Peaks. To get to the Bulls Eye mine, however, you want to go straight up the old mine road.

As you continue your climb for about another mile, you will start to see debris from area mining operations and long-ago camping outings: metal scraps, ancient rusted cans, fragments of timbers, and mine pits. Much of the final stretch (about a mile's worth) is loose talus, but the trail is a long-established lane that saw plenty of travel during the mine's heyday, so it's always visible and relatively easy to navigate.

A rock shelter at the end of the trail

Around the time you hit timberline, you'll begin to notice the remains of the Bulls Eye on a steep hillside overlooking a tiny tributary of Wahatoya Creek. The trail passes over a massive pile of tailings, their yellowish and rust colors being the only thing that distinguishes them from the loose talus you will be scrambling up for the rest of the hike. Below the tailings you can make out further evidence of the mining that went on here, in the form of scattered timbers and hunks of rusted metal, including an old boiler, that have inched their way down toward the creek over the decades. The mine is privately owned, so please stay on the trail.

From here the trail narrows considerably, and it's about another 0.5 mile to its end inside a cirque near the mountain's summit. The near-vertical walls of the cirque surround you in a boulder-strewn alpine environment. At the trail's end is a stone shelter, perched atop a rise. The shelter consists of little more than a set of partial walls piled up to a height of about 5 feet, complete with makeshift fireplace and chimney. The only sounds that accompany you up here are the squawks of many marmots, the cheeps of curious swifts as they nosedive and flit over your head, and the whistling wind. Looking back the way you came, enjoy the view of the Wet Mountains to the north and the High Plains to the northeast.

Bear Lake

TROUBLE'S BRUIN

For as long as people have ranched and recreated in forestlands, those people have met up with bears. The bear is "the most impressive animal on the continent," wrote naturalist and Rocky Mountain National Park founder Enos Mills, who was especially fascinated by grizzlies. Mills lamented the dwindling numbers of bears due to their ever-increasing encounters with humans. "The grizzly bear is rapidly verging on extermination," he wrote in 1914. "The lion and the tiger oftentimes are rapacious, cruel, sneaking, bloodthirsty and cowardly, and it may be better for other wild folks if they are exterminated; but the grizzly deserves a better fate." He based his reasoning on his own observation that the grizzly, counter to its reputation, was a remarkably sensitive animal. "If you are invariably kind, gentle and playful, he always responds in the same manner," Mills wrote.

Still, early 20th-century newspapers and literary journals abound with tales both true and fanciful of violent incidents involving bears—incidents both happy-in-the-end and otherwise. Western papers regularly printed grisly accounts of bear attacks, tall tales of bear hunts, and reports of forest rangers' efforts to dispatch particularly problematic bruins. Sometimes the headline says it all: "Grizzly Bear Eats Man Alive, Dragging Him Asleep from Bed." "Bear Hunts Lion, Man Captures Both." "Forest Ranger Kills Bears He Finds Wrecking Cabin." Even "Beat a Bear to Death with the Heel of a Boot" and "Bear Kisses Him on Face; He Gets Gun and Kills It." Each of these accounts appeared between 1903 and 1917, and there were many others from Colorado alone.

Asa Arnold's capture of a troublesome bear on the shores of a lake that would become Bear Lake is the stuff of local legend.

One of the most legendary bear tales of the San Isabel National Forest tells of ranger Asa Arnold and his 1907 encounter with the bear that gave Bear Lake its name. The bear, which the principal account of the incident describes simply as "extremely large," had killed several cattle in the rangeland around the Blue Lakes. In an era that pre-dated bear-protection laws, it fell to Arnold, the first ranger for the San Carlos Ranger District of the newly created national forest, to deal with the cattle-killing omnivore.

Arnold set a trap at the northernmost of the Blue Lakes, affixing the trap firmly to a log. The trap did its job and the bear was ensnared. In its struggle to free itself, though, the bear loosed the log from its resting spot. The bear was so big that it dragged the trap—log and all—into the lake before drowning. "Asa used his saddle horse and pack horse to pull the bear, trap, and log out of the water," the account of the incident relates. "From that time on, the lake was known as Bear Lake."

When he wasn't battling bears, Arnold kept busy building trails, and he built a lot of them in his brief three years as ranger. In the Bear Lake area he created the Blue Lakes Trail, Indian Creek Trail, Apishapa Trail, Chaparral Trail, and others. Arnold knew what he was doing: Along these trails, gradual up-and-down hikes pass through lovely woods of aspen and pine, taking advantage of natural opportunities to climb to views of the spectacular Spanish Peaks—the scenic high points of the national forest over which he stood guard.

LOCATION:	Cuchara River Recreation Area, San Isabel National Forest
DESCRIPTION:	A short loop circles a secluded lake where a bear met its match in 1907, giving the lake its name.
DISTANCE:	1-mile loop (or a number of longer, moderate hikes)
HIKING TIME:	1 hour
RATING:	Easy
TRAILHEAD ELEVATION:	10,400 feet
MAXIMUM ELEVATION:	10,400 feet
MAP:	*Colorado Atlas & Gazetteer*, p. 92, B1
CONTACT:	San Carlos Ranger District, (719) 269-8500, www.fs.fed.us/r2/psicc/sanc/

GETTING THERE:	Bear Lake is about 35 miles southwest of Walsenburg or 55 miles northwest of Trinidad, in either case via CO 12, the Scenic Highway of Legends. From Walsenburg, drive west and then south on CO 12 (also marked as US 160 at Walsenburg) about 32 miles to the Bear Lake/Blue Lakes turnoff, just past Cuchara. Turn right and drive 5 miles up a good-quality, winding gravel road to the parking area and campground at Bear Lake. If you're coming from Trinidad, take CO 12 about 51 miles to the Bear Lake/Blue Lakes turnoff just beyond Cucharas Pass; turn left and drive the 5 miles to the parking area and campground.
	If you are coming from Trinidad you'll see a few historical points of interest along the way. First you'll pass through the historic coal-mining district of Cokedale, with its rows of coke ovens visible from the highway. Just past Bosque del Oso ("Bear Forest") State Wildlife Area, when you've gone about 27 miles from Trinidad, watch on your right for the famous "house on the bridge"—a tiny adobe home built on a stone bridge over a creek. You will also pass the town of Stonewall, so named for its dramatic backdrop—a massive volcanic dike.
GOOD TO KNOW:	Bear Lake lies along the eastern flank of the Sangre de Cristo Mountains within the scenic 1.1-million-acre San Isabel National Forest. The Bear Lake Trailhead/campground has toilets, picnic tables, and grills (and bugs). You'll need to pay a day-use fee of about $5 to hike on the trails. Bear Lake is a supreme trout-fishing and boating spot. No camping or fires are permitted around the lake.

THE WALK

The deep blue waters of Bear Lake lie below the level of the campground, nestled among the evergreens. After parking at the campground, walk down to the lake and around it via the Fisherman's Trail. It's an easy loop around the edge of the lake. Once you get down to the water's edge, the hike is about 0.5 mile around the lake's circumference.

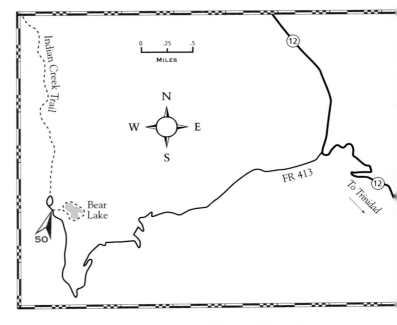

True to its name, the trail is there for people who are trout fishing, of whom there might be many, depending on the season.

For more of a challenge, drive or walk through the campground to its end, where you'll find another parking area (with restrooms and picnic tables) and the Indian Creek Trailhead. From here you can explore a number of the trails established by Asa Arnold during his tenure as forest ranger from 1907 to 1910.

Trail 1300 (open to hikers, horses, bikes, and ATVs but not four-wheel-drive vehicles) leads straight north, through aspens and pines, for many miles. You can stay on it to your heart's content as it follows the base of the Sangre de Cristos.

Or, a convenient loop hike leads back to the Indian Creek Trailhead via short stretches of the Dodgeton and Spring Creek Trails. Take the Indian Creek Trail (Trail 1300) north 5.6 miles to the Dodgeton Trail (1302); then go east a few miles to the Spring Creek Trail, which leads back south to the Indian Creek Trail and the trailhead. This is a long up-and-down hike with views of Cuchara Valley (including its ski resort) and the Spanish Peaks. A popular destination along the way is Cuchara Overlook, a side trail (at about 1 mile past the trailhead) toward the east that leads to a rise with a beautiful view of the peaks and the valley. Along this loop hike, a few well-marked shortcuts—the Baker Creek Trail (1301) or the "Shortcut Trail" (1300A)—cut east from the Indian Creek Trail to the Spring Creek Trail to shave a few miles off the walk.

Yet another option is to hike down to Bear Lake from the Spring Creek Trailhead at Cuchara, a few miles north of the Bear Lake/Blue Lakes turnoff on CO 12. This is a moderate hike of about 6 miles one way.

Along all of these trails, you're likely to see some deer grazing in the woods. And, whichever route you choose, take a cue from Asa Arnold and watch for bears.

Appendix A: Hikes by Difficulty Rating

EASY

MODERATE

Appendix B: Further Reading

We owe a debt of gratitude to the dozens of historians who wrote the books, articles, survey reports, and national and state register forms we relied on for our research. Among those sources were some true standouts.

For a beautifully illustrated trailhead-to-summit tale of Longs Peak, see Dougald MacDonald's *Longs Peak: The Story of Colorado's Favorite Fourteener*, also from Westcliffe Publishers. Norman Fry offers a personal narrative of Cache la Poudre history in *The River: As Seen From 1889*. Oliver Toll's *Arapaho Names and Trails: A Report of a 1914 Pack Trip* tells Gun Griswold's story. For Boulder County history, consult Joanna Sampson's many publications and *Once a Coal Miner: The Story of Colorado's Northern Coal Field* by Phyllis Smith. For a history of the U.S. Forest Service in Colorado, see Len Shoemaker's *Saga of a Forest Ranger: A Biography of William R. Kreutzer*. C.W. Buchholtz's *Rocky Mountain National Park: A History* is still the best general work on the park, and Betty D. Freudenburg adds a personal touch with *Facing the Frontier: The Story of the MacGregor Ranch*. For more on the Cripple Creek Mining District, see Elizabeth Jameson, *All That Glitters: Class, Conflict, and Community in Cripple Creek*; Frank Waters, *Midas of the Rockies: The Story of Stratton and Cripple Creek*; and Marshall Sprague, *Money Mountain: The Story of Cripple Creek Gold*. Susan Consola Appleby's *Fading Past: The Story of Douglas County, Colorado* is local history at its finest, and Kenneth Jessen's *Ghost Towns: Colorado Style* series was indispensable.

Anyone exploring the southern Colorado coal camps needs F. Dean Sneed's self-published *Las Animas County Ghost Towns and Mining Camps*; pick up a copy at the Trinidad History Museum. For the northern gold and silver camps, see John K. Aldrich's *Ghosts of Boulder County: A Guide to the Ghost Towns and Mining Camps of Boulder County, Colorado* and *Ghosts of Clear Creek County: A Guide to the Ghost Towns and Mining Camps of Clear Creek County, Colorado*; Donald C. Kemp's *Silver, Gold, and Black Iron: A Story of the Grand Island Mining District of Boulder County, Colorado*; Perry Eberhart's *Guide to the Colorado Ghost Towns and Mining Camps*; and Duane A. Smith's *Silver Saga: The Story of Caribou, Colorado*. Muriel Sibell Wolle's 1949 classic, *Stampede to Timberline: The Ghost Towns and Mining Camps of Colorado*, is still a delight.

Forrest Crossen's *The Switzerland Trail of America* is a hefty look at that rail line with a wealth of photographs. And Herbert W. Meyer, Steven W. Veatch, and Amanda Cook's *Field Guide to the Paleontology and Volcanic Setting of the Florissant Fossil Beds, Colorado*, Field Guide 5 of the Geological Society of America (available at the Florissant visitor center), is a surprisingly good read.

Appendix C: Photography Credits

All contemporary photographs were taken by Steve Grinstead, Dan Fogelberg, or Ben Fogelberg. Historic photographs, listed here, were provided courtesy of the Fort Collins Public Library (FCPL), Denver Public Library (DPL), and Colorado Historical Society (CHS). All rights reserved. When known, historic photographers are also listed.

Region 1: Fort Collins

p. 15: FCPL H06949

2. Pingree Valley Loop to the Ramsey-Koenig Ranch, p. 23: FCPL H0490

Region 2: Rocky Mountain National Park

4. Lulu City Historic Site, p. 30: DPL 10012238

8. Ute Trail to Tombstone Ridge, p. 45: CHS 10025974

11. Agnes Vaille Shelter on Longs Peak, p. 56: CHS 10036052

Region 3: Boulder

p. 62: Photo by A.E. Dickerson; DPL 10011721

13. Switzerland Trail, p. 68: Photo by J.B. Sturtevant; CHS 10036054

14. The Fourth of July Mine, p. 73: Photo by Muriel Sibell Wolle; DPL 10003218

15. Caribou, p. 77: Photo by Alexander Martin; DPL 10061537

16. Hessie to Lost Lake, p. 81: CHS 10027082

17. Chautauqua Trail, p. 85: DPL 10011717

20. Crags Mountain Resort and Moffat Road, p. 97: Photo by L.C. McClure; DPL 00071391

21. Marshall Mesa Trail, p. 101: DPL 10062772

Region 4: Denver

p.106: Photo by L.C. McClure; DPL 00070692

24. Waldorf and the Argentine Central Railroad, p. 114: DPL 10013982

26. Lookout Mountain and Buffalo Bill Trails, p. 123: Photo by Elliott and Fry; DPL 11002395

29. Mount Falcon Park, p. 137: CHS 10036055

31. Fountain Valley Trail to Persse Place, p. 144: Photo by William Henry Jackson; CHS 20100103

32. Castlewood Dam, p. 149: Photo by Harry H. Buckwalter; CHS 20031339

Region 5: Colorado Springs

p.158: Photo by Harry H. Buckwalter; CHS 20030858

36. Petrified Forest Loop, p. 169: Photo by Harry H. Buckwalter; CHS 20030061

38. Gold Camp Trail, p. 177: Photo by Underwood and Underwood; DPL 10062463

39. Vindicator Valley Loop, p. 182: CHS 20004607

Region 6: Pueblo

p.192: Photo by Charles E. Rose; DPL 11002395

42. Conduit–Arkansas Point Trails, p. 198: Photo by F.M. Steele; DPL 11005049

Region 7: La Junta

p.208: CHS 10036056

Region 8: Trinidad

p.222: CHS 20004829

47. Berwind Canyon, p. 224: CHS 20005002

Index

Note: Citations followed by the letter "m" denote maps.

About the Authors/Photographers

photo by Noah Fogelberg

BEN FOGELBERG edits *Colorado History NOW*, the membership newsletter of the Colorado Historical Society. An avid hiker and runner, he spends his free time on the trails near his home in Loveland. He is a regular contributor to *Colorado Heritage* magazine and has written for several Front Range publications. Along with Steve Grinstead, he co-edited the 2004 anthology *Western Voices: 125 Years of Colorado Writing*, which won a Certificate of Commendation from the American Association for State and Local History.

Ben's father, Dan Fogelberg, took many of the photographs in this book. He taught high school photography for 27 years before retiring in 2003 to pursue his artwork full time in his Boulder County studio.

STEVE GRINSTEAD is the editor of *Colorado Heritage*, the quarterly magazine of the Colorado Historical Society, and is the former editor of the society's *Colorado History* journal. Born and raised in eastern Kansas, he moved west in 1980 and has lived, hiked, and photographed in Wyoming and Colorado ever since. He is the author of *Trinidad History Museum: A Capsule History and Guide* and several features for *Colorado Heritage*. He is a longtime editor of Colorado histories and field guides, including several for Westcliffe Publishers.

photo by Leigh Grinstead